EAT LIKE A PRESIDENT:
THE WHITE HOUSE COOKBOOK

(BOOK ONE)

EAT LIKE A PRESIDENT: THE WHITE HOUSE COOKBOOK

(BOOK ONE)

COOKING, MENUS, DINNERS, TABLE ETIQUETTE FIT FOR A PRESIDENT

HUGO ZIEMANN
Former Steward of the White House
and
Fanny Lemira Gillette

The New
Atlantian Library

The New Atlantian Library
is an imprint of
ABSOLUTELY AMAZING eBOOKS

Published by Whiz Bang LLC, 926 Truman Avenue, Key West, Florida 33040, USA.

Eat Like a President: The White House Cookbook (Book One) copyright © 2017 by Gee Whiz Entertainment LLC. Electronic compilation/paperback edition copyright © 2017 by Whiz Bang LLC. *The White House Cook Book* was originally published in 1887. This edition edited by Rosemary Mason.

All rights reserved. No part of this book may be reproduced, scanned, or transmitted in any form or by any means, electronic or mechanical, including photocopying, recording, or any information storage and retrieval system, without permission in writing from the publisher. Please do not participate in or encourage piracy of copyrighted materials in violation of the author's rights. Purchase only authorized ebook editions.

While the authors and publisher have made every effort to provide accurate information at the time of publication, neither assumes any responsibility for errors, or for changes that occur after publication. Further, the publisher does not have any control over and does not assume any responsibility for author or third-party websites or their contents.

Statement by Archivist: *This book is in the public domain because it was published in the United States before 1923.*

For information contact:
Publisher@AbsolutelyAmazingEbooks.com

ISBN-13: 978-1945772337 (The New Atlantian Library)
ISBN-10: 1945772336

To the wives of our presidents, those noble women who have graced the white house, and whose names and memories are dear to all Americans, this volume is affectionately dedicated by the author.

EAT LIKE A PRESIDENT: THE WHITE HOUSE COOKBOOK

(BOOK ONE)

PUBLISHERS' PREFACE

In presenting to the public *The White House Cookbook*, the publishers believe they can justly claim that it represents a perfection of the culinary art. Hugo Ziemann was at one time caterer for that Prince Napoleon who was killed while fighting the Zulus in Africa. He was afterwards steward of the famous Hotel Splendide in Paris. Later he conducted the celebrated Brunswick Café in New York, and still later he gave to the Hotel Richelieu in Chicago a cuisine that won the applause of even the gourmets of foreign lands.

Mrs. F.L. Gillette is no less proficient and capable, having made a life-long and thorough study of cookery.

The book has been prepared with great care. Every recipe has been *tried* and *tested*. The subject of carving has been given a prominent place, not only because of its special importance in a work of this kind, but particularly because it contains entirely new and original designs, and is so far a departure from the usual mode of treating the subject.

Interesting information is given concerning the White House: how its hospitality is conducted, the menus served on special occasions, etc.

— The Publisher

Editor's Note

In republishing this fascinating cookbook by one-time White House steward Hugo Ziemann for a modern-day audience, we chose to shift its focus slightly, approaching the subject more from the standpoint of what a US president eats rather than presenting a hardcore collection of recipes. Also we divided the thick tome into two parts (Book One and Book Two), the first sticking more with entrees and the second concerning itself more with desserts.

For simplicity we omitted a few recipes from the original printing, but were careful not to add any new ones. Admittedly, a few recipes we allowed to remain for their quaintness (we can't imagine a sophisticated US President slurping squirrel soup, but there it was among the expected culinary fare -- dishes like braised veal and Lobster á la Newburg and Macaroni á la Italienne).

We've also taken the liberty of shuffling things around.

Furthermore, we dressed this new edition up with some new food photographs, mindful of the visual age we live in today.

As noted, these recipes were tested and found satisfactory for the palate of the leader of the Free World. You can make most of them in your own kitchen. And "Eat like a President."

- Rosemary Mason
2017

WHITE HOUSE COOKBOOK

MANAGEMENT AND DIRECTION

OF☐DINNERS AND RECEPTIONS☐ ON☐STATE OCCASIONS AT THE WHITE HOUSE

Etiquette as observed in European courts is not known at the White House.

The President's Secretary issues invitations by direction of the President to the distinguished guests.

The Usher in charge of the cloak-room hands to the gentleman on arrival an envelope containing a diagram of the table (as shows below), whereon the name and seat of the respective guest and the lady he is to escort to dinner are marked.

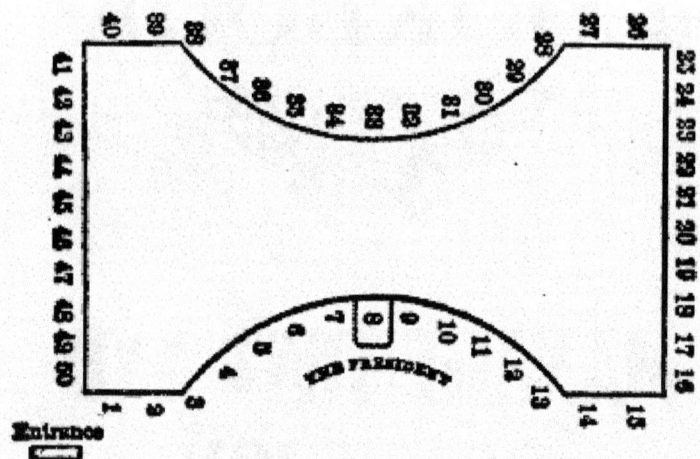

A card corresponding with his name is placed on the napkin belonging to the cover of the seat he will occupy.

The President's seat is in the middle of the table. The most distinguished guests sit on his right and left. If their wives are present they will occupy these seats, and the gentlemen will be seated next to the President's wife whose seat is directly opposite the President.

Official dinners all over the world are always served after the French fashion, and are divided into three distinct parts. Two of them are served from the kitchen, and the third from the pantry.

The first part of the dinner served French style includes from oysters on the shell to the sherbets.

The second service continues to the sweet dishes.

The third includes ice, cakes, fruits, cheeses, which are all understood as desserts, and are dressed in the pantry.

All principal dishes which are artistically decorated are shown to the President first, then are carried around the table before being carved by the Steward in the pantry.

Fancy folding of the napkins is considered out of fashion; plain square folded, so as to show monogram in the middle, is much preferred.

The following diagram will illustrate the arrangement of the glasses on the table. (See diagram.)

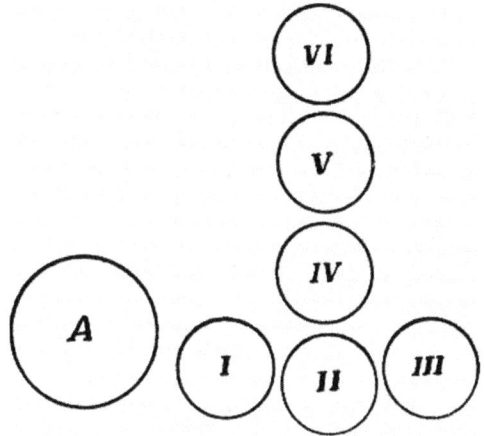

DIAGRAM ILLUSTRATING HOW TO ARRANGE GLASSES ON TABLE

A – Plate.
I – Glass for Sauterne.
II – Glass for Sherry.
III – Glass for Rhine Wine.
IV – Glass for Water.
V – Glass for Champagne.
VI – Glass for Burgundy.

Flower decorations on the table are to be in flat designs, so as not to obscure the view of the guests.

Corsage bouquets for ladies consist of not more than eight large roses tied together by silk ribbon, with the name of the lady stamped on in gold letters.

Gentlemen's boutonnieres consist only of one rosebud.

Bouquets for ladies are to be placed on the right side; for gentlemen, on the napkin next to card bearing his name.

Printed menus are never used on any official occasion.

The private dinners menus are either printed or written on a plain card and placed on each cover.

Liquors, cordials, cigars are served on a separate table after the ladies have retired to the parlor.

Eat Like a President: Book I

Lincoln China

THE LAYING OF THE TABLE

AND THE TREATMENT OF GUESTS

In giving "dinners," the apparently trifling details are of great importance when taken as a whole.

We gather around our board agreeable persons, and they pay us and our dinner the courtesy of dressing for the occasion, and this reunion should be a time of profit as well as pleasure. There are certain established laws by which "dinner giving" is regulated in polite society; and it may not be amiss to give a few observances in relation to them. One of the first is that an invited guest should arrive at the house of his host at least a quarter of an hour before the time appointed for dinner. In laying the table for dinner *all* the linen should be a spotless white throughout, and underneath the linen tablecloth should be spread one of thick cotton-flannel or baize, which gives the linen a heavier and finer appearance, also deadening the sound of moving dishes. Large and neatly folded napkins (ironed without starch), with pieces of bread three or four inches long, placed between the folds, but not to completely conceal it, are laid on each plate. An ornamental centerpiece, or a vase filled with a few rare flowers, is put on the center of the table, in place of the large table-castor, which has gone into disuse, and is rarely seen now on well-appointed tables. A few choice flowers make a charming variety in the appearance of even the most simply laid table, and a pleasing variety at table is quite as essential to the enjoyment of the repast as is a good choice of dishes, for the eye in fact should be gratified as much as the palate.

All dishes should be arranged in harmony with the decorations of the flowers, such as covers, relishes, confectionery, and small sweets. Garnishing of dishes has also a great deal to do with the appearance of a dinner-table, each dish garnished sufficiently to be in good taste without looking absurd.

Beside each plate should be laid as many knives, forks and spoons as will be required for the several courses, unless the hostess prefers to have them brought on with each change. A glass of water, and when wine is served glasses for it, and individual saltcellars may be placed at every plate. Water bottles are now much in vogue with corresponding tumblers to cover them; these, accompanied with dishes of broken ice, may be arranged in suitable places. When butter is served a special knife is used, and that, with all other required service, may be left to the judgment and taste of the hostess, in the proper placing of the various aids to her guests' comfort.

The dessert plates should be set ready, each with a doily and a finger-glass partly filled with water, in which is dropped a slice of lemon; these with extra knives, forks and spoons, should be on the side-board ready to be placed beside the guest between the courses when required.

If preferred, the "dinner" may all be served from the side-table, thus relieving the host from the task of carving. A plate is set before each guest, and the dish carved is presented by the waiter on the left-hand side of each guest. At the end of each course the plates give way for those of the next. If not served from the side-table, the dishes are brought in ready carved, and placed before the host and hostess, then served and placed upon the waiter's salver, to be laid by that attendant before the guest.

Soup and fish being the first course, plates of soup are usually placed on the table before the dinner is announced; or if the hostess wishes the soup served at the table, the soup-tureen, containing *hot* soup, and the *warm* soup-plates are placed before the seat of the hostess. Soup and fish being disposed of, then come the joints or roasts, *entrees* (made dishes), poultry, etc., also relishes.

After dishes have been passed that are required no more, such as vegetables, hot sauces, etc., the dishes containing them may be set upon the side-board, ready to be taken away.

Jellies and sauces, when not to be eaten as a dessert, should be helped on the dinner-plate, not on a small side dish as was the former usage.

If a dish be on the table, some parts of which are preferred to others, according to the taste of the individuals, all should have the opportunity of choice. The host will simply ask each one if he has any preference for a particular part; if he replies in the negative, you are not to repeat the question, nor insist that he must have a preference.

Do not attempt to eulogize your dishes, or apologize that you cannot recommend them – this is extreme bad taste; as also is the vaunting of the excellence of your wines, etc., etc.

Do not insist upon your guests partaking of particular dishes. Do not ask persons more than once, and never force a supply upon their plates. It is ill-bred, though common, to press any one to eat; and, moreover, it is a great annoyance to many.

In winter, plates should always be warmed, but not made hot. Two kinds of animal food, or two kinds of dessert, should not be eaten *off* of one plate, and there should never be more than two kinds of vegetables with one course. Asparagus, green corn, cauliflower and raw tomatoes comprise one course in place of a salad. All meats should be cut across the grain in very thin slices. Fish, at dinner, should be baked or boiled, never fried or broiled. Baked ham may be used in every course after fish, sliced thin and handed after the regular course is disposed of.

The hostess should retain her plate, knife and fork, until her guests have finished.

The crumb-brush is not used until the preparation for bringing in the dessert; then all the glasses are removed, except the flowers, the water-tumblers, and the glass of wine which the guest wishes to retain with his dessert. The dessert plate containing the finger-bowl, also a dessert knife and fork, should then be set before each guest, who at once removes the finger-bowl and its doily, and the knife and fork to the table, leaving the plate ready to be used for any dessert chosen.

Finely sifted sugar should always be placed upon the table to be used with puddings, pies, fruit, etc., and if cream is required, let it stand by the dish it is to be served with.

To lay a dessert for a small entertainment and a few guests outside of the family, it may consist simply of two dishes of fresh fruit in season, two of dried fruits and two each of cakes and nuts.

Coffee and tea are served *lastly*, poured into tiny cups and served clear, passed around on a tray to each guest, then the sugar and cream passed that each person may be allowed to season his black coffee or *café noir* to suit himself.

A *family dinner*, even with a few friends, can be made quite attractive and satisfactory without much display or expense; consisting first of good soup, then fish garnished with suitable additions, followed by a roast; then vegetables and some made dishes, a salad, crackers, cheese and olives, then dessert. This sensible meal, well cooked and neatly served, is pleasing to almost any one, and is within the means of any housekeeper in ordinary circumstances.

Eat Like a President: Book I

ARTICLES REQUIRED FOR THE KITCHEN

The following list will show what articles are necessary for the kitchen, and will be quite an aid to young housekeepers when about commencing to furnish the utensils needed in the kitchen department, and may prove useful to many.

    3 Sweeping brooms and 1 dustpan.
        1 Whiskbroom.
        1 Breadbox.
        2 Cake boxes.
        1 Large flour box.
        1 Dredging box.
        1 Large-sized tin pepperbox.
        1 Spice box containing smaller spice boxes.
        2 Cake pans, two sizes.
        4 Bread pans.
        2 Square biscuit pans.

1 Apple corer.
1 Lemon squeezer.
1 Meat cleaver.
3 Kitchen knives and forks.
1 Large kitchen fork and 4 kitchen spoons, two sizes.
1 Wooden spoon for cake making.
1 Large bread knife.
1 Griddlecake turner, also 1 griddle.
1 Potato masher.
1 Meat board.
1 Dozen patty pans; and the same number otartlet pans.
1 Large tin pail and 1 wooden pail.
2 Small tin pails.
1 Set of tin basins.
1 Set of tin measures.
1 Wooden butter ladle.
1 Tin skimmer.
1 Tin steamer.
2 Dippers, two sizes.
2 Funnels, two sizes.
1 Set of jelly cake tins.
4 Pie pans.
3 Pudding molds, one for boiling, two for baking, two sizes.
2 Dishpans, two sizes.
2 Cake or biscuit cutters, two sizes.
2 Graters, one large and one small.
1 Coffee canister.
1 Tea canister.

1 Tin or graniteware teapot.
1 Tin or graniteware coffeepot.
4 Milk pans, 1 milk strainer.
1 Dozen iron gem pans or muffin rings.
1 Coarse gravy strainer, 1 fine strainer.
1 Colander.
1 Flour sifter.
2 Scoops, one for flour, one for sugar.
2 Jelly molds, two sizes.
1 Can opener, 1 eggbeater.
1 Corkscrew.
1 Chopping-knife.
2 Wooden chopping-bowls, two sizes.
1 Meat saw.
2 Large earthen bowls.
4 Stone jars.
1 Coffee mill.
1 Candlestick.
2 Market baskets, two sizes.
1 Clock.
1 Ash bucket.
1 Gridiron.
2 Frying pans or spiders, two sizes.
4 Flatirons, 2 number 8 & 2 number 6
2 Dripping pans, two sizes.
3 Iron kettles, porcelain lined if possible.
1 Corn beef or fish kettle.
1 Teakettle.
2 Graniteware stew pans two sizes.

1 Wire toaster.
1 Double kettle for cooking custards, grains.
2 Sugar boxes - one for coarse, one for fine.
1 Waffle iron.
1 Stepladder.
1 Stove, 1 coal shovel.
1 Pair of scales.
2 Coal hods or buckets.
1 Kitchen table, 2 kitchen chairs.
1 Large clothesbasket.
1 Wash boiler, 1 washboard.
8 Dozen clothespins.
1 Large nail hammer and one small tack hammer.
1 Bean pot.
1 Clothes wringer.

An ingenious housewife will manage to do with less conveniences, but these articles, if they can be purchased in the commencement of housekeeping, will save time and labor, making the preparation of food more easy – and it is always economy in the end to get the best material in all wares, as, for instance, the double plate tin will last for years, whereas the poor kind has to be replaced in a short time; the low-priced earthenware is soon broken up, whereas the strong stoneware, costing but a trifle more, lasts almost a lifetime.

In relation to the economy and management of the kitchen, I might suggest that the most essential thing is cleanliness in cooking, and also cleanliness with your person as well as in the keeping of the kitchen.

The hands of the cook should be always thoroughly cleansed before touching or handling anything pertaining to the cooking. Next there should never be anything wasted or thrown away that can be turned to account, either for your own family or some family in poor circumstances. Bread that has become hard can be used for toasting, or for stuffing and pudding. In warm weather any gravies or soups that are left from the preceding day should be boiled up and poured into clean pans. This is particularly necessary where vegetables have been added to the preparation, as it then so soon turns sour. In cooler weather, every other day will be often enough to warm up these things. In cooking, clear as you go; that is to say, do not allow a host of basins, plates, spoons, and other utensils, to accumulate on the dressers and tables whilst you are engaged in preparing the dinner. By a little management and forethought, much confusion may be saved in this way. It is as easy to put a thing in its place when it is done with, as it is to keep continually moving it to find room for fresh requisites. For instance, after making a pudding, the flour-tub, pasteboard, and rolling pin, should be put away, and any basins, spoons, etc., should be neatly packed up near the sink, to be washed when the proper time arrives. Neatness, order and method should be always observed.

Never let your stock of spices, salt, seasoning, herbs, etc., dwindle down so low that some day, in the midst of preparing a large dinner, you find yourself minus a very important ingredient, thereby causing much confusion and annoyance.

After you have washed your saucepans, fish-kettle, etc., stand them before the fire for a few minutes to get thoroughly dry inside, before putting them away. They should then be kept in a dry place, in order that they may escape the deteriorating influence of rust, and thereby be quickly destroyed. Never leave saucepans dirty from one day's use to be cleaned the next; it is slovenly and untidy.

Do not be afraid of hot water in washing up dishes and dirty cooking utensils. As these are essentially greasy, lukewarm water cannot possibly have the effect of cleansing them effectually. Do not be chary also of changing and renewing the water occasionally. You will thus save yourself much time and labor in the long run.

Keep a cake of sapolio always on hand in the kitchen – always convenient for rubbing off stains from earthenware, tin, glass, in fact, almost everything but silver; it is a cheap and valuable article, and can be purchased at nearly every grocery in the United States.

WHITE HOUSE RECIPES

Eat Like a President: Book I

MEAT SOUPS

Preparations

Consommé, or Stock, forms the basis of all meat soups, and also of all principal sauces. It is, therefore, essential to the success of these culinary operations to know the most complete and economical method of extracting from a certain quantity of meat the best possible stock or broth. Fresh, uncooked beef makes the best stock, with the addition of cracked bones, as the glutinous matter contained in them renders it important that they should be boiled with the meat, which adds to the strength and thickness of the soup. They are composed of an earthy substance – to which they owe their solidity – of gelatin, and a fatty fluid, something like marrow. *Two ounces* of them contain as much gelatin as *one pound* of meat; but, in them, this is so encased in the earthy substance, that boiling water can dissolve only the surface of the whole bones, but by breaking them they can be dissolved more. When there is an abundance of it, it causes the stock, when cold, to become a jelly. The flesh of old animals contains more flavor than the flesh of young ones. Brown meats contain more flavor than white.

Mutton is too strong in flavor for good stock, while veal, although quite glutinous, furnishes very little nutriment.

Some cooks use meat that has once been cooked; this renders little nourishment and destroys the flavor. It might answer for ready soup, but for stock to keep it is not as good, unless it should be roasted meats. Those contain higher fragrant properties; so by putting the remains of roast meats in the stockpot you obtain a better flavor.

The shinbone is generally used, but the neck or "sticking-piece," as the butchers call it, contains more of the substance that you want to extract, makes a stronger and more nutritious soup, than any other part of the animal. Meats for soup should always be put on to cook in *cold* water, in a covered pot, and allowed to simmer slowly for several hours, in order that the essence of the meat may be drawn out thoroughly, and should be carefully skimmed to prevent it from becoming turbid, never allowed to *boil fast* at any time, and if more water is needed, use boiling water from the tea-kettle; cold or lukewarm water spoils the flavor. Never salt it before the meat is tender (as that hardens and toughens the meat), especially if the meat is to be eaten. Take off every particle of scum as it rises, and before the vegetables are put in.

Allow a little less than a quart of water to a pound of meat and bone, and a teaspoonful of salt. When done, strain through a colander. If for clear soups, strain again through a hair sieve, or fold a clean towel in a colander set over an earthen bowl, or any dish large enough to hold the stock. As stated before, stock is not as good when made entirely from cooked meats, but in a family where it requires a large joint roasted every day, the bones, and bits and underdone pieces of beef, or the bony structure of turkey or chicken that has been left from carving, bones of roasted poultry, these all assist in imparting a rich dark color to soup, and would be sufficient, if stewed as above, to furnish a family, without buying fresh meat for the purpose; still, with the addition of a little fresh meat it would be more nutritious. In cold weather you can gather them up for several days and put them to cook in cold water, and when done, strain, and put aside until needed.

Soup will be as good the second day as the first if heated to the boiling point. It should never be left in the pot, but should be turned into a dish or shallow pan, and set aside to get cold. Never cover it up, as that will cause it to turn sour very quickly.

Before heating a second time, remove all the fat from the top. If this is melted in, the flavor of the soup will certainly be spoiled.

Thickened soups require nearly double the seasoning used for thin soups or broth.

Coloring is used in some brown soups, the chief of which is brown burnt sugar, which is known as caramel by French cooks.

Pounded spinach leaves give a fine green color to soup. Parsley, or the green leaves of celery put in soup, will serve instead of spinach.

Pound a large handful of spinach in a mortar, then tie it in a cloth, and wring out all the juice; put this in the soup you wish to color green five minutes before taking it up.

Mock turtle, and sometimes veal and lamb soups, should be this color.

Okras give a green color to soup.

To color soup red, skin six red tomatoes, squeeze out the seeds, and put them into the soup with the other vegetables – or take the juice only, as directed for spinach.

For white soups, which are of veal, lamb or chicken, none but white vegetables are used; rice, pearl barley, vermicelli, or macaroni, for thickening.

Grated carrot gives a fine amber color to soup; it must be put in as soon as the soup is free from scum.

Hotel and private house stock is quite different.

Hotels use meat in such large quantities that there is always more or less trimmings and bones of meat to add to fresh meats; that makes very strong stock, which they use in most all soups and gravies and other made dishes.

The meat from which soup has been made is good to serve cold thus: Take out all the bones, season with pepper and salt, and ketchup, if liked, then chop it small, tie it in a cloth, and lay it between two plates, with a weight on the upper one; slice it thin for luncheon or supper; or make sandwiches of it; or make a hash for breakfast; or make it into balls, with the addition of a little wheat flour and an egg, and serve them fried in fat, or boil in the soup.

An agreeable flavor is sometimes imparted to soup by sticking some cloves into the meat used for making stock; a few slices of onions fried very brown in butter are nice; also flour browned by simply putting it into a saucepan over the fire and stirring it constantly until it is a dark brown.

Clear soups must be perfectly transparent, and thickened soups about the consistency of cream. When soups and gravies are kept from day to day in hot weather, they should be warmed up every day, and put into fresh-scalded pans or tureens, and placed in a cool cellar. In temperate weather, every other day may be sufficient.

HERBS AND VEGETABLES USED IN SOUPS

Of vegetables the principal ones are carrots, tomatoes, asparagus, green peas, okra, macaroni, green corn, beans, rice, vermicelli, Scotch barley, pearl barley, wheat flour, mushroom, or mushroom ketchup, parsnips, beetroot, turnips, leeks, garlic, shallots and onions; sliced onions fried with butter and flour until they are browned, then rubbed through a sieve, are excellent to heighten the color and flavor of brown sauces and soups. The herbs usually used in soups are parsley, common thyme, summer savory, knotted marjoram, and other seasonings, such as bay-leaves, tarragon, allspice, cinnamon, nutmeg, cloves, mace, black and white pepper, red pepper, lemon peel and juice, orange peel and juice. The latter imparts a finer flavor and the acid much milder. These materials, with wine, and the various ketchups, combined in various proportions, are, with other ingredients, made into almost an endless variety of excellent soups and gravies. Soups that are intended for the principal part of a meal certainly ought not to be flavored like sauces, which are only intended to give relish to some particular dish.

STOCK

Six pounds of shin of beef, or six pounds of knuckle of veal; any bones, trimmings of poultry, or fresh meat; one-quarter pound of lean bacon or ham, two ounces of butter, two large onions, each stuck with cloves; one turnip, three carrots, one head of celery, two ounces of salt, one-half teaspoonful of whole pepper, one large blade of mace, one bunch of savory herbs except sage, four quarts and one-half-pint of cold water.

Cut up the meat and bacon, or ham, into pieces of about three inches square; break the bones into small pieces, rub the butter on the bottom of the stew pan; put in one-half a pint of water, the broken bones, then meat and all other ingredients. Cover the stew pan, and place it on a sharp fire, occasionally stirring its contents. When the bottom of the pan becomes covered with a pale, jelly-like substance, add the four quarts of cold water, and simmer very gently for five or six hours. As we have said before, do not let it boil quickly. When nearly cooked, throw in a tablespoonful of salt to assist the scum to rise. Remove every particle of scum whilst it is doing, and strain it through a fine hair sieve; when cool remove all grease. This stock will keep for many days in cold weather.

Stock is the basis of many of the soups afterwards mentioned, and this will be found quite strong enough for ordinary purposes. Keep it in small jars, in a cool place. It makes a good gravy for hash meats; one tablespoonful of it is sufficient to impart a fine flavor to a dish of macaroni and various other dishes. Good soups of various kinds are made from it at short notice; slice off a portion of the jelly, add water, and whatever vegetables and thickening preferred. It is best to partly cook the vegetables before adding to the stock, as much boiling injures the flavoring of the soup. Season and boil a few moments and serve hot.

WHITE STOCK

White stock is used in the preparation of white soups,

and is made by boiling six pounds of a knuckle of veal, cut up in small pieces, poultry trimmings, and four slices of lean ham. Proceed according to directions given in STOCK, on opposite page.

TO CLARIFY STOCK

Place the stock in a clean saucepan, set it over a brisk fire. When boiling, add the white of one egg to each quart of stock, proceeding as follows: beat the whites of the eggs up well in a little water; then add a little hot stock; beat to a froth and pour gradually into the pot; then beat the whole hard and long; allow it to boil up once, and immediately remove and strain through a thin flannel cloth.

BEEF SOUP

Select a small shin of beef of moderate size, crack the bone in small pieces, wash and place it in a kettle to boil, with five or six quarts of *cold* water. Let it boil about two hours, or until it begins to get tender, then season it with a tablespoonful of salt, and a teaspoonful of pepper; boil it one hour longer, then add to it one carrot, two turnips, two tablespoonfuls of rice or pearl barley, one head of celery, and a teaspoonful of summer savory powdered fine; the vegetables to be minced up in small pieces like dice. After these ingredients have boiled a quarter of an hour, put in two potatoes cut up in small pieces, let it boil half an hour longer; take the meat from the soup, and if intended to be served with it, take out the bones and lay it closely and neatly on a dish, and garnish with sprigs of parsley.

Serve made mustard and ketchup with it. It is very nice pressed and eaten cold with mustard and vinegar, or ketchup. Four hours are required for making this soup. Should any remain over the first day, it may be heated, with the addition of a little boiling water, and served again. Some fancy a glass of brown sherry added just before being served. Serve very hot.

VEAL SOUP (Excellent)

Put a knuckle of veal into three quarts of cold water, with a small quantity of salt, and one small tablespoonful of uncooked rice. Boil slowly, hardly above simmering, four hours, when the liquor should be reduced to half the usual quantity; remove from the fire. Into the tureen put the yolk of one egg, and stir well into it a teacupful of cream, or, in hot weather, new milk; add a piece of butter the size of a hickory nut; on this strain the soup, boiling hot, stirring all the time. Just at the last, beat it well for a minute.

SCOTCH MUTTON BROTH

Six pounds neck of mutton, three quarts water, five carrots, five turnips, two onions, four tablespoonfuls barley, a little salt. Soak mutton in water for an hour, cut off scrag, and put it in stew pan with three quarts of water. As soon as it boils, skim well, and then simmer for one and one-half hours. Cut best end of mutton into cutlets, dividing it with two bones in each; take off nearly all fat before you put it into broth; skim the moment the meat boils, and every ten minutes afterwards; add carrots, turnips and onions, all cut into two or three pieces, then put them into soup soon enough to be thoroughly done; stir in barley; add salt to taste; let all stew together for three and one-half hours; about one-half hour before sending it to table, put in little chopped parsley and serve.

Cut the meat off the scrag into small pieces, and send it to table in the tureen with the soup. The other half of the mutton should be served on a separate dish, with whole turnips boiled and laid round it. Many persons are fond of mutton that has been boiled in soup.

You may thicken the soup with rice or barley that has first been soaked in cold water, or with green peas, or with young corn, cut down from the cob, or with tomatoes, scalded, peeled and cut into pieces.

GAME SOUP

Two grouse or partridges, or, if you have neither, use a pair of rabbits; half a pound of lean ham; two medium-sized onions; one pound of lean beef; fried bread; butter for frying; pepper, salt and two stalks of white celery cut into inch lengths; three quarts of water.

Joint your game neatly; cut the ham and onions into small pieces, fry all in butter to a light brown. Put into a soup pot with the beef, cut into strips, add a little pepper. Pour on the water; heat slowly, and stew gently two hours. Take out the pieces of bird, and cover in a bowl; cook the soup an hour longer; strain; cool; drop in the celery and simmer ten minutes. Pour upon fried bread in the tureen.

Venison soup made the same, with the addition of a tablespoonful of brown flour wet into a paste with cold water, adding a tablespoonful of ketchup, Worcestershire, or other pungent sauce, and a glass of Madeira or brown sherry.

CONSOMMÉ SOUP

Take good strong stock, remove all fat from the surface, and for each quart of the stock allow the white and shell of one egg and a tablespoonful of water, well whipped together. Pour this mixture into a saucepan containing the stock; place it over the fire and heat the contents gradually, stirring often to prevent the egg from sticking to the bottom of the saucepan. Allow it to boil gently until the stock looks perfectly clear under the egg, which will rise and float upon the surface in the form of a thick white scum. Now remove it and pour it into a folded towel laid in a colander set over an earthen bowl, allowing it to run through without moving or squeezing it. Season with more salt if needed, and quickly serve very hot. This should be a clear amber color.

CHICKEN CREAM SOUP

An old chicken for soup is much the best. Cut it up into quarters, put it into a soup kettle with half a pound of corned ham, and an onion; add four quarts of cold water. Bring slowly to a gentle boil, and keep this up until the liquid has diminished one-third, and the meat drops from the bones; then add half a cup of rice. Season with salt, pepper and a bunch of chopped parsley.

Cook slowly until the rice is tender, then the meat should be taken out. Now stir in two cups of rich milk thickened with a little flour. The chicken could be fried in a spoonful of butter and a gravy made, reserving some of the white part of the meat, chopping it and adding it to the soup.

PLAIN ECONOMICAL SOUP

Take a cold roast-beef bone, pieces of beefsteak, the rack of a cold turkey or chicken. Put them into a pot with three or four quarts of water, two carrots, three turnips, one onion, a few cloves, pepper and salt. Boil the whole gently four hours; then strain it through a colander, mashing the vegetables so that they will all pass through. Skim off the fat, and return the soup to the pot. Mix one tablespoonful of flour with two of water, stir it into the soup and boil the whole ten minutes. Serve this soup with sippits of toast.

Sippits are bits of dry toast cut into a triangular form.

A seasonable dish about the holidays.

OX-TAIL SOUP

Two ox-tails, two slices of ham, one ounce of butter, two carrots, two turnips, three onions, one leek, one head of celery, one bunch of savory herbs, pepper, a tablespoonful of salt, two tablespoonfuls of ketchup, one-half glass of port wine, three quarts of water.

Cut up the tails, separating them at the joints; wash them, and put them in a stew pan with the butter. Cut the vegetables in slices and add them with the herbs. Put in one-half pint of water, and stir it over a quick fire till the juices are drawn. Fill up the stew pan with water, and, when boiling, add the salt. Skim well, and simmer very gently for four hours, or until the tails are tender. Take them out, skim and strain the soup, thicken with flour, and flavor with the ketchup and port wine. Put back the tails, simmer for five minutes and serve.

Another way to make an appetizing ox-tail soup. You should begin to make it the day before you wish to eat the soup. Take two tails, wash clean, and put in a kettle with nearly a gallon of cold water; add a small handful of salt; when the meat is well cooked, take out the bones. Let this stand in a cool room, covered, and next day, about an hour and a half before dinner, skim off the crust or cake of fat which has risen to the top. Add a little onion, carrot, or any vegetables you choose, chopping them fine first; summer savory may also be added.

SQUIRREL SOUP

Wash and quarter three or four good sized squirrels; put them on, with a small tablespoonful of salt, directly after breakfast, in a gallon of cold water. Cover the pot close, and set it on the back part of the stove to simmer gently, *not* boil. Add vegetables just the same as you do in case of other meat soups in the summer season, but especially good will you find corn, Irish potatoes, tomatoes and Lima beans. Strain the soup through a coarse colander when the meat has boiled to shreds, so as to get rid of the squirrels' troublesome little bones. Then return to the pot, and after boiling a while longer, thicken with a piece of butter rubbed in flour. Celery and parsley leaves chopped up are also considered an improvement by many. Toast two slices of bread, cut them into dice one-half inch square, fry them in butter, put them into the bottom of your tureen, and then pour the soup boiling hot upon them.

GREEN PEA SOUP (with Meat)

Wash a small quarter of lamb in cold water, and put it into a soup pot with six quarts of cold water; add to it two tablespoonfuls of salt, and set it over a moderate fire – let it boil gently for two hours, then skim it clear; add a quart of shelled peas, and a teaspoonful of pepper; cover it, and let it boil for half an hour; then having scraped the skins from a quart of small young potatoes, add them to the soup; cover the pot and let it boil for half an hour longer; work quarter of a pound of butter and a dessertspoonful of flour together, and add them to the soup ten or twelve minutes before taking it off the fire.

Serve the meat on a dish with parsley sauce over it, and the soup in a tureen.

MACARONI SOUP

To a rich beef or other soup, in which there is no seasoning other than pepper or salt, take half a pound of small pipe macaroni, boil it in clear water until it is tender, then drain it and cut it in pieces of an inch length; boil it for fifteen minutes in the soup and serve.

MULLAGATAWNY SOUP (as made in India)

Cut four onions, one carrot, two turnips, and one head of celery into three quarts of liquor, in which one or two fowls have been boiled; keep it over a brisk fire till it boils, then place it on a corner of the fire, and let it simmer twenty minutes; add one tablespoonful of curry powder, and one tablespoonful of flour; mix the whole well together, and let it boil three minutes; pass it through a colander; serve with pieces of roast chicken in it; add boiled rice in a separate dish. It must be of good yellow color, and not too thick. If you find it too thick, add a little boiling water and a teaspoonful of sugar. Half veal and half chicken answers as well.

A dish of rice, to be served separately with this soup, must be thus prepared: put three pints of water in a saucepan and one tablespoonful of salt; let this boil. Wash well, in three waters, half a pound of rice; strain it, and put it into the boiling water in saucepan. After it has come to the boil – which it will do in about two minutes – let it boil twenty minutes; strain it through a colander, and pour over it two quarts of cold water. This will separate the grains of rice. Put it back in the saucepan, and place it near the fire until hot enough to send to the table. This is also the proper way to boil rice for curries. If these directions are strictly carried out every grain of the rice will separate, and be thoroughly cooked.

PHILADELPHIA PEPPER POT

Put two pounds of tripe and four calves' feet into the soup pot and cover them with cold water; add a red pepper, and boil closely until the calves' feet are boiled very tender; take out the meat, skim the liquid, stir it, cut the tripe into small pieces, and put it back into the liquid; if there is not enough liquid, add boiling water; add half a teaspoonful of sweet marjoram, sweet basil, and thyme, two sliced onions, sliced potatoes, salt. When the vegetables have boiled until almost tender, add a piece of butter rolled in flour, drop in some egg balls, and boil fifteen minutes more. Take up and serve hot.

MOCK TURTLE SOUP

Scald a well-cleansed calf's head, remove the brain, tie it up in a cloth, and boil an hour, or until the meat will easily slip from the bone; take out, save the broth; cut it in small square pieces, and throw them into cold water; when cool, put it in a stew pan, and cover with some of the broth; let it boil until quite tender, and set aside.

In another stew pan melt some butter, and in it put a quarter of a pound of lean ham, cut small, with fine herbs to taste; also parsley and one onion; add about a pint of the broth; let it simmer for two hours, and then dredge in a small quantity of flour; now add the remainder of the broth, and a quarter bottle of Madeira or sherry; let all stew quietly for ten minutes and rub it through a medium sieve; add the calf's head, season with a very little cayenne pepper, a little salt, the juice of one lemon, and, if desired, a quarter teaspoonful pounded mace and a dessert-spoon sugar.

Having previously prepared force meatballs, add them to the soup, and five minutes after serve hot.

GREEN TURTLE SOUP

One turtle, two onions, a bunch of sweet herbs, juice of one lemon, five quarts of water, a glass of Madeira.

After removing the entrails, cut up the coarser parts of the turtle meat and bones. Add four quarts of water, and stew four hours with the herbs, onions, pepper and salt. Stew very slowly, do not let it cease boiling during this time. At the end of four hours strain the soup, and add the finer parts of the turtle and the green fat, which has been simmered one hour in two quarts of water. Thicken with brown flour; return to the soup pot, and simmer gently for an hour longer. If there are eggs in the turtle, boil them in a separate vessel for four hours, and throw into the soup before taking up. If not, put in force meatballs; then the juice of the lemon, and the wine; beat up at once and pour out.

Some cooks add the finer meat before straining, boiling all together five hours; then strain, thicken and put in the green fat, cut into lumps an inch long. This makes a handsomer soup than if the meat is left in.

Green turtle can now be purchased preserved in airtight cans.

Force Meat Balls for the Above – Six tablespoonfuls of turtle meat chopped very fine. Rub to a paste, with the yolk of two hard-boiled eggs, a tablespoonful of butter, and, if convenient, a little oyster liquor. Season with cayenne, mace, half a teaspoonful of white sugar and a pinch of salt. Bind all with a well-beaten egg; shape into small balls; dip in egg, then powdered cracker; fry in butter, and drop into the soup when it is served.

TURKEY SOUP

Take the turkey bones and boil three-quarters of an hour in water enough to cover them; add a little summer savory and celery chopped fine. Just before serving, thicken with a little flour (browned), and season with pepper, salt and a small piece of butter. This is a cheap but good soup, using the remains of cold turkey which might otherwise be thrown away.

GUMBO OR OKRA SOUP

Fry out the fat of a slice of bacon or fat ham, drain it off, and in it fry the slices of a large onion brown; scald, peel and cut up two quarts fresh tomatoes, when in season (use canned tomatoes otherwise), and cut thin one quart okra; put them, together with a little chopped parsley, in a stew-kettle with about three quarts of hot broth of any kind; cook slowly for three hours, season with salt and pepper. Serve hot.

In chicken broth the same quantity of okra pods, used for thickening instead of tomatoes, forms a chicken gumbo soup.

FORCE MEAT BALLS FOR SOUP

One cupful of cooked veal or fowl meat, minced; mix with this a handful of fine breadcrumbs, the yolks of four hard-boiled eggs rubbed smooth together with a tablespoon of milk; season with pepper and salt; add a half teaspoon of flour, and bind all together with two beaten eggs; the hands to be well floured, and the mixture to be made into little balls the size of a nutmeg; drop into the soup about twenty minutes before serving.

FISH STOCK

Place a saucepan over the fire with a good-sized piece of sweet butter and a sliced onion; put into that some sliced tomatoes, then add as many different kinds of fish as you can get – oysters, clams, smelts, pawns, crabs, shrimps and all kinds of pan-fish; cook all together until the onions are well browned; then add a bunch of sweet herbs, salt and pepper, and sufficient water to make the required amount of stock. After this has cooked for half an hour pound it with a wooden pestle, then strain and cook again until it jellies.

FISH SOUP

Select a large, fine fish, clean it thoroughly, put it over the fire with a sufficient quantity of water, allowing for each pound of fish one quart of water; add an onion cut fine and a bunch of sweet herbs. When the fish is cooked, and is quite tasteless, strain all through a colander, return to the fire, add some butter, salt and pepper to taste.

A small tablespoonful of Worcestershire sauce may be added if liked. Serve with small squares of fried bread and thin slices of lemon.

OYSTER SOUP, No. 1

Two quarts of oysters, one quart of milk, two tablespoonfuls of butter, one teacupful of hot water; pepper, salt.

Strain all the liquor from the oysters; add the water, and heat. When near the boil, add the seasoning, then the oysters. Cook about five minutes from the time they begin to simmer, until they "ruffle." Stir in the butter, cook one minute, and pour into the tureen. Stir in the boiling milk and send to table. Some prefer all water in place of milk.

OYSTER SOUP. No. 2

Scald one gallon of oysters in their own liquor. Add one quart of rich milk to the liquor, and when it comes to a boil, skim out the oysters and set aside. Add the yolks of four eggs, two good tablespoonfuls of butter, and one of flour, all mixed well together, but in this order – first, the milk, then, after beating the eggs, add a little of the hot liquor to them gradually, and stir them rapidly into the soup. Lastly, add the butter and whatever seasoning you fancy besides plain pepper and salt, which must both be put in to taste with caution.

Celery salt most persons like extremely; others would prefer a little marjoram or thyme; others again mace and a bit of onion. Use your own discretion in this regard.

CLAM SOUP (French Style)

Mince two-dozen hard-shell clams very fine. Fry half a minced onion in an ounce of butter; add to it a pint of hot water, a pinch of mace, four cloves, one allspice and six whole peppercorns. Boil fifteen minutes and strain into a saucepan; add the chopped clams and a pint of clam-juice or hot water; simmer slowly two hours; strain and rub the pulp through a sieve into the liquid. Return it to the saucepan and keep it lukewarm. Boil three half-pints of milk in a saucepan (previously wet with cold water, which prevents burning) and whisk it into the soup. Dissolve a teaspoonful of flour in cold milk, add it to the soup, taste for seasoning; heat it gently to near the boiling point; pour into a tureen previously heated with hot water, and serve with or without pieces of fried bread – called *croutons* in kitchen French.

CLAM SOUP

Twenty-five clams chopped fine. Put over the fire the liquor that was drained from them, and a cup of water; add the chopped clams and boil half an hour; then season to taste with pepper and salt and a piece of butter as large as an egg; boil up again and add one quart of milk boiling hot, stir in a tablespoon of flour made to a cream with a little cold milk, or two crackers rolled fine. Some like a little mace and lemon juice in the seasoning.

Eat Like a President: Book I

SOUPS WITHOUT MEAT

SPRING VEGETABLE SOUP

Half pint green peas, two shredded lettuces, one onion, a small bunch of parsley, two ounces butter, the yolks of three eggs, one pint of water, one and a half quarts of soup stock. Put in a stew pan the lettuce, onion, parsley and butter, with one pint of water, and let them simmer till tender. Season with salt and pepper. When done, strain off the vegetables, and put two-thirds of the liquor with the stock. Beat up the yolks of the eggs with the other third, toss it over the fire, and at the moment of serving add this with the vegetables to the strained-off soup.

WINTER VEGETABLE SOUP

Scrape and slice three turnips and three carrots and peel three onions, and fry all with a little butter until a light yellow; add a bunch of celery and three or four leeks cut in pieces; stir and fry all the ingredients for six minutes; when fried, add one clove of garlic, two stalks of parsley, two cloves, salt, pepper and a little grated nutmeg; cover with three quarts of water and simmer for three hours, taking off the scum carefully. Strain and use. Croutons, vermicelli, Italian pastes, or rice may be added.

SWISS WHITE SOUP

A sufficient quantity of broth for six people; boil it; beat up three eggs well, two spoonfuls of flour, one cup milk; pour these gradually through a sieve into the boiling soup; salt and pepper.

CELERY SOUP

Celery soup may be made with *white stock*. Cut down the white of half a dozen heads of celery into little pieces and boil it in four pints of white stock, with a quarter of a pound of lean ham and two ounces of butter. Simmer gently for a full hour, then strain through a sieve, return the liquor to the pan, and stir in a few spoonfuls of cream with great care. Serve with toasted bread, and if liked, thicken with a little flour. Season to taste.

IRISH POTATO SOUP

Peel and boil eight medium-sized potatoes with a large onion sliced, some herbs, salt and pepper; press all through a colander; then thin it with rich milk and add a lump of butter, more seasoning, if necessary; let it heat well and serve hot.

CORN SOUP

Cut the corn from the cob, and boil the cobs in water for at least an hour, then add the grains, and boil until they are thoroughly done; put one dozen ears of corn to a gallon of water, which will be reduced to three quarts by the time the soup is done; then pour on a pint of new milk, two well-beaten eggs, salt and pepper to your taste; continue the boiling a while longer, and stir in, to season and thicken it a little, a tablespoonful of good butter rubbed up with two tablespoonfuls of flour. Corn soup may also be made nicely with water in which a pair of grown fowls have been boiled or parboiled, instead of having plain water for the foundation.

PEA SOUP

Put a quart of dried peas into five quarts of water; boil for four hours; then add three or four large onions, two heads of celery, a carrot, two turnips, all cut up rather fine. Season with pepper and salt. Boil two hours longer, and if the soup becomes too thick add more water. Strain through a colander and stir in a tablespoonful of cold butter. Serve hot, with small pieces of toasted bread placed in the bottom of the tureen.

SPLIT PEA SOUP

Wash well a pint of split peas and cover them well with cold water, adding a third of a teaspoonful of soda; let them remain in it over night to swell. In the morning put them in a kettle with a close fitting cover. Pour over them three quarts of cold water, adding half a pound of lean ham or bacon cut into slices or pieces; also a teaspoonful of salt and a little pepper, and some celery chopped fine. When the soup begins to boil, skim the froth from the surface. Cook slowly from three to four hours, stirring occasionally till the peas are all dissolved, adding a little more boiling water to keep up the quantity as it boils away. Strain through a colander, and leave out the meat. It should be quite quick. Serve with small squares of toasted bread, cut up and added. If not rich enough, add a small piece of butter.

CREAM OF ASPARAGUS

For making two quarts of soup, use two bundles of fresh asparagus. Cut the tops from one of the bunches and cook them twenty minutes in salted water, enough to cover them. Cook the remainder of the asparagus about twenty minutes in a quart of stock or water. Cut an onion into thin slices and fry in three tablespoonfuls of butter ten minutes, being careful not to scorch it; then add the asparagus that has been boiled in the stock; cook this five minutes, stirring constantly; then add three tablespoonfuls of dissolved flour, cook five minutes longer. Turn this mixture into the boiling stock and boil twenty minutes. Rub through a sieve; add the milk and cream and the asparagus heads. If water is used in place of stock, use all cream.

DRIED BEAN SOUP

Put two quarts of dried white beans to soak the night before you make the soup, which should be put on as early in the day as possible.

Take two pounds of the lean of fresh beef – the coarse pieces will do. Cut them up and put them into your soup pot with the bones belonging to them (which should be broken in pieces), and a pound of lean bacon, cut very small. If you have the remains of a piece of beef that has been roasted the day before, and so much underdone that the juices remain in it, you may put it into the pot and its bones along with it. Season the meat with pepper only, and pour on it six quarts of water. As soon as it boils, take off the scum, and put in the beans (having first drained them) and a head of celery cut small, or a tablespoonful of pounded celery seed. Boil it slowly till the meat is done to shreds, and the beans all dissolved. Then strain it through a colander into the tureen, and put into it small squares of toasted bread with the crust cut off.

TURTLE SOUP (from Beans)

Soak over night one quart of black beans; next day boil them in the proper quantity of water, say a gallon, then dip the beans out of the pot and strain them through a colander. Then return the flour of the beans, thus pressed, into the pot in which they were boiled. Tie up in a thin cloth some thyme, a teaspoonful of summer savory and parsley, and let it boil in the mixture. Add a tablespoonful of cold butter, salt and pepper. Have ready four hard-boiled yolks of eggs quartered, and a few force meatballs; add this to the soup with a sliced lemon, and half a glass of wine just before serving the soup.

This approaches so near in flavor to the real turtle soup that few are able to distinguish the difference.

JULIENNE SOUP

Cut carrots and turnips into quarter-inch pieces the shape of dice; also celery into thin slices. Cover them with boiling water; add a teaspoonful of salt, half a teaspoonful pepper, and cook until soft. In another saucepan have two quarts of boiling stock (see pages 27 and 30), to which add the cooked vegetables, the water and more seasoning if necessary. Serve hot.

In the spring and summer season use asparagus, peas and string beans – all cut into small uniform thickness.

CREAM OF SPINACH

Pick, wash and boil enough spinach to measure a pint, when cooked, chopped and pounded into a soft paste. Put it into a stew pan with four ounces of fresh butter, a little grated nutmeg, a teaspoonful of salt. Cook and stir it about ten minutes. Add to this two quarts of strong stock; let boil up, then rub it through a strainer. Set it over the fire again, and, when on the point of boiling, mix with it a tablespoonful of butter, and a teaspoonful of granulated sugar.

VERMICELLI SOUP

Swell quarter of a pound of vermicelli in a quart of warm water, then add it to a good beef, veal, lamb, or chicken soup or broth, with quarter of a pound of sweet butter; let the soup boil for fifteen minutes after it is added.

TAPIOCA CREAM SOUP

One quart of white stock; one pint of cream or milk; one onion; two stalks celery; one-third of a cupful of tapioca; two cupfuls of cold water; one tablespoonful of butter; a small piece of mace; salt, pepper. Wash the tapioca and soak over night in cold water. Cook it and the stock together very gently for one hour. Cut the onion and celery into small pieces, and put on to cook for twenty minutes with the milk and mace. Strain on the tapioca and stock. Season with salt and pepper, add butter and serve.

NOODLES FOR SOUP

Beat up one egg light, add a pinch of salt, and flour enough to make a *very stiff* dough; roll out very thin, like thin pie crust, dredge with flour to keep from sticking. Let it remain on the breadboard to dry for an hour or more; then roll it up into a tight scroll, like a sheet of music. Begin at the end and slice it into slips as thin as straws. After all are cut, mix them lightly together, and to prevent them sticking, keep them floured a little until you are ready to drop them into your soup which should be done shortly before dinner, for if boiled *too long* they will go to pieces.

EGG BALLS FOR SOUP

Take the yolks of six hard-boiled eggs and half a tablespoonful of wheat flour, rub them smooth with the yolks of two raw eggs and a teaspoonful of salt; mix all well together; make it in balls, and drop them into the boiling soup a few minutes before taking it up.

Used in green turtle soup.

EGG DUMPLINGS FOR SOUP

To half a pint of milk put two well-beaten eggs, and as much wheat flour as will make a smooth, rather *thick* batter free from lumps; drop this batter, a tablespoonful at a time, into boiling soup.

Another Mode – One cupful of sour cream and one cupful of sour milk, three eggs, well beaten, whites and yolks separately; one teaspoonful of salt, one level teaspoonful of soda, dissolved in a spoonful of water, and enough flour added to make a *very stiff* batter. To be dropped by spoonfuls into the broth and boiled twenty minutes, or until no raw dough shows on the outside.

SUET DUMPLINGS FOR SOUP

Three cups of sifted flour in which three teaspoonfuls of baking powder have been sifted; one cup of finely chopped suet, well rubbed into the flour, with a teaspoonful of salt. Wet all with sweet milk to make a dough as stiff as biscuit. Make into small balls as large as peaches, well floured. Drop into the soup three-quarters of an hour before being served. This requires steady boiling, being closely covered, and the cover not to be removed until taken up to serve. A very good form of potpie.

CROUTONS FOR SOUP

In a frying pan have the depth of an inch of boiling fat; also have prepared slices of stale bread cut up into little half-inch squares; drop into the frying pan enough of these bits of bread to cover the surface of the fat. When browned, remove with a skimmer and drain; add to the hot soup and serve.

Some prefer them prepared in this manner:

Take very thin slices of bread, butter them well; cut them up into little squares three-fourths of an inch thick, place them in a baking pan, buttered side up, and brown in a quick oven.

Eat Like a President: Book I

FAVORITE SOUPS

TOMATO SOUP No. 1

Place in a kettle four pounds of beef. Pour over it one gallon of cold water. Let the meat and water boil slowly for three hours, or until the liquid is reduced to about one-half. Remove the meat and put into the broth a quart of tomatoes, and one chopped onion; salt and pepper to taste. A teaspoonful of flour should be dissolved and stirred in, then allowed to boil half an hour longer. Strain and serve hot. Canned tomatoes in place of fresh ones may be used.

TOMATO SOUP No. 2

Place over the fire a quart of peeled tomatoes, stew them soft with a pinch of soda. Strain it so that no seeds remain, set it over the fire again, and add a quart of hot boiled milk; season with salt and pepper, a piece of butter the size of an egg, add three tablespoonfuls of rolled cracker, and serve hot. Canned tomatoes may be used in place of fresh ones.

TOMATO SOUP No. 3

Peel two quarts of tomatoes, boil them in a saucepan with an onion, and other soup vegetables; strain and add a level tablespoonful of flour dissolved in a third of a cup of melted butter; add pepper and salt. Serve very hot over little squares of bread fried brown and crisp in butter.

An excellent addition to a cold meat lunch.

ONION SOUP

One quart of milk, six large onions, yolks of four eggs, three tablespoonfuls of butter, a large one of flour, one cup full of cream, salt, pepper. Put the butter in a frying pan. Cut the onions into thin slices and drop in the butter. Stir until they begin to cook; then cover tight and set back where they will simmer, but not burn, for half an hour. Now put the milk on to boil, and then add the dry flour to the onions and stir constantly for three minutes over the fire; then turn the mixture into the milk and cook fifteen minutes. Rub the soup through a strainer, return to the fire, season with salt and pepper. Beat the yolks of the eggs well, add the cream to them and stir into the soup. Cook three minutes, stirring constantly. If you have no cream, use milk, in which case add a tablespoonful of butter at the same time. Pour over fried croutons in a soup tureen.

This is a refreshing dish when one is fatigued.

LOBSTER BISQUE

Have ready a good broth made of three pounds of veal boiled slowly in as much water as will cover it, till the meat is reduced to shreds. It must then be well strained.

Having boiled one fine middle-sized lobster, extract all

the meat from the body and claws. Bruise part of the coral in a mortar, and also an equal quantity of the meat. Mix them well together. Add mace, cayenne, salt and pepper, and make them up into force meatballs, binding the mixture with the yolk of an egg slightly beaten.

Take three quarts of the veal broth and put it into the meat of the lobster cut into mouthfuls. Boil it together about twenty minutes. Then thicken it with the remaining coral (which you must first rub through a sieve), and add the force meatballs and a little butter rolled in flour. Simmer it gently for ten minutes, but do not let it come to a boil, as that will injure the color. Serve with small dice of bread fried brown in butter.

Eat Like a President: Book I

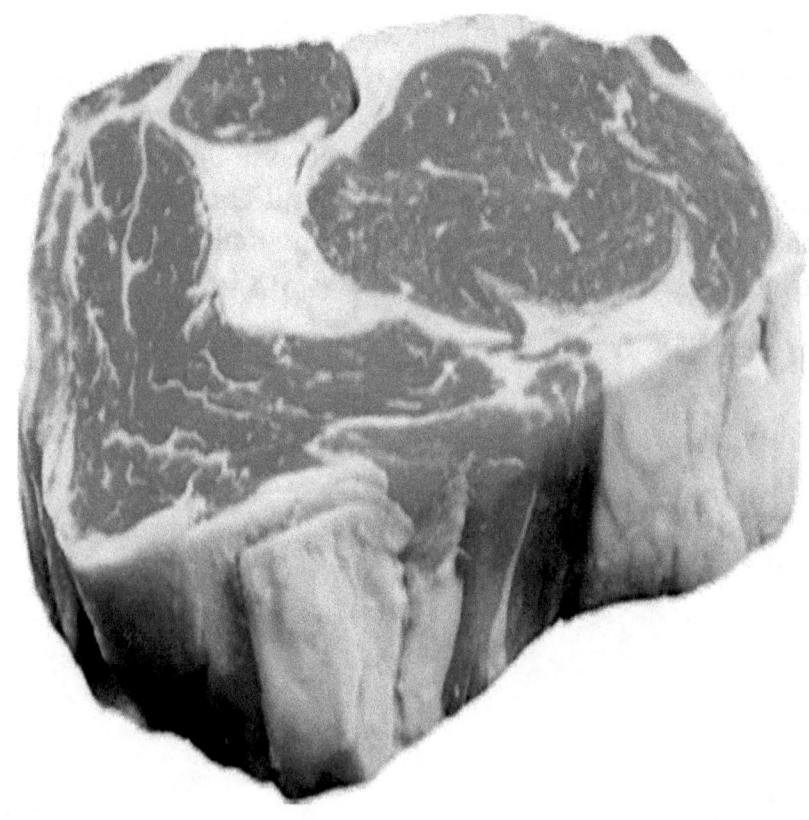

MEATS

Preparations

In the selection of meat it is most essential that we understand how to choose it; in beef it should be a smooth, fine grain, of a clear bright red color, the fat white, and will feel tender when pinched with the fingers. Will also have abundant kidney fat or suet. The choicest pieces for roast are the sirloin, fore and middle ribs.

Veal, to be good, should have the flesh firm and dry, fine grained and a delicate pinkish color, and plenty of kidney fat; the joints stiff.

Mutton is good when the flesh is a bright red, firm and juicy and a close grain, the fat firm and white.

Pork, if young, the lean will break on being pinched smooth when nipped with the fingers, also the skin will break and dent; if the rind is rough and hard it is old.

In roasting meat, allow from fifteen to twenty minutes to the pound, which will vary according to the thickness of the roast. A great deal of the success in roasting depends on the heat and goodness of the fire; if put into a cool oven it loses its juices, and the result is a tough, tasteless roast;

whereas, if the oven is of the proper heat, it immediately sears up the pores of the meat and the juices are retained.

The oven should be the hottest when the meat is put into it, in order to quickly crisp the surface and close the pores of the meat, thereby confining its natural juices. If the oven is too hot to hold the hand in for only a moment, then it is right to receive the meat. The roast should first be washed in pure water, then wiped dry with a clean dry cloth, placed in a baking pan without any seasoning; some pieces of suet or cold drippings laid under it, but *no water* should be put into the pan, for this would have a tendency to soften the outside of the meat. The water can never get so hot as the hot fat upon the surface of the meat, and the generating of the steam prevents its crispness, so desirable in a roast.

It should be frequently basted with its own drippings, which flow from the meat when partly cooked, and well seasoned. Lamb, veal and pork should be cooked rather slower than beef, with a more *moderate* fire, covering the fat with a piece of paper, and *thoroughly* cooked till the flesh parts from the bone, and nicely browned, without being burned. An onion sliced and put on top of a roast while cooking, especially roast of pork, gives a nice flavor. Remove the onion before serving.

Larding meats is drawing ribbons of fat pork through the upper surface of the meat, leaving both ends protruding. This is accomplished by the use of a larding needle, which may be procured at house-furnishing stores.

Boiling or stewing meat, if fresh, should be put into *boiling* water, closely covered and boiled *slowly*, allowing twenty minutes to each pound, and, when partly cooked, or when it begins to get tender, salted, adding spices and vegetables.

Salt meats should be covered with *cold* water, and require thirty minutes *very slow* boiling, from the time the water boils, for each pound; if it is very salt, pour off the first water and put it in another of boiling water, or it may be soaked one night in cold water. After meat commences to boil the pot should *never stop* simmering and always be replenished from the *boiling* teakettle.

Frying may be done in two ways. One method, which is most generally used, is by putting one ounce or more (as the case requires) of beef drippings, lard or butter into a frying pan, and when at the *boiling point* lay in the meat, cooking both sides a nice brown. The other method is to *completely immerse* the article to be cooked in sufficient *hot* lard to cover it, similar to frying doughnuts.

Broiled meats should be placed over clear, red coals free from smoke, giving out a good heat, but not too brisk, or the meat will be hardened and scorched; but if the fire is dead the gravy will escape and drop upon the coals, creating a blaze, which will blacken and smoke the meat. Steaks and chops should be turned often, in order that every part should be evenly done – never sticking a fork into the lean part, as that lets the juices escape; it should be put into the outer skin or fat. When the meat is sufficiently broiled it should be laid on a *hot* dish and seasoned. The best pieces for steak are the porterhouse, sirloin and rump.

THAWING FROZEN MEAT, ETC.

If meat, poultry, fish, vegetables, or any other article of food, when found frozen, is thawed by putting it into *warm water* or placing it before the fire, it will most certainly spoil by that process, and be rendered unfit to eat.

The only way to thaw these things is by immersing them in *cold* water. This should be done as soon as they are brought in from market, that they may have time to be well thawed before they are cooked.

If meat that has been frozen is to be boiled, put it on in cold water. If to be roasted, begin by setting it at a distance from the fire, for if it should not chance to be thoroughly thawed all through to the center, placing it at first too near the fire will cause it to spoil. If it is expedient to thaw the meat or poultry the night before cooking, lay it in cold water early in the evening, and change the water at bedtime. If found crusted with ice in the morning, remove the ice, and put the meat in fresh cold water, letting it lie in it till wanted for cooking.

Potatoes are injured by being frozen. Other vegetables are not the worse for it, provided they are always thawed in cold water.

TO KEEP MEAT FROM FLIES

Put in sacks, with enough straw around it so the flies cannot reach through. Three-fourths of a yard of yard-wide muslin is the right size for the sack. Put a little straw in the bottom, then put in the ham and lay straw in all around it; tie it tightly and hang it in a cool, dry place. Be sure the straw is all around the meat, so the flies cannot reach through to deposit the eggs. (The sacking must be done early in the season before the fly appears.) Muslin lets the air in and is much better than paper. Thin muslin is as good as thick, and will last for years if washed when laid away when emptied.

Hugo Ziemann and Fanny Lemira Gillette

National Stockman.

TO FRY BEEFSTEAKS

Beefsteak for frying should be cut much thinner than for broiling. Take from the ribs or sirloin and remove the bone. Put some butter or nice beef dripping into a frying pan and set it over the fire, and when it has boiled and become hot lay in the steaks; when cooked quite enough, season with salt and pepper, turn and brown on both sides. Steaks when fried should be thoroughly done. Have ready a hot dish, and when they are done take out the steaks and lay them on it, with another dish cover the top to keep them hot. The gravy in the pan can be turned over the steaks, first adding a few drops of boiling water, or a gravy to be served in a separate dish made by putting a large tablespoonful of flour into the hot gravy left in the pan after taking up the steaks. Stir it smooth, then pour in a pint of cream or sweet rich milk, salt and pepper, let it boil up once until it thickens, pour hot into a gravy dish and send to the table with the steaks.

TO CURE HAMS AND BACON (A Prize Recipe)

For each hundred pounds of hams, make a pickle of ten pounds of salt, two pounds of brown sugar, two ounces of saltpeter, one ounce of red pepper, and from four to four and a half gallons of water, or just enough to cover the hams, after being packed in a water-tight vessel, or enough salt to make a brine to float a fresh egg high enough, that is to say, out of water. First rub the hams with common salt and lay them into a tub. Take the above ingredients, put them into a vessel over the fire, and heat it hot, stirring it frequently;

remove all the scum, allow it to boil ten minutes, let it cool and pour over the meat. After laying in this brine five or six weeks, take out, drain and wipe, and smoke from two to three weeks. Small pieces of bacon may remain in this pickle two weeks, which would be sufficient.

TO SMOKE HAMS AND FISH AT HOME

Take an old hogshead, stop up all the crevices, and fix a place to put a cross-stick near the bottom, to hang the article to be smoked on. Next, in the side, cut a hole near the top, to introduce an iron pan filled with hickory wood sawdust and small pieces of green wood. Having turned the hogshead upside down, hang the articles upon the cross-stick, introduce the iron pan in the opening, and place a piece of red-hot iron in the pan, cover it with sawdust, and all will be complete. Let a large ham remain ten days, and keep up a good smoke.

The best way for keeping hams is to sew them in coarse cloths, whitewashed on the outside.

TO CURE ENGLISH BACON

This process is called the "dry cure," and is considered far preferable to the New England or Yankee style of putting prepared brine or pickle over the meat. First the hog should not be too large or too fat, weighing not over two hundred pounds, then after it is dressed and cooled cut it up into proper pieces; allow to every hundred pounds a mixture of four quarts of common salt, one quarter of a pound of saltpeter and four pounds of sugar. Rub this preparation thoroughly over and into each piece, then place them into a tight tub or suitable cask; there will a brine form of itself from the juices of the meat, enough at least to baste it with, which should be done two or three times a week; turning each piece every time.

In smoking this bacon, the sweetest flavor is derived from black birch chips, but if these are not to be had, the next best wood is hickory; the smoking with corncobs imparts a rank flavor to this bacon, which is very distasteful to English people visiting this country. It requires three weeks or a month to smoke this bacon properly.

Berkshire Recipe.

TO TRY OUT LARD

Skin the leaf lard carefully, cut it into small pieces, and put it into a kettle or saucepan; pour in a cupful of water to prevent burning; set it over the fire where it will melt slowly. Stir it frequently and let it simmer until nothing remains but brown scraps. Remove the scraps with a perforated skimmer, throw in a little salt to settle the fat, and, when clear, strain through a coarse cloth into jars. Remember to watch it constantly, stirring it from the bottom until the salt is thrown in to settle it; then set it back on the range until clear. If it scorches it gives it a very bad flavor.

Eat Like a President: Book I

MODES OF FRYING

The usual custom among professional cooks is to entirely immerse the article to be cooked in boiling fat, but from inconvenience most households use the half-frying method of frying in a small amount of fat in a frying pan. For the first method a shallow iron frying kettle, large at the top and small at the bottom, is best to use. The fat should half fill the kettle, or an amount sufficient to float whatever is to be fried; the heat of the fat should get to such a degree that, when a piece of bread or a teaspoonful of the batter is dropped in it, it will become brown almost instantly, but should not be so hot as to burn the fat. Some cooks say that the fat should be smoking, but my experience is, that is a mistake, as that soon ruins the fat. As soon as it begins to smoke it should be removed a little to one side, and still be kept at the boiling point. If fritters, crullers, croquettes, etc., are dropped into fat that is too hot, it crusts over the outside before the inside has fully risen, making a heavy, hard article, and also ruining the fat, giving it a burnt flavor.

Many French cooks prefer beef fat or suet to lard for frying purposes, considering it more wholesome and digestible, does not impart as much flavor, or adhere or soak into the article cooked as pork fat.

In families of any size, where there is much cooking required, there are enough drippings and fat remnants from roasts of beef, skimmings from the soup kettle, with the addition of occasionally a pound of suet from the market, to amply supply the need. All such remnants and skimmings should be clarified about twice a week, by boiling them all together in water. When the fat is all melted, it should be strained with the water and set aside to cool. After the fat on the top has hardened, lift the cake from the water on which it lies, scrape off all the dark particles from the bottom, then melt over again the fat; while hot strain into a small clean stone jar or bright tin pail, and then it is ready for use. Always after frying anything, the fat should stand until it settles and has cooled somewhat; then turn off carefully so as to leave it clear from the sediment that settles at the bottom.

Refined cottonseed oil is now being adopted by most professional cooks in hotels, restaurants and many private households for culinary purposes, and will doubtless in future supersede animal fats, especially for frying, it being quite as delicate a medium as frying with olive oil. It is now sold by leading grocers, put up in packages of two and four quarts.

The second mode of frying, using a frying pan with a small quantity of fat or grease, to be done properly, should, in the first place, have the frying pan hot over the fire, and the fat in it *actually boiling* before the article to be cooked is placed in it, the intense heat quickly searing up the pores of the article and forming a brown crust on the lower side, then turning over and browning the other the same way.

Still, there is another mode of frying; the process is somewhat similar to broiling, the hot frying pan or spider replacing the hot fire. To do this correctly, a thick-bottomed frying pan should be used. Place it over the fire, and when it is so hot that it will siss, oil over the bottom of the pan with a piece of suet, that is if the meat is all lean; if not, it is not necessary to grease the bottom of the pan. Lay in the meat quite flat, and brown it quickly, first on one side, then on the other; when sufficiently cooked, dish on a *hot* platter and season the same as broiled meats.

Eat Like a President: Book I

MEAT RECIPES

ROAST BEEF

One very essential point in roasting beef is to have the oven well heated when the beef is first put in; this causes the pores to close up quickly, and prevents the escape of the juices.

Take a rib piece or loin roast of seven or eight pounds. Wipe it thoroughly all over with a clean wet towel. Lay it in a dripping-pan, and baste it well with butter or suet fat. Set it in the oven.

Baste it frequently with its own drippings, which will make it brown and tender. When partly done season with salt and pepper, as it hardens any meat to salt it when raw, and draws out its juices, then dredge with sifted flour to give it a frothy appearance.

It will take a roast of this size about two hours' time to be properly done, leaving the inside a little rare or red – half an hour less would make the inside quite rare. Remove the beef to a heated dish, set where it will keep hot; then skim the drippings from all fat, add a tablespoonful of sifted flour, a little pepper and a teacupful of boiling water. Boil up once and serve hot in a gravy boat.

Some prefer the clear gravy without the thickening. Serve with mustard or grated horseradish and vinegar.

YORKSHIRE PUDDING

This is a very nice accompaniment to a roast of beef; the ingredients are, one pint of milk, four eggs, whites and yolks beaten separately, one teaspoonful of salt, and two teaspoonfuls of baking powder sifted through two cups of flour. It should be mixed very smooth, about the consistency of cream. Regulate your time when you put in your roast, so that it will be done half an hour or forty minutes before dishing up. Take it from the oven, set it where it will keep hot. In the meantime have this pudding prepared. Take two common biscuit tins, dip some of the drippings from the dripping-pan into these tins, pour half of the pudding into each, set them into the hot oven, and keep them in until the dinner is dished up; take these puddings out at the last moment and send to the table hot. This I consider much better than the old way of baking the pudding under the meat.

BEEFSTEAK No. 1

The first consideration in broiling is to have a clear, glowing bed of coals. The steak should be about three-quarters of an inch in thickness, and should be pounded only in extreme cases, *i.e.*, when it is cut *too* thick and is "stringy." Lay it on a buttered gridiron, turning it often, as it begins to drip, attempting nothing else while cooking it. Have everything else ready for the table; the potatoes and vegetables dished and in the warming closet. Do not season it until it is done, which will be in about ten to twelve minutes. Remove it to a warm platter, pepper and salt it on both sides and spread a liberal lump of butter over it. Serve at once while hot.

No definite rule can be given as to the *time* of cooking steak, individual tastes differ so widely in regard to it, some only liking it when well done, others so rare that the blood runs out of it. The best pieces for broiling are the porterhouse and sirloin.

BEEFSTEAK No. 2

Take a smooth, thick-bottomed frying pan, scald it out with hot water, and wipe it dry; set it on the stove or range, and when *very* hot, rub it over the bottom with a rag dipped in butter; then place your steak or chops in it, turn often until cooked through, take up on a warm platter, and season both sides with salt, pepper and butter. Serve hot.

Many prefer this manner of cooking steak rather than broiling or frying in a quantity of grease.

BEEFSTEAK AND ONIONS

Prepare the steak in the usual way. Have ready in a frying pan a dozen onions cut in slices and fried brown in a little beef drippings or butter. Dish your steak, and lay the onions thickly over the top. Cover and let stand five minutes, then send to the table hot.

BEEFSTEAK AND OYSTERS

Broil the steak the usual way. Put one quart of oysters with very little of the liquor into a stew pan upon the fire; when it comes to a boil, take off the scum that may rise, stir in three ounces of butter mixed with a tablespoonful of sifted flour, let it boil one minute until it thickens, pour it over the steak. Serve hot.

Palace Hotel, San Francisco.

POT ROAST (Old Style)

This is an old-fashioned dish, often cooked in our grandmothers' time. Take a piece of fresh beef weighing about five or six pounds. It must not be *too fat*. Wash it and put it into a pot with barely sufficient water to cover it. Set it over a slow fire, and after it has stewed an hour salt and pepper it. Then stew it slowly until tender, adding a little onion if liked. Do not replenish the water at the last, but let all nearly boil away. When tender all through take the meat from the pot and pour the gravy in a bowl. Put a large lump of butter in the bottom of the pot, then dredge the piece of meat with flour and return it to the pot to brown, turning it often to prevent its burning. Take the gravy that you have poured from the meat into the bowl and skim off all the fat; pour this gravy in with the meat and stir in a large spoonful of flour wet with a little water; let it boil up ten or fifteen minutes and pour into a gravy dish. Serve both hot, the meat on a platter. Some are very fond of this way of cooking a piece of beef which has been previously placed in spiced pickle for two or three days.

SPICED BEEF (Excellent)

For a round of beef weighing twenty or twenty-four pounds, take one-quarter of a pound of saltpeter, one-quarter of a pound of coarse brown sugar, two pounds of salt, one ounce of cloves, one ounce of allspice and half an ounce of mace; pulverize these materials, mix them well together, and with them rub the beef thoroughly on every part; let the beef lie for eight or ten days in the pickle thus made, turning and rubbing it every day; then tie it around with a broad tape, to keep it in shape; make a coarse paste of flour and water, lay a little suet finely chopped over and under the beef, enclose the beef entirely in the paste, and bake it six hours. When you take the beef from the oven, remove the paste, but do not remove the tape until you are ready to send it to the table. If you wish, to eat the beef cold, keep it well covered that it may retain its moisture.

BEEF Á LA MODE

Mix together three teaspoonfuls of salt, one of pepper, one of ginger, one of mace, one of cinnamon, and two of cloves. Rub this mixture into ten pounds of the upper part of a round of beef. Let this beef stand in this state over night. In the morning, make a dressing or stuffing of a pint of fine breadcrumbs, half a pound of fat salt pork cut in dice, a teaspoonful of ground thyme or summer savory, two teaspoonfuls sage, half a teaspoonful of pepper, one of nutmeg, a little cloves, an onion minced fine, moisten with a little milk or water. Stuff this mixture into the place from whence you took out the bone. With a long skewer fasten the two ends of the beef together, so that its form will be circular, and bind it around with tape to prevent the skewers giving way. Make incisions in the beef with a sharp knife; fill these incisions very closely with the stuffing, and dredge the whole with flour.

Put it into a dripping-pan and pour over it a pint of hot water; turn a large pan over it to keep in the steam, and roast slowly from three to four hours, allowing a quarter of an hour to each pound of meat. If the meat should be tough, it may be stewed first in a pot, with water enough to cover it, until tender, and then put into a dripping-pan and browned in the oven.

If the meat is to be eaten hot, skim off the fat from the gravy, into which, after it is taken off the fire, stir in the beaten yolks of two eggs. If onions are disliked you may omit them and substitute minced oysters.

TENDERLOIN OF BEEF

To serve tenderloin as directed below, the whole piece must be extracted before the hindquarter of the animal is cut out. This must be particularly noted, because not commonly practiced, the tenderloin being usually left attached to the roasting pieces, in order to furnish a tidbit for a few.

To dress it whole, proceed as follows: Washing the piece well, put it in an oven; add about a pint of water, and chop up a good handful of each of the following vegetables as an ingredient of the dish, *viz.*, Irish potatoes, carrots, turnips and a large bunch of celery. They must be washed, peeled and chopped up raw, then added to the meat; blended with the juice, they form and flavor the gravy. Let the whole slowly simmer, and when nearly done, add a teaspoonful of pounded allspice. To give a richness to the gravy, put in a tablespoonful of butter. If the gravy should look too greasy, skim off some of the melted suet. Boil also a lean piece of beef, which, when perfectly done, chop fine, flavoring with a very small quantity of onion, besides pepper and salt to the taste. Make into small balls, wet them on the outside with eggs, roll in grated cracker or fine breadcrumbs. Fry these force meat balls a light brown. When serving the dish, put these around the tenderloin, and pour over the whole the rich gravy. This dish is a very handsome one, and, altogether, fit for an epicurean palate. A sumptuous dish.

STEWED STEAK WITH OYSTERS

Two pounds of rump steak, one pint of oysters, one tablespoonful of lemon juice, three of butter, one of flour, salt, pepper, one cupful of water. Wash the oysters in the water and drain into a stew pan. Put this liquor on to heat. As soon as it comes to a boil, skim and set back. Put the butter in a frying pan, and when hot, put in a steak. Cook ten minutes. Take up the steak, and stir the flour into the butter remaining in the pan. Stir until a dark brown. Add the oyster liquor and boil one minute. Season with salt and pepper. Put back the steak, cover the pan, and simmer half an hour or until the steak seems tender, then add the oysters and lemon juice. Boil one minute. Serve on a hot dish with points of toast for a garnish.

SMOTHERED BEEFSTEAK

Take *thin* slices of steak from the upper part of the round or one large thin steak. Lay the meat out smoothly and wipe it dry. Prepare a dressing, using a cupful of fine breadcrumbs, half a teaspoonful of salt, some pepper, a tablespoonful of butter, half a teaspoonful of sage, the same of powdered summer savory, and enough milk to moisten it all into a stiff mixture. Spread it over the meat, roll it up carefully, and tie with a string, securing the ends well. Now fry a few thin slices of salt pork in the bottom of a kettle or saucepan, and into the fat that has fried out of this pork, place this roll or rolls of beef, and brown it on all sides, turning it until a rich color all over, then add half a pint of water, and stew until tender. If the flavor of onion is liked, a slice may be chopped fine and added to the dressing. When cooked sufficiently, take out the meat, thicken the gravy, and turn over it. To be carved cutting crosswise, in slices, through beef and stuffing.

BEEFSTEAK ROLLS

This mode is similar to the above recipe, but many might prefer it.

Prepare a good dressing, such as you like for turkey or duck; take a round steak, pound it, but not very hard, spread the dressing over it, sprinkle in a little salt, pepper, and a few bits of butter, lap over the ends, roll the steak up tightly and tie closely; spread two great spoonfuls of butter over the steak after rolling it up, then wash with a well-beaten egg, put water in the bake-pan, lay in the steak so as not to touch the water, and bake as you would a duck, basting often. A half-hour in a brisk oven will bake. Make a brown gravy and send to the table hot.

TO COLLAR A FLANK OF BEEF

Procure a well-corned flank of beef – say six pounds. Wash it, and remove the inner and outer skin with the gristle. Prepare a seasoning of one teaspoonful each of sage, parsley, thyme, pepper and cloves. Lay your meat upon a board and spread this mixture over the inside. Roll the beef up tight, fasten it with small skewers, put a cloth over it, bandage the cloth with tape, put the beef into the stewpot, cover it with water to the depth of an inch, boil gently six hours; take it out of the water, place it on a board without undoing it; lay a board on top of the beef, put a fifty pound weight upon this board, and let it remain twenty-four hours. Take off the bandage, garnish with green pickles and curled parsley, and serve.

DRIED BEEF

Buy the best of beef, or that part which will be the most lean and tender. The tender part of the round is a very good piece. For every twenty pounds of beef use one pint of salt, one teaspoonful of saltpeter, and a quarter of a pound of brown sugar. Mix them well together, and rub the beef well with one-third of the mixture for three successive days. Let it lie in the liquor it makes for six days, then hang up to dry.

A large crock or jar is a good vessel to prepare the meat in before drying it.

BEEF CORNED OR SALTED (Red)

Cut up a quarter of beef. For each hundredweight take half a peck of coarse salt, a quarter of a pound of saltpeter, the same weight of saleratus and a quart of molasses, or two pounds of coarse brown sugar. Mace, cloves and allspice may be added for spiced beef.

Strew some of the salt in the bottom of a pickle-tub or barrel, then put in a layer of meat, strew this with salt, then add another layer of meat, and salt and meat alternately, until all is used. Let it remain one night. Dissolve the saleratus and saltpeter in a little warm water, and put it to the molasses or sugar; then put it over the meat, add water enough to cover the meat, lay a board on it to keep it under the brine. The meat is fit for use after ten days. This recipe is for winter beef. Rather more salt may be used in warm weather.

Towards spring take the brine from the meat, make it boiling hot, skim it clear, and when it is cooled, return it to the meat.

Beef tongues and smoking pieces are fine pickled in this brine. Beef liver put in this brine for ten days, and then wiped dry and smoked, is very fine. Cut it in slices, and fry or broil it. The brisket of beef, after being corned, may be smoked, and is very good for boiling.

Lean pieces of beef, cut properly from the hindquarter, are the proper pieces for being smoked. There may be some fine pieces cut from the forequarter.

After the beef has been in brine ten days or more, wipe it dry, and hang it in a chimney where wood is burned, or make a smothered fire of sawdust or chips, and keep it smoking for ten days; then rub fine black pepper over every part to keep the flies from it, and hang it in a *dry, dark, cool place*. After a week it is fit for use. A strong, coarse brown paper, folded around the beef, and fastened with paste, keeps it nicely.

Tongues are smoked in the same manner. Hang them by a string put through the root end. Spiced brine for smoked beef or tongues will be generally liked.

ROAST BEEF PIE WITH POTATO CRUST

When you have a cold roast of beef, cut off as much as will half fill a baking dish suited to the size of your family; put this sliced beef into a stew pan with any gravy that you may have also saved, a lump of butter, a bit of sliced onion and a seasoning of pepper and salt, with enough water to make plenty of gravy; thicken it, too, by dredging in a tablespoonful of flour; cover it up on the fire, where it may stew gently, but not be in danger of burning.

Meanwhile there must be boiled a sufficient quantity of potatoes to fill up your baking dish, after the stewed meat has been transferred to it. The potatoes must be boiled done, mashed smooth, and beaten up with milk and butter, as if they were to be served alone, and placed in a thick layer on top of the meat. Brush it over with egg, place the dish in an oven, and let it remain there long enough to be brown. There should be a goodly quantity of gravy left with the beef, that the dish be not dry and tasteless. Serve with it tomato sauce, Worcestershire sauce or any other kind that you prefer. A good, plain dish.

ROAST BEEF PIE

Cut up roast beef, or beefsteak left from a previous meal, into thin slices, lay some of the slices into a deep dish which you have lined *on the sides* with rich biscuit dough, rolled very thin (say a quarter of an inch thick); now sprinkle over this layer a little pepper and salt; put in a small bit of butter, a few slices of cold potatoes, a little of the cold gravy, if you have any left from the roast. Make another layer of beef, another layer of seasoning, and so on, until the dish is filled; cover the whole with paste leaving a slit in the center, and bake half an hour.

BEEFSTEAK PIE

Cut up rump or flank steak into strips two inches long and about an inch wide. Stew them with the bone, in just enough water to cover them, until partly cooked; have half a dozen of cold boiled potatoes sliced. Line a baking dish with pie paste, put in a layer of the meat with salt, pepper, and a little of thinly-sliced onion, then one of the sliced potatoes, with bits of butter dotted over them. Then the steak, alternated with layers of potato, until the dish is full. Add the gravy or broth, having first thickened it with brown flour. Cover with a top crust, making a slit in the middle; brush a little beaten egg over it, and bake until quite brown.

FRIZZLED BEEF

Shave off *very thin* slices of smoked or dried beef, put them in a frying pan, cover with cold water, set it on the back of the range or stove, and let it come to a very slow heat, allowing it time to swell out to its natural size, but not to boil. Stir it up, then drain off the water. Melt one ounce of sweet butter in the frying pan and add the wafers of beef. When they begin to frizzle or turn up, break over them three eggs; stir until the eggs are cooked; add a little white pepper, and serve on slices of buttered toast.

FLANK STEAK

This is cut from the boneless part of the flank and is secreted between an outside and inside layer of creamy fat. There are two ways for broiling it. One is to slice diagonally across the grain; the other is to broil it whole. In either case brush butter over it and proceed as in broiling other steaks. It is considered by butchers to be the finest steak, which they frequently reserve for themselves.

TO BOIL CORNED BEEF

The aitch-bone and the brisket are considered the best pieces for boiling. If you buy them in the market already corned, they will be fit to put over the fire without a previous soaking in water. If you corn them in the brine in which you keep your beef through the winter, they must be soaked in cold water over night. Put the beef into a pot, cover with sufficient *cold* water, place over a brisk fire, let it come to a boil in half an hour; just before boiling remove all the scum from the pot, place the pot on the back of the fire, let it boil very slowly until quite tender.

A piece weighing eight pounds requires two and a half hours' boiling. If you do not wish to eat it hot, let it remain in the pot after you take it from the fire until nearly cold, then lay it in a colander to drain, lay a cloth over it to retain its fresh appearance; serve with horse-radish and pickles.

If vegetables are to accompany this, making it the old-fashioned "boiled dinner," about three-quarters of an hour before dishing up skim the liquor free from fat and *turn part of it out into another kettle,* into which put a cabbage carefully prepared, cutting it into four quarters; also half a dozen peeled medium-sized white turnips, cut into halves; scrape four carrots and four parsnips each cut into four pieces. Into the kettle with the meat, about half an hour before serving, pour on more water from the boiling teakettle, and into this put peeled medium-sized potatoes. This dinner should also be accompanied by boiled beets, sliced hot, cooked separate from the rest, with vinegar over them. Cooking the cabbage separately from the meat prevents the meat from having the flavor of cabbage when cold. The carrots, parsnips and turnips will boil in about an hour. A piece of salt pork was usually boiled with a "New

England boiled dinner."

SPICED BEEF RELISH

Take two pounds of raw, tender beefsteak, chop it *very fine*, put into it salt, pepper and a little sage, two tablespoonfuls of melted butter; add two rolled crackers made very fine, also two well-beaten eggs. Make it up into the shape of a roll and bake it; baste with butter and water before baking. Cut in slices when cold.

FRIED BEEF LIVER

Cut it in rather thin slices, say a quarter of an inch thick; pour over it *boiling* water, which closes the pores of the meat, makes it impervious to the fat, and at the same time seals up the rich juice of the meat. It may be rolled in flour or breadcrumbs, seasoned with salt and pepper, dipped in egg and fried in hot fat mixed with one-third butter.

PRESSED BEEF

First have your beef nicely pickled; let it stay in pickle a week; then take the thin, flaky pieces, such as will not make a handsome dish of themselves, put on a large potful, and let them boil until perfectly done; then pull to pieces, and season just as you do souse, with pepper, salt and allspice; only put it in a coarse cloth and press down upon it some very heavy weight.

The advantage of this recipe is that it makes a most acceptable, presentable dish out of a part of the beef that otherwise might be wasted.

FRENCH STEW

Grease the bottom of an iron pot, and place in it three or four pounds of beef; be very careful that it does not burn, and turn it until it is nicely browned. Set a muffin ring under the beef to prevent its sticking. Add a few sliced carrots, one or two sliced onions, and a cupful of hot water; keep covered and stew slowly until the vegetables are done. Add pepper and salt. If you wish more gravy, add hot water, and thicken with flour. Serve on a dish with the vegetables.

TO POT BEEF

The round is the best piece for potting, and you may use both the upper and under part. Take ten pounds of beef, remove all the fat, cut the lean into square pieces, two inches thick. Mix together three teaspoonfuls of salt, one of pepper, one of cloves, one of mace, one of cinnamon, one of allspice, one of thyme, and one of sweet basil. Put a layer of the pieces of beef into an earthen pot, sprinkle some of this spice mixture over this layer, add a piece of fat salt pork, cut as thin as possible, sprinkle a little of the spice mixture over the pork, make another layer of the beef with spices and pork, and so on, until the pot is filled. Pour over the whole three tablespoonfuls of Tarragon vinegar, or, if you prefer it, half a pint of Madeira wine; cover the pot with a paste made of flour and water, so that no steam can escape.

Put the pot into an oven, moderately heated, and let it stand there eight hours; then set it away to use when wanted.

Beef cooked in this manner will keep good for a fortnight in moderate weather.

It is an excellent relish for breakfast, and may be eaten either warm or cold. When eaten warm, serve with slices of lemon.

STEWED BRISKET OF BEEF

Put the part that has the hard fat into a stewpot with a small quantity of water; let it boil up and skim it thoroughly; then add carrots, turnips, onions, celery and a few peppercorns. Stew till extremely tender; then take out all the flat bones and remove all the fat from the soup. Either serve that and the meat in tureen, or the soup alone, and the meat on a dish garnished with some vegetables. The following sauce is much admired served with the beef: Take half a pint of the soup and mix it with a spoonful of ketchup, a teaspoonful of made mustard, a little flour, a bit of butter and salt; boil all together a few minutes, then pour it round the meat.

DRIED BEEF WITH CREAM

Shave your beef *very fine*. Put it into a suitable dish on the back of the stove; cover with cold water and give it time to soak out to its original size before being dried. When it is quite soft and the water has become hot (it must not boil) take it off, turn off the water, pour on a cup of cream; if you do not have it use milk and butter, a pinch of pepper; let it come to a boil, thicken with a tablespoonful of flour wet up in a little milk. Serve on dipped toast or not, just as one fancies. A nice breakfast dish.

BEEF CROQUETTES No. 1

Chop fine one cup of cold, cooked, lean beef, half a cup of fat, half a cup of cold boiled or fried ham; cold pork will do if you have not the ham. Also mince up a slice of onion. Season all with a teaspoonful of salt, half a teaspoonful of pepper, and a teaspoonful of powdered sage or parsley if liked. Heat together with half a cup of stock or milk; when cool add a beaten egg. Form the mixture into balls, slightly flattened, then roll in egg and breadcrumbs, or flour and egg. Fry in hot lard or beef drippings. Serve on a platter and garnish with sprigs of parsley. Almost any cold meats can be used instead of beef.

BEEF CROQUETTES No. 2

Take cold roast or corned beef. Put it into a wooden bowl and chop it fine. Mix with it about twice the quantity of hot mashed potatoes well seasoned with butter and salt. Beat up an egg and work it into the potato and meat, then form the mixture into little cakes the size of fish balls. Flatten them a little, roll in flour or egg and cracker crumbs, fry in butter and lard mixed, browning on both sides. Serve piping hot.

MEAT AND POTATO CROQUETTES

Put in a stew pan an ounce of butter and a slice of onion minced fine; when this simmers add a level tablespoonful of sifted flour; stir the mixture until it becomes smooth and frothy; then add half of a cupful of milk, some seasoning of salt and pepper; let all boil, stirring it all the while. Now add a cupful of cold meat chopped fine, and a cupful of cold or hot mashed potato. Mix all thoroughly and spread on a plate to cool. When it is cool enough, shape it with your hands into balls or rolls. Dip them in beaten egg and roll in cracker or breadcrumbs. Drop them into hot lard and fry about two minutes a delicate brown; take them out with a skimmer and drain them on a piece of brown paper. Serve immediately while hot. These are very nice.

Cold rice or hominy may be used in place of the potato; or a cupful of cold fish minced fine in place of the meat.

COLD ROAST (warmed) No. 1

Cut from the remains of a cold roast the lean meat from the bones into small, thin slices. Put over the fire a frying pan containing a spoonful of butter or drippings. Cut up a quarter of an onion and fry it brown, then remove the onion, add the meat gravy left from the day before, and if not thick enough add a little flour; salt and pepper. Turn the pieces of meat into this and let them *simmer* a few minutes. Serve hot.

COLD ROAST (warmed) No. 2

Cold rare roast beef may be made as good as when freshly cooked by slicing, seasoning with salt, pepper and bits of butter; put it in a plate or pan with a spoonful or two of water, covering closely, and set in the oven until hot, but no longer. Cold steak may be shaved very fine with a knife and used the same way.

Or, if the meat is in small pieces, cover them with buttered letter paper, twist each end tightly, and boil them on the gridiron, sprinkling them with finely chopped herbs.

Still another nice way of using cold meats is to mince the lean portions very fine and add to a batter made of one pint of milk, one cup of flour and three eggs. Fry like fritters and serve with drawn butter or sauce.

COLD MEAT AND POTATO (Baked)

Put in a frying pan a round tablespoonful of cold butter;

when it becomes hot, stir into it a teaspoonful of chopped onion and a tablespoonful of flour, stirring it constantly until it is smooth and frothy; then add two-thirds of a cupful of cold milk or water. Season this with salt and pepper and allow it to come to a boil; then add a cupful of cold meat finely chopped and cleared from bone and skin; let this all heat thoroughly; then turn it into a shallow dish well buttered. Spread hot or cold mashed potatoes over the top, and cook for fifteen or twenty minutes in a moderate hot oven.

Cold hominy, or rice may be used in place of mashed potatoes, and is equally as good.

BEEF HASH No. 1

Chop rather finely cold roast beef or pieces of beefsteak, also chop twice as much cold boiled potatoes. Put over the fire a stew pan or frying pan, in which put a piece of butter as large as required to season it well, add pepper and salt, moisten with beef gravy if you have it, if not, with hot water; cover and let it steam and heat through thoroughly, stirring occasionally, so that the ingredients be evenly distributed, and to keep the hash from sticking to the bottom of the pan. When done it should not be at all watery, nor yet dry, but have sufficient adhesiveness to stand well on a dish or buttered toast. Many like the flavor of onion; if so, fry two or three slices in the butter before adding the hash. Corned beef makes excellent hash.

BEEF HASH No. 2

Chop cold roast beef, or pieces of beefsteak; fry half an onion in a piece of butter; when the onion is brown, add the chopped beef; season with a little salt and pepper; moisten with the beef gravy, if you have any, if not, with sufficient water and a little butter; cook long enough to be hot, but no longer, as much cooking toughens the meat. An excellent breakfast dish.

Prof. Blot.

Some prefer to let a crust form on the bottom and turn the hash brown side uppermost. Served with poached eggs on top.

HAMBURGER STEAK

Take a pound of raw flank or round steak, without any fat, bone or stringy pieces. Chop it until a perfect mince, it cannot be chopped too fine. Also chop a small onion quite fine and mix well with the meat. Season with salt and pepper; make into cakes as large as a biscuit, but quite flat, or into one large flat cake a little less than half an inch thick. Have ready a frying pan with butter and lard mixed; when boiling hot put in the steak and fry brown. Garnish with celery top around the edge of the platter and two or three slices of lemon on the top of the meat.

A brown gravy made from the grease the steak was fried in and poured over the meat enriches it.

TO ROAST BEEF HEART

Wash it carefully and open it sufficiently to remove the ventricles, then soak it in cold water until the blood is discharged; wipe it dry and stuff it nicely with dressing, as for turkey; roast it about an hour and a half. Serve it with the gravy, which should be thickened with some of the stuffing and a glass of wine. It is very nice hashed. Served with currant jelly.

Palmer House, Chicago.

STEWED BEEF KIDNEY

Cut the kidney into slices, season highly with pepper and salt, fry it a light brown, take out the slices, then pour a little warm water into the pan, dredge in some flour, put in slices of kidney again; let them stew very gently; add some parsley if liked. Sheep's kidneys may be split open, broiled over a clear fire and served with a piece of butter placed on each half.

BEEFS HEART STEWED

After washing the heart thoroughly cut it up into squares half an inch long; put them into a saucepan with water enough to cover them. If any scum rises skim it off. Now take out the meat, strain the liquor and put back the meat, also add a sliced onion, some parsley, a head of celery chopped fine, pepper and salt and a piece of butter. Stew until the meat is very tender. Stir up a tablespoonful of browned flour with a small quantity of water and thicken the whole. Boil up and serve.

BOILED BEEF TONGUE

Wash a fresh tongue and just cover it with water in the pot; put in a pint of salt and a small red pepper; add more water as it evaporates, so as to keep the tongue nearly covered until done – when it can be easily pierced with a fork; take it out, and if wanted soon, take off the skin and set it away to cool. If wanted for future use, do not peel until it is required. A cupful of salt will do for three tongues, if you have that number to boil; but do not fail to keep water enough in the pot to keep them covered while boiling. If salt tongues are used, soak them over night, of course omitting the salt when boiling. Or, after peeling a tongue, place it in a saucepan with one cup of water, half a cup vinegar, four tablespoonfuls sugar, and cook until the liquor is evaporated.

SPICED BEEF TONGUE

Rub into each tongue a mixture made of half a pound of brown sugar, a piece of saltpeter the size of a pea and a tablespoonful of ground cloves, put it in a brine made of three-quarters of a pound of salt to two quarts of water and keep covered. Pickle two weeks, then wash well and dry with a cloth; roll out a thin paste made of flour and water, smear it all over the tongue and place in a pan to bake slowly; baste well with lard and hot water; when done scrape off the paste and skim.

TO BOIL TRIPE

Wash it well in warm water, and trim it nicely, taking off all the fat. Cut into small pieces, and put it on to boil five hours before dinner in water enough to cover it very well. After it has boiled four hours, pour off the water, season the tripe with pepper and salt, and put it into a pot with milk and water mixed in equal quantities. Boil it an hour in the milk and water.

Boil in a saucepan ten or a dozen onions. When they are quite soft, drain them in a colander and mash them. Wipe out your saucepan and put them on again, with a bit of butter rolled in flour and a wineglass of cream or milk.

Let them boil up, and add them to the tripe just before you send it to table. Eat it with pepper, vinegar and mustard.

It is best to give tripe its first and longest boiling the day before it is wanted.

TO FRY TRIPE

Boil the tripe the day before till it is quite tender, which it will not be in less than four or five hours. Then cover it and set it away. Next day cut it into long slips, and dip each piece into beaten yolk of egg, and afterwards roll them in grated breadcrumbs. Have ready in a frying pan over the fire some good beef drippings. When it is boiling hot put in the tripe, and fry it about ten minutes, till of a light brown.

You may serve it with onion sauce.

Boiled tripe that has been left from the dinner of the preceding day may be fried in this manner.

FRICASSEED TRIPE

Cut a pound of tripe in narrow strips, put a small cup of water or milk to it, add a bit of butter the size of an egg, dredge in a large teaspoonful of flour, or work it with the butter; season with pepper and salt, let it simmer gently for half an hour, serve hot. A bunch of parsley cut small and put with it is an improvement.

Some put in oysters five minutes before dishing up.

TRIPE LYONNAISE

Cut up half a pound of cold boiled tripe into neat squares. Put two ounces of butter and a tablespoonful of chopped onion in a frying pan and fry to a delicate brown;

add to the tripe a teaspoonful of chopped parsley and a little strong vinegar, salt and cayenne; stir the pan to prevent burning. Cover the bottom of a platter with tomato sauce, add the contents of the pan and serve.

TO CLARIFY BEEF DRIPPINGS

Drippings accumulated from different cooked meats of beef or veal can be clarified by putting it into a basin and slicing into it a raw potato, allowing it to boil long enough for the potato to brown, which causes all impurities to disappear. Remove from the fire, and when cool drain it off from the sediment that settles at the bottom. Turn it into basins or small jars and set it in a cool place for future use. When mixed with an equal amount of butter it answers the same purpose as clear butter for frying and basting any meats except game and poultry.

Mutton drippings impart an unpleasant flavor to anything cooked outside of its kind.

ROAST LOIN OF VEAL

Prepare it the same as any roast, leaving in the kidney, around which put considerable salt. Make a dressing the same as for fowls; unroll the loin, put the stuffing well around the kidney, fold and secure with several coils of white cotton twine wound around in all directions; place in a dripping-pan with the thick side down, and put in a rather hot oven, graduated after it commences to roast to moderate; in half an hour add a little hot water to the pan, and baste often; in another half hour turn over the roast, and when about done dredge lightly with flour and baste with melted butter.

Before serving carefully remove the twine. A roast of four to five pounds will bake in about two hours. For a gravy, skim off some of the fat if there is too much in the drippings; dredge in some flour, stir until brown, add some hot water if necessary; boil a few minutes, stir in such sweet herbs as fancied, and put in a gravy boat. Serve with green peas and lemon jelly. Is very nice sliced cold for lunch, and Worcestershire or Chili sauce forms a fine relish.

ROAST FILLET OF VEAL

Select a nice fillet, take out the bone, fill up the space with stuffing, and also put a good layer under the fat. Truss it of a good shape by drawing the fat round and tie it up with tape. Cook it rather moderately at first, and baste with butter. It should have careful attention and frequent basting, that the fat may not burn. Roast from three to four hours, according to the size. After it is dished pour melted butter over it; serve with ham or bacon, and fresh cucumbers if in season. Veal, like all other meat, should be well washed in cold water before cooking and wiped thoroughly dry with a clean cloth. Cold fillet of veal is very good stewed with tomatoes and an onion or two.

In roasting veal, care must be taken that it is not at first placed in too hot an oven; the fat of a loin, one of the most delicate joints of veal, should be covered with greased paper; a fillet, also, should have on the caul until nearly done enough.

BOILED FILLET OF VEAL

Choose a small, delicate fillet; prepare as for roasting, or stuff it with an oyster force meat; after having washed it thoroughly, cover it with water and let it boil very gently three and a half or four hours, keeping it well skimmed. Send it to the table with a rich white sauce, or, if stuffed with oysters, a tureen of oyster sauce. Garnish with stewed celery and slices of bacon. A boiled tongue should be served with it.

VEAL PUDDING

Cut about two pounds of lean veal into small collops a quarter of an inch in thickness; put a piece of butter the size of an egg into a very clean frying pan to melt; then lay in the veal and a few slices of bacon, a small sprig of thyme and a seasoning of pepper and salt; place the pan over a slow fire for about ten minutes, then add two or three spoonfuls of warm water. Just boil it up and then let it stand to cool. Line a pudding-dish with a good suet crust, lay in the veal and bacon, pour the gravy over it; roll out a piece of paste to form a lid, place it over, press it close with the thumb, tie the basin in a pudding cloth and put it into a saucepan of boiling water, keeping continually boiling until done, or about one hour.

FRIED VEAL CUTLETS

Put into a frying pan two or three tablespoonfuls of lard or beef drippings. When boiling hot lay in the cutlets, well seasoned with salt and pepper and dredged with flour. Brown nicely on both sides, then remove the meat, and if you have more grease than is necessary for the gravy put it aside for further use. Reserve a tablespoonful or more and rub into it a tablespoonful of flour, with the back of the spoon, until it is a smooth, rich brown color; then add gradually a cup of *cold water* and season with pepper and salt. When the gravy is boiled up well return the meat to the pan and gravy. Cover it closely and allow it to stew gently on the back of the range for fifteen minutes. This softens the meat, and with this gravy it makes a nice breakfast dish.

Another mode is to simply fry the cutlets, and afterwards turning off some of the grease they were fried in and then adding to that left in the pan a few drops of hot water, turning the whole over the fried chops.

FRIED VEAL CHOPS (Plain)

Sprinkle over them salt and pepper, then dip them in beaten egg and cracker crumbs, and fry in drippings, or hot lard and butter mixed. If you wish a gravy with them, add a tablespoonful of flour to the gravy they were fried in and turn in cream or milk; season to taste with salt and pepper. Boil up and serve hot with the gravy in separate dish. This dish is very fine accompanied with a few sound fresh tomatoes, sliced and fried in the same grease the cutlets were, and all dished on the same platter.

VEAL COLLOPS

Cut veal from the leg or other lean part into pieces the size of an oyster. Season with pepper, salt and a little mace; rub some over each piece; dip in egg, then into cracker crumbs and fry. They both look and taste like oysters.

VEAL OLIVES

Cut up a slice of a fillet of veal, about half an inch thick, into squares of three inches. Mix up a little salt pork, chopped with breadcrumbs, one onion, a little pepper, salt, sweet marjoram, and one egg well beaten; put this mixture upon the pieces of veal, fastening the four corners together with little bird skewers; lay them in a pan with sufficient veal gravy or light stock to cover the bottom of the pan, dredge with flour and set in a hot oven. When browned on top, put a small bit of butter on each, and let them remain until quite tender, which will take twenty minutes. Serve with horseradish.

VEAL CHEESE

Prepare equal quantities of boiled sliced veal and smoked tongue. Pound the slices separately in a mortar, moistening with butter as you proceed; then pack it in a jar or pail, mixing it in alternate layers; first the tongue and then the veal, so that when cut it will look variegated. Press it down hard and pour melted butter over the top. Keep it well covered and in a dry place. Nice for sandwiches, or sliced cold for lunch.

VEAL CROQUETTES

Mince a coffee cup of cold veal in a chopping bowl, adding a little cold ham and two or three slices of onion, a pinch of mace, powdered parsley and pepper, some salt. Let a pint of milk or cream come to the boiling point, then add a tablespoonful of cold butter, then the above mixture. Beat up two eggs and mix with a teaspoonful of cornstarch or flour, and add to the rest; cook it all about ten minutes, stirring with care. Remove from the fire, and spread it on a platter, roll it into balls, when cooled flatten each; dip them in egg and breadcrumbs, and fry in a wire basket, dipped in hot lard.

BROILED VEAL CUTLETS (Fine)

Two or three pounds of veal cutlets, egg and breadcrumbs, two tablespoonfuls of minced savory herbs, salt and pepper to taste, a little grated nutmeg.

Cut the cutlets about three-quarters of an inch in thickness; flatten them, and brush them over with the yolk of an egg; dip them into breadcrumbs and minced herbs, season with pepper and salt, and fold each cutlet in a piece of white letter paper well buttered; twist the ends, and broil over a clear fire; when done remove the paper. Cooked this way, they retain all the flavor.

VEAL POTPIE

Procure a nice breast or brisket of veal, well jointed, put the pieces into the pot with one quart of water to every five pounds of meat; put the pot over a slow fire; just before it comes to a boil, skim it well and pour in a teacupful of cold water; then turn over the meat in order that all the scum may rise; remove all the scum, boil quite hard, season with pepper and salt to your taste, always remembering that the crust will take up part of the seasoning; when this is done cut off your crust in pieces of equal size, but do not roll or mold them; lay them on top of the meat, so as to cover it; put the lid on the pot closely, let the whole boil slowly one hour. If the lid does not fit the pot closely, wrap a cloth around it, in order that no steam shall escape; and by no means allow the pot to *stop boiling.*

The crust for potpie should be raised with yeast. To three pints of flour add two ounces of butter, a little salt, and wet with milk sufficient to make a soft dough; knead it well and set it away to rise; when quite light, mold and knead it again, and let it stand, in winter, one hour, in summer, one-half hour, when it will be ready to cut.

In summer you had better add one-half a teaspoonful of soda when you knead it the second time, or you may wet it with water and add another bit of butter.

VEAL PIE

Cut the veal into rather small pieces or slices, put it in a stew pan with hot water to cover it; add to it a tablespoonful of salt and set it over the fire; take off the scum as it rises; when the meat is tender turn it into a dish to cool; take out all the small bones, butter a tin or earthen basin or pudding-pan, line it with pie paste, lay some of the parboiled meat in to half fill it; put bits of butter in the size of a hickory nut all over the meat; shake pepper over, dredge wheat flour over until it looks white, then fill it nearly to the top with some of the water in which the meat was boiled; roll a cover for the top of the crust, puff-paste it, giving it two or three turns, and roll it to nearly half an inch thickness; cut a slit in the center and make several small incisions on either side of it, put the crust on, trim the edges neatly with a knife; bake one hour in a quick oven. A breast of veal will make two two-quart basin pies; half a pound of nice corned pork, cut in thin slices and parboiled with the meat, will make it very nice, and very little, if any, butter will be required for the pie; when pork is used not other salt will be necessary. Many are fond of thin slices of sweet ham cooked with the veal for pie.

VEAL STEW

Cut up two or three pounds of veal into pieces three inches long and one thick. Wash it, put it into your stew pan with two quarts of water, let it boil, skim it well, and when all the scum is removed, add pepper and salt to your taste, and a small piece of butter; pare and cut in halves twelve small Irish potatoes, put them into the stew pan; when it boils, have ready a batter made with two eggs, two spoonfuls of cream or milk, a little salt, and flour enough to make it a little thicker than for pancakes; drop this into the stew, a spoonful at a time, while it is boiling; when all is in, cover the pan closely so that no steam can escape; let it boil twenty minutes and serve in a deep dish.

VEAL LOAF

Three pounds of raw veal chopped very fine, butter the size of an egg, three eggs, three tablespoonfuls of cream or milk; if milk use a small piece of butter; mix the eggs and cream together; mix with the veal four pounded crackers, one teaspoonful of black pepper, one large tablespoonful salt, one large tablespoonful of sage; mix well together and form into a loaf. Bake two and one-half hours, basting with butter and water while baking. Serve cut in thin slices.

VEAL FOR LUNCH

Butter a good-sized bowl, and line it with thin slices of hard-boiled eggs; have veal and ham both in very thin slices; place, in the bowl a layer of veal, with pepper and salt, then a layer of ham, omitting the salt, then a layer of veal, and so on, alternating with veal and ham, until the bowl is filled; make a paste of flour and water as stiff as it can be rolled out; cover the contents of the bowl with the paste, and over this tie a double cotton cloth; put the bowl into a saucepan, or other vessel, with water just up to the rim of the bowl, and boil three hours; then take it from the fire, remove the cloth and paste, and let it stand until the next day, when it may be turned out and served in very thin slices. An excellent lunch in traveling.

VEAL PATTIES

Cut portions of the neck or breast of veal into small pieces, and, with a little salt pork cut fine, stew gently for ten or fifteen minutes; season with pepper and salt, and a small piece of celery chopped coarsely, also of the yellow top, picked (not chopped) up; stir in a paste made of a tablespoonful of flour, the yolk of one egg, and milk to form a thin batter; let all come to a boil, and it is ready for the patties. Make the patties of a light, flaky crust, as for tarts, cut round, the size of a small sauce plate; the center of each, for about three inches, cut half way through, to be raised and serve as a cover. Put a spoonful of the stew in each crust, lay on the top and serve. Stewed oysters or lamb may be used in place of veal.

BRAISED VEAL

Take a piece of the shoulder weighing about five pounds. Have the bone removed and tie up the meat to make it firm. Put a piece of butter the size of half an egg, together with a few shavings of onion, into a kettle or stone crock and let it get hot. Salt and pepper the veal and put it into the kettle, cover it tightly and put it over a medium fire until the meat is brown on both sides, turning it occasionally. Then set the kettle back on the stove, where it will simmer slowly for about two hours and a half. Before setting the meat back on the stove, see if the juice of the meat together with the butter do not make gravy enough, and if not, put in about two tablespoonfuls of hot water. When the gravy is cold it will be like jelly. It can be served hot with the hot meat, or cold with the cold meat.

BAKED CALF'S HEAD

Boil a calf's head (after having cleaned it) until tender, then split it in two, and keep the best half (bone it if you like); cut the meat from the other in uniform pieces, the size of an oyster; put bits of butter, the size of a nutmeg, all over the best half of the head; sprinkle pepper over it, and dredge on flour until it looks white, then set it on a trivet or muffin rings in a dripping-pan; put a cup of water into the pan, and set it in a hot oven; turn it that it may brown evenly; baste once or twice. Whilst this is doing, dip the prepared pieces of the head in wheat flour or batter, and fry in hot lard or beef drippings a delicate brown; season with pepper and salt and slices of lemon, if liked. When the roast is done put it on a hot dish, lay the fried pieces around it, and cover it with a tin cover; put the gravy from the dripping-pan into the pan in which the pieces were fried, with the slices of lemon, and a tablespoonful of browned flour, and, if necessary, a little hot water. Let it boil up once, and strain it into a gravy boat, and serve with the meat.

CALF'S HEAD CHEESE

Boil a calf's head in water enough to cover it, until the meat leaves the bones; then take it with a skimmer into a wooden bowl or tray; take from it every particle of bone;

chop it small; season with pepper and salt, a heaping tablespoonful of salt and a teaspoonful of pepper will be sufficient; if liked, add a tablespoonful of finely chopped sweet herbs; lay in a cloth in a colander, put the minced meat into it, then fold the cloth closely over it, lay a plate over, and on it a gentle weight. When cold it may be sliced thin for supper or sandwiches. Spread each slice with made mustard.

BRAIN CUTLETS

Well wash the brains and soak them in cold water until white. Parboil them until tender in a small saucepan for about a quarter of an hour; then thoroughly drain them and place them on a board. Divide them into small pieces with a knife. Dip each piece into flour, and then roll them in egg and breadcrumbs, and fry them in butter or well-clarified drippings. Serve very hot with gravy. Another way of doing brains is to prepare them as above, and then stew them gently in rich stock, like stewed sweetbreads. They are also nice plainly boiled and served with parsley and butter sauce.

CALFS HEAD (Boiled)

Put the head into boiling water and let it remain about five minutes; take it out, hold it by the ear, and with the back of the knife scrape off the hair (should it not come off easily dip the head again in boiling water.) When perfectly clean take out the eyes, cut off the ears and remove the brain, which soak for an hour in warm water. Put the head to soak in hot water a few minutes to make it look white, and then have ready a stew pan, into which lay the head; cover it with cold water and bring it gradually to boil. Remove the scum and add a little salt, which increases it and causes it to rise to the top. Simmer it very gently from two and a half to three hours, or until the bones will slip out easily, and when nearly done, boil the brains fifteen or twenty minutes; skin and chop them (not too finely), add a tablespoonful of minced parsley which has been previously scalded; also a pinch of pepper, salt; then stir into this four tablespoonfuls of melted butter; set it on the back of the range to keep it hot.

When the head is done, take it up and drain very dry. Score the top and rub it over with melted butter; dredge it with flour and set it in the oven to brown.

When you serve the head, have it accompanied with a gravy boat of melted butter and minced parsley.

CALF'S LIVER AND BACON

Slice the liver a quarter of an inch thick; pour hot water over it and let it remain for a few minutes to clear it from blood; then dry it in a cloth. Take a pound of bacon, or as much as you require, and cut the same number of thin slices as you have of liver; fry the bacon to a nice crisp; take it out and keep it hot; then fry the liver in the same pan, having first seasoned it with pepper and salt and dredged in a little flour; lay it in the hot bacon fat and fry it a nice brown. Serve it with a slice of bacon on the top of each slice of liver.

If you wish a gravy with it, pour off most of the fat from the frying pan, put in about two ounces of butter, a tablespoonful of flour well rubbed in, add a cup of water, salt and pepper, give it one boil and serve in a gravy boat.

Another Way – Cut the liver in nice thin slices, pour boiling water over it and let it stand about five minutes;

then drain and put in a dripping-pan with three or four thin slices of salt pork or bacon; pepper and salt and put in the oven, letting it cook until thoroughly done, then serve with a cream or milk gravy poured over it.

Calf's liver and bacon are very good broiled after cutting each in thin slices. Season with butter, pepper and salt.

CROQUETTES OF SWEETBREADS

Take four veal sweetbreads, soak them for an hour in cold salted water, first removing the pipes and membranes; then put them into boiling salted water with a tablespoonful of vinegar, and cook them twenty minutes, then drop them again into cold water to harden. Now remove them, chop them very fine, almost to a paste. Season with salt, pepper and a teaspoonful of grated onion; add the beaten yolks of three raw eggs, one tablespoonful of butter, half a cupful of cream, and sufficient fine cracker crumbs to make stiff enough to roll out into little balls or cork-shaped croquettes. Have ready a frying kettle half full of fat over the fire, a dish containing three smoothly beaten eggs, a large platter of cracker dust; wet the hands with cold water and make the mixture in shape; afterwards rolling them in the cracker dust, then into the beaten egg, and again in the cracker dust; smooth them on the outside and drop them carefully in the hot fat. When the croquettes are fried a nice golden brown, put them on a brown paper a moment to free them from grease. Serve hot with sliced lemon or parsley.

SWEETBREADS

Sweetbreads are the thymus gland. There are two in a calf, which are considered delicacies. Select the largest. The color should be clear and a shade darker than the fat. Before cooking in any manner let them lie for half an hour in tepid water; then throw into hot water to whiten and harden, after which draw off the outer casing, remove the little pipes, and cut into thin slices. They should always be thoroughly cooked.

FRIED SWEETBREADS

After preparing them as above they are put into hot fat and butter, and fried the same as lamb chops, also broiled the same, first rolling them in egg and cracker crumbs.

BAKED SWEETBREADS

Three sweetbreads, egg and breadcrumbs, oiled butter, three slices of toast, brown gravy.

Choose large, white sweetbreads, put them into warm water to draw out the blood, and to improve their color; let them remain for rather more than one hour; then put them into boiling water, and allow them to simmer for about ten minutes which renders them firm. Take them up, drain them, brush over the egg, sprinkle with breadcrumbs; dip them in egg again, and then into more breadcrumbs. Drop on them a little oiled butter, and put the sweetbreads into a moderately heated oven, and let them bake for nearly three-quarters of an hour. Make three pieces of toast; place the sweetbreads on the toast, and pour round, but not over, them a good brown gravy.

FRICASSEED SWEETBREADS

If they are uncooked, cut into thin slices, let them simmer in a rich gravy for three-quarters of an hour, add a well-beaten egg, two tablespoonfuls of cream and a tablespoonful of chopped parsley; stir all together for a few minutes and serve immediately.

Eat Like a President: Book I

MUTTON AND LAMB

ROAST MUTTON.

The pieces mostly used for roasting are the hindquarter of the sheep, called the loin and leg, the fore-quarter, the shoulder, also the chine or saddle, which is the two loins together. Every part should be trimmed off that cannot be eaten; then wash well and dry with a clean cloth; lay it in your dripping-pan and put in a little water to baste it with at first; then afterward with its own gravy. Allow, in roasting, about twelve minutes to the pound; that is, if your fire is strong, which it should be. It should not be salted at first, as that tends to harden it, and draws out too much of the blood or juices; but salt soon after it begins to roast well. If there is danger of its browning too fast, cover it with a sheet of white paper. Baste it often, and about a quarter of an hour before you think it will be done dredge the meat very lightly with flour and baste it with butter. Skim the gravy well and thicken very slightly with brown flour. Serve with currant jelly or other tart sauce.

BONED LEG OF MUTTON ROASTED

Take the bone out of a small leg of mutton, without spoiling the skin if possible, then cut off most of the fat. Fill the hole whence the bone was taken with a stuffing made the same as for fowls, adding to it part of an onion finely minced. Sew the leg up underneath to prevent the dressing or stuffing from falling out. Bind and tie it up compactly; put it in a roasting pan, turn in a cup of hot water and place it in a moderately hot oven, basting it occasionally. When partly cooked, season with salt and pepper. When thoroughly cooked, remove and place the leg on a warm platter; skim the grease from the top of the drippings, add a cup of water and thicken with a spoonful of dissolved flour. Send the gravy to the table in a gravy dish, also a dish of currant jelly.

BOILED LEG OF MUTTON

To prepare a leg of mutton for boiling, wash it clean, cut a small piece off the shank bone, and trim the knuckle. Put it into a pot with water enough to cover it, and boil gently from two to three hours, skimming well. Then take it from the fire, and keeping the pot well covered, let it finish by remaining in the steam for ten or fifteen minutes. Serve it up with a sauceboat of melted butter, into which a teacupful of capers or nasturtiums have been stirred. If the broth is to be used for soup, put in a little salt while boiling; if not, salt it well when partly done, and boil the meat in a cloth.

BRAISED LEG OF MUTTON

This recipe can be varied either by preparing the leg with a stuffing, placed in the cavity after having the bone removed, or cooking it without. Having lined the bottom of a thick iron kettle or stew pan with a few thin slices of bacon, put over the bacon four carrots, three onions, a bunch of savory herbs; then over these place the leg of mutton. Cover the whole with a few more slices of bacon, then pour over half a pint of water. Cover with a tight cover and stew very gently for four hours, basting the leg occasionally with its own liquor, and seasoning it with salt and pepper as soon as it begins to be tender. When cooked strain the gravy, thicken with a spoonful of flour (it should be quite brown), pour some of it over the meat and send the remainder to the table in a tureen, to be served with the mutton when carved. Garnish the dish around the leg with potatoes cut in the shape of olives and fried a light brown in butter.

LEG OF MUTTON Á LA VENISON

Remove all the rough fat from the mutton and lay it in a deep earthen dish; rub into it thoroughly the following: One tablespoonful of salt, one each of celery-salt, brown sugar, black pepper, English mustard, allspice, and some sweet herbs, all powdered and mixed; after which pour over it slowly a teacup of good vinegar, cover tightly, and set in a cool place four or five days, turning it and basting often with the liquid each day. To cook, put in a kettle a quart of boiling water, place over it an inverted shallow pan, and on it lay the meat just as removed from the pickle; cover the kettle tightly and stew for four hours. Do not let the water touch the meat. Add a cup of hot water to the pickle remaining and baste with it. When done, thicken the liquid with flour and strain through a fine sieve, to serve with the meat; also a relish of currant jelly, the dame as for venison.

This is a fine dish when the directions are faithfully followed.

STEAMED LEG OF MUTTON

Wash and put the leg in a steamer and cook it until tender, then place in a roasting pan, salt and dredge well with flour and set it in a hot oven until nicely browned; the water that remains in the bottom of the steamer may be used for soup. Serve with currant jelly.

HASHED MUTTON

Cut into small pieces the lean of some cold mutton that has been underdone, and season it with pepper and salt. Take the bones and other trimmings, put them in a saucepan with as much water as will cover them, and some sliced onions, and let them stew till you have drawn from them a good gravy. Having skimmed it well, strain the gravy into a stew-pan, and put the mutton into it. Have ready-boiled some carrots, turnips, potatoes and onions. Slice them and add to the meat and gravy. Set the pan on the fire and let it simmer till the meat is warmed through, but do not allow it to boil, as it has been once cooked already. Cover the bottom of the dish with slices of buttered toast. Lay the meat and vegetables upon it, and pour over them the gravy.

Tomatoes will be found an improvement.

If green peas or Lima beans are in season, you may boil them and put them to the hashed mutton, leaving out the other vegetables, or serving them up separately.

BROILED MUTTON CHOPS

Loin of mutton, pepper and salt, a small piece of butter. Cut the chops from a tenderloin of mutton, remove a portion of the fat, and trim them into a nice shape; slightly beat and level them; place the gridiron over a bright clear fire, rub the bars with a little fat, and lay on the chops. While broiling frequently turn them, and in about eight minutes they will be done. Season with pepper and salt, dish them on a very hot dish, rub a small piece of butter on each chop, and serve very hot and expeditiously. Nice with tomato sauce poured over them.

FRIED MUTTON CHOPS NO. 1

Put in a frying-pan a tablespoonful of cold lard and butter mixed; have some fine mutton chops without much fat; trim off the skin. Dip into wheat flour, or rolled cracker, and beaten egg, then lay them into the hot grease, sprinkle with salt and pepper, fry on both sides a fine brown. When dine, take them up and place on a hot dish. If you wish a made gravy, turn off the superfluous grease, if any. Stir into the hot gravy remaining a heaping spoonful of cold water or milk; season with pepper and salt, let it boil up thick. You can serve it in a separate dish or pour it over the chops. Tomato sauce is considered fine, turned over a dish of hot fried or broiled chops.

FRIED MUTTON CHOPS NO. 2

Prepare the chops by trimming off all extra fat and skin, season them with salt and pepper; dip each chop in beaten egg, then in rolled cracker or bread-crumbs; dip again in the egg and crumbs, and so on until they are well coated with the crumb. Have ready a deep spider containing a pound or more of lard, hot enough to fry crullers. Drop into this hot lard the chops, frying only a few at a time, as too many cool the fat. Fry them brown, and serve them up hot and dry, on a warm platter.

MUTTON CUTLETS (Baked)

Prepare them the same as for frying, lay them in a dripping-pan with a *very* little water at the bottom. Bake quickly, and baste often with butter and water. Make a little brown gravy and turn over them when they are served.

BAKED MUTTON CHOPS AND POTATOES

Wash and peel some good potatoes and cut them into slices the thickness of a penny-piece. The quantity of potatoes must, of course, be decided according to the number of persons to whom they have to be served; but it is a safe plan to allow two, or even three, potatoes for each person. After the potatoes are sliced, wash them in two or three waters to thoroughly cleanse them, then arrange them neatly (in layers) in a brown stone dish proper for baking purposes. Sprinkle a little salt and pepper between each layer, and add a sufficient quantity of cold water to prevent their burning. Place the dish in a very hot oven – oil the top shelf – so as to brown the potatoes in a few minutes. Have ready some nice loin chops (say one – for each person); trim off most of the fat; make them into a neat round shape by putting a small skewer through each. When the potatoes are nicely browned, remove the dish from the oven, and place the chops on the top. Add a little more salt and pepper, and water if required, and return the dish to a cooler part of the oven, where it may be allowed to remain until sufficiently cooked, which will be in about three-quarters of an hour. When the upper sides of the chops are a nice crisp brown, turn them over so as to brown the other side also. If, in the cooking, the potatoes appear to be getting too dry, a little more water may be gently poured in at one corner of the dish, only care must be taken to see that the water is hot this time – not cold as at first. The dish in which the chops and potatoes are baked must be as neat looking as possible, as it has to be sent to the table; turning the potatoes out would, of course, spoil their appearance. Those who have never tasted this dish have no idea how delightful it is. While the chops are baking the gravy drips from them among the potatoes, rendering the whole most delicious.

MUTTONETTES

Cut from a leg of mutton slices about half an inch thick. On each slice lay a spoonful of stuffing made with breadcrumbs, beaten egg, butter, salt, pepper, sage and summer savory. Roll up the slices, pinning with little skewers or small wooden toothpicks to keep the dressing in. Put a little butter and water in a baking-pan with the muttonettes, and cook in hot oven three-quarters of an hour. Baste often, and when done thicken the gravy, pour over the meat, garnish with parsley, and serve on hot platter.

IRISH STEW

Time about two hours. Two and a half pounds of chops, eight potatoes, four turnips, four small onions, nearly a quart of water. Take some chops from loin of mutton, place them in stew pan in alternate layers of sliced potatoes and chops; add turnips and onions cut into pieces, pour in nearly a quart of cold water; cover stew pan closely, let it stew gently till vegetables are ready to mash and the greater part of the gravy is absorbed; then place in a dish; serve it up hot.

MUTTON PUDDING

Line a two-quart pudding basin with some beef suet paste; fill the lining with thick mutton cutlets, slightly trimmed, or, if preferred, with steaks cut from the leg; season with pepper and salt some parsley, a little thyme and two slices of onion chopped fine, and between each layer of meat, put some slices of potatoes. When the pudding is filled, wet the edges of the paste around the top of the basin, and cover with a piece of paste rolled out the size of the basin. Fasten down the edge by bearing all around with the thumb; and then with the thumb and forefinger twist the edges of the paste over so as to give it a corded appearance. This pudding can be set in a steamer and steamed, or boiled. The time required for cooking is about three hours. When done, turn it out carefully on a platter and serve with a rich gravy under it.

This is a very good recipe for cooking small birds.

SCRAMBLED MUTTON

Two cups of chopped cold mutton, two tablespoonfuls of hot water, and a piece of butter as large as an English walnut. When the meat is hot, break in three eggs, and constantly stir until the eggs begin to stiffen. Season with pepper and salt.

SCALLOPED MUTTON AND TOMATOES

Over the bottom of an earthen baking dish place a layer of breadcrumbs, and over it alternate layers of cold roast mutton cut in thin slices, and tomatoes peeled and sliced; season each with salt, pepper and bits of butter, as laid in. The top layer should be of tomatoes, spread over with breadcrumbs. Bake three-quarters of an hour, and serve immediately.

LAMB SWEETBREADS AND TOMATO SAUCE

Lamb sweetbreads are not always procurable, but a stroll through the markets occasionally reveals a small lot of them, which can invariably be had at a low price, owing to their excellence being recognized by but few buyers. Wash them well in salted water and parboil fifteen minutes; when cool, trim neatly and put them in a pan with just butter enough to prevent their burning; toss them about until a delicate color; season with salt and pepper and serve, surrounded with tomato sauce. (See SAUCES.)

ROAST QUARTER OF LAMB.

Procure a nice hind-quarter, remove some of the fat that is around the kidney, skewer the lower joint up to the fillet, place it in a moderate oven, let it heat through slowly, then dredge it with salt and flour; quicken the fire, put half a pint of water into the dripping-pan, with a teaspoonful of salt. With this liquor baste the meat occasionally; serve with lettuce, green peas and mint sauce.

A quarter of lamb weighing seven or eight pounds will require two hours to roast.

A breast of lamb roasted is very sweet and is considered by many as preferable to hindquarter. It requires nearly as long a time to roast as the quarter, and should be served in the same manner.

Make the gravy from the drippings, thickened with flour.

The mint sauce is made as follows: Take fresh, young spearmint leaves stripped from stems; wash and drain them or dry on a cloth, chop very fine, put in a gravy tureen, and to three tablespoonfuls of mint add two of finely powdered cut-loaf sugar; mix, and let it stand a few minutes, then pour over it six tablespoonfuls good cider or white-wine vinegar. The sauce should be made some time before dinner, so that the flavor of the mint may be well extracted.

TO BROIL THE FORE-QUARTER OF LAMB

Take off the shoulder and lay it upon the gridiron with the breast; cut in two parts, to facilitate its cooking; put a tin sheet on top of the meat, and a weight upon that; turn the meat around frequently to prevent its burning; turn over as soon as cooked on one side; renew the coals occasionally, that all parts may cook alike; when done, season with butter, pepper and salt – exactly like beefsteak. It takes some time to broil it well; but when done it will be found to be equal to broiled chicken, the flavor being more delicate than when cooked otherwise. Serve with cream sauce, made as follows: Heat a tablespoonful of butter in a saucepan, add a teaspoonful of flour and stir until perfectly smooth; then add, slowly stirring in, a cup of cold milk; let it boil up once, and season to taste with salt and pepper and a teaspoonful of finely chopped fresh parsley. Serve in a gravy boat, all hot.

LAMB STEW

Cut up the lamb into small pieces (after removing all the fat) say about two inches square. Wash it well and put it over the fire, with just enough cold water to cover it well, and let it heat gradually. It should stew gently until it is partly done; then add a few thin slices of salt pork, one or two onions sliced up fine, some pepper and salt if needed, and two or three raw potatoes cut up into inch pieces. Cover it closely and stew until the meat is tender. Drop in a few made dumplings, made like short biscuit, cut out *very* small. Cook fifteen minutes longer. Thicken the gravy with a little flour moistened with milk. Serve.

PRESSED LAMB

The meat, either shoulder or leg, should be put to boil in the morning with water just enough to cover it; when tender, season with salt and pepper, then keep it over the fire until *very* tender and the juice nearly boiled out. Remove it from the fireplace in a wooden chopping bowl, season more if necessary, chop it up like hash. Place it in a bread-pan, press out all the juice, and put it in a cool place to harden. The pressing is generally done by placing a dish over the meat and putting a flatiron upon that. Nice cut up cold into thin slices, and the broth left from the meat would make a nice soup served with it, adding vegetables and spices.

CROQUETTES OF ODDS AND ENDS

These are made of any scraps or bits of good food that happen to be left from one or more meals, and in such small quantities that they cannot be warmed up separately. As, for example, a couple of spoonfuls of frizzled beef and cream, the lean meat of one mutton chop, one spoonful of minced beef, two cold hard-boiled eggs, a little cold chopped potato, a little mashed potato, a chick's leg, all the gristle and hard outside taken from the meat. These things well chopped and seasoned, mixed with one raw egg, a little flour and butter, and boiling water; then made into round cakes, thick like fish-balls and browned well with butter in a frying pan or on a griddle.

Scraps of hash, cold rice, boiled oatmeal left from breakfast, every kind of fresh meat, bits of salt tongue, bacon, pork or ham, bits of poultry, and crumbs of bread may be used. They should be put together with care, so as not to have them too dry to be palatable, or too moist to cook in shape. Most housekeepers would be surprised at the result, making an addition to the breakfast or lunch table. Serve on small squares of buttered toast, and with cold celery if in season.

PORK

The best parts, and those usually used for roasting, are the loin, the leg, the shoulder, the sparerib and chine. The hams, shoulders and middlings are usually salted, pickled and smoked. Pork requires more thorough cooking than most meats; if the least underdone it is unwholesome.

To choose pork: If the rind is thick and tough, and cannot be easily impressed with the finger, it is old; when fresh, it will look cool and smooth, and only corn-fed pork is good; swill or still-fed pork is unfit to cure. Fresh pork is in season from October to April. When dressing or stuffing is used, there are more or less herbs used for seasoning – sage, summer savory, thyme and sweet marjoram; these can be found (in the dried, pulverized form, put up in small, light packages) at most of the best druggists; still those raised and gathered at home are considered more fresh.

ROAST PIG

Prepare your dressing as for DRESSING FOR FOWLS, adding half an onion, chopped fine; set it inside. Take a young pig about six weeks old, wash it thoroughly inside and outside; and in another water put a teaspoonful of baking soda, and rinse out the inside again; wipe it dry with a fresh towel, salt the inside and stuff it with the prepared dressing; making it full and plump, giving it its original size and shape. Sew it up, place it in a kneeling posture in the dripping-pan, tying the legs in proper position. Pour a little hot salted water into the dripping-pan, baste with butter and water a few times as the pig warms, afterwards with gravy from the dripping-pan.

When it begins to smoke all over rub it often with a rag dipped in melted butter. This will keep the skin from cracking and it still will be crisp. It will take from two to three hours to roast. Make the gravy by skimming off most of the grease; stir into that remaining in the pan a good tablespoonful of flour, turn in water to make it the right consistency, season with pepper and let all boil up once. Strain, and if you like wine in it, add half a glass; turn it into a gravy boat.

Place the pig upon a large, hot platter, surrounded with parsley or celery tops; place a green wreath around the neck, and a sprig of celery in its mouth. In carving, cut off its head first; split down the back, take off its hams and shoulders, and separate the ribs.

ROAST LOIN OF PORK.

Score the skin in strips about a quarter of an inch apart; place it in a dripping-pan with a *very little* water under it; cook it moderately at first, as a high heat hardens the rind before the meat is heated through. If it is very lean, it should be rubbed with fresh lard or butter when put into the pan. A stuffing might be made of breadcrumbs, chopped sage and onions, pepper and salt, and baked separately on a pie dish; this method is better than putting it in the meat, as many persons have a great aversion to its flavor. A loin weighing about six pounds will roast in two hours; allow more time if it should be very fat. Make a gravy with flour stirred into the pork drippings. Serve with applesauce and pickles.

ROAST LEG OF PORK.

Choose a small leg of fine young pork; cut a slit in the knuckle with a sharp knife, and fill the space with sage and onion chopped, and a little pepper and salt. When half done, score the skin in slices, but do not cut deeper than the outer rind. Applesauce and potatoes should be served with it. The gravy is to be made the same way as for beef roast, by turning off all the superfluous fat and adding a spoonful of flour stirred with a little water; add water to make the right consistency. Serve in a gravy boat.

BOILED LEG OF PORK

For boiling, choose a small, compact, well-filled leg, and rub it well with salt; let it remain in pickle for a week or ten days, turning and rubbing it every day. An hour before dressing it put it into cold water for an hour, which improves the color. If the pork is purchased ready salted, ascertain how long the meat has been in pickle and soak it accordingly.

Put it into a boiling pot, with sufficient cold water to cover it, let it gradually come to a boil, and remove the scum as it rises. Simmer it very gently until tender, and do not allow it to boil fast, or the knuckle will fall to pieces before the middle of the leg is done. Carrots, turnips or parsnips may be boiled with the pork, some of which should be laid around the dish as a garnish.

Time – A leg of pork weighing eight pounds, three hours after the water boils, and to be simmered very gently.

ROAST SPARE RIB

Trim off the rough ends neatly, crack the ribs across the middle, rub with salt and sprinkle with pepper, fold over, stuff with turkey dressing, sew up tightly, place in a dripping-pan with a pint of water, baste frequently, turning over once so as to bake both sides equally until a rich brown.

PORK TENDERLOINS

The tenderloins are unlike any other part of the pork in flavor. They may be either fried or broiled; the latter being drier, butter well before serving, which should be done on a hot platter before the butter becomes oily. Fry them in a little lard, turning them to have them cooked through; when done, remove, and keep hot while making a gravy by dredging a little flour into the hot fat; if not enough add a little butter or lard, stir until browned, and add a little milk or cream, stir briskly, and pour over the dish. A little Worcestershire sauce may be added to the gravy if desired.

PORK CUTLETS

Cut them from the leg, and remove the skin; trim them and beat them, and sprinkle on salt and pepper. Prepare some beaten egg in a pan, and on a flat dish a mixture of breadcrumbs, minced onion and sage. Put some lard or drippings into a frying pan over the fire, and when it boils put in the cutlets, having dipped every one first in the egg, and then in the seasoning. Fry them twenty or thirty minutes, turning them often. After you have taken them out of the frying pan, skim the gravy, dredge in a little flour, give it one boil, and then pour it on the dish round the cutlets.

Have applesauce to eat with them.

Pork cutlets prepared in this manner may be stewed instead of being fried. Add to them a little water, and stew them slowly till thoroughly done, keeping them closely covered, except when you remove the lid to skim them.

FRIED PORK CHOPS

Fry them the same as mutton chops. If a sausage flavor is liked, sprinkle over them a little powdered sage or summer savory, pepper and salt, and if a gravy is liked, skim off some of the fat in the pan and stir in a spoonful of flour; stir it until free from lumps, then season with pepper and salt and turn in a pint of sweet milk. Boil up and serve in a gravy boat.

PORK CHOPS AND FRIED APPLES.

Season the chops with salt and pepper and a little powdered sage; dip them into breadcrumbs. Fry about twenty minutes or until they are done. Put them on a hot dish; pour off part of the gravy into another pan to make a gravy to serve with them, if you choose. Then fry apples which you have sliced about two-thirds of an inch thick, cutting them around the apple so that the core is in the center of each piece; then cut out the core. When they are browned on one side and partly cooked, turn them carefully with a pancake turner, and finish cooking; dish around the chops or on a separate dish.

PORK PIE

Make a good plain paste. Take from two and a half to three pounds of the thick ends of a loin of pork, with very little fat on it; cut into very thin slices three inches long by two inches wide; put a layer at the bottom of a pie-dish. Wash and chop finely a handful of parsley, also an onion. Sprinkle a small portion of these over the pork, and a little pepper and salt. Add another layer of pork, and over that some more of the seasoning, only be sparing of the nutmeg. Continue this till the dish is full. Now pour into the dish a cupful of stock or water, and a spoonful or two of ketchup. Put a little paste around the edge of the dish; put on the cover and place the pie in a rather hot oven. When the paste has risen and begins to take color, place the pie at the bottom of the oven, with some paper over it, as it will require to be baked at least two hours. Some prefer to cook the meat until partly done, before putting into the crust.

Palmer House, Chicago.

PORK POTPIE

Take pieces of ribs of lean salt pork, also a slice or two of the fat of salt pork; scald it well with hot water so as to wash out the briny taste. Put it into a kettle and cover it with cold water, enough for the required want. Cover it and boil an hour, season with pepper; then add half a dozen potatoes cut into quarters. When it all commences to boil again, drop in dumplings made from this recipe:

One pint of sour or buttermilk, two eggs, well beaten, a teaspoonful of salt, a level teaspoonful of soda; dissolve in a spoonful of water as much flour as will make a very stiff batter. Drop this into the kettle or broth by spoonfuls, and cook forty minutes, closely covered.

FRESH PORK POTPIE

Boil a sparerib, after removing all the fat and cracking the bones, until tender; remove the scum as it rises, and when tender season with salt and pepper; half an hour before time for serving the dinner thicken the gravy with a little flour. Have ready another kettle, into which remove all the bones and most of the gravy, leaving only sufficient to cover the pot half an inch above the rim that rests on the stove; put in the crust, cover tight, and boil steadily forty-five minutes. To prepare the crust, work into light dough a *small* bit of butter, roll it out thin, cut it in small, square cakes, and lay them on the molding-board until very light. No steam should possibly escape while the crust is cooking, and by no means allow the pot to cease boiling.

PORK AND BEANS (Baked)

Take two quarts of white beans, pick them over the night before, put to soak in cold water; in the morning put them in fresh water and let them scald, then turn off the water and put on more, hot; put to cook with them a piece of salt pork, gashed, as much as would make five or six slices; boil slowly till soft (not mashed), then add a tablespoonful of molasses, half a teaspoonful of soda, stir in well, put in a deep pan, and bake one hour and a half. If you do not like to use pork, salt the beans when boiling, and add a lump of butter when preparing them for the oven.

BOSTON PORK AND BEANS

Pick over carefully a quart of small, white beans; let them soak over night in cold water; in the morning wash and drain in another water. Put on to boil in plenty of cold water with a piece of soda the size of a bean; let them come to a boil, then drain again, cover with water once more, and boil them fifteen minutes, or until the skin of the beans will crack when taken out and blown upon. Drain the beans again, put them into an earthen pot, adding a tablespoonful of salt; cover with hot water, place in the center a pound of salt pork, first scalding it with hot water, and scoring the rind across the top, a quarter of an inch apart to indicate where the slices are to be cut. Place the pot in the oven, and bake six hours or longer. Keep the oven a moderate heat; add hot water from the teakettle as needed, on account of evaporation, to keep the beans moist. When the meat becomes crisp and looks cooked, remove it, as too long baking the pork destroys its solidity.

FRIED SALT PORK

Cut in thin slices, and freshen in cold water, roll in flour, and fry crisp. If required quickly pour boiling water over the slices, let stand a few minutes, drain and roll in flour as before; drain off most of the grease from the frying pan; stir in while hot one or two tablespoonfuls of flour, about half a pint of milk, a little pepper, and salt if over freshened; let it boil, and pour into a gravy dish. A teaspoonful of finely chopped parsley will add pleasantly to the appearance of the gravy.

GRILLED SALT PORK

Take quite thin slices of the thick part of side pork, of a

clear white, and thinly streaked with lean; hold one on a toasting fork before a brisk fire to grill; have at hand a dish of cold water, in which immerse it frequently while cooking, to remove the superfluous fat and render it more delicate. Put each slice as cooked in a warm covered pan; when all are done, serve hot.

FRIED HAM AND EGGS

Cut slices of ham quite thin, cut off the rind or skin, put them into a hot frying pan, turning them often until crisp, taking care not to burn the slices; three minutes will cook them well. Dish them on a hot platter; then turn off the top of the grease, rinse out the pan, and put back the clear grease to fry the eggs. Break the eggs separately in a saucer, that in case a bad one should be among them it may not mix with the rest. Slip each egg gently into the frying pan. Do not turn them while they are frying, put keep pouring some of the hot lard over them with a kitchen spoon; this will do them sufficiently on the upper side. They will be done enough in about three minutes; the white must retain its transparency so that the yolk will be seen through it. When done take them up with a tin slice; drain off the lard, and if any part of the white is discolored or ragged, trim it off. Lay a fried egg upon each slice of the ham, and send to table hot.

COLD BACON AND EGGS

An economical way of using bacon and eggs that have been left from a previous meal is to put them in a wooden bowl and chop them quite fine, adding a little mashed or cold chopped potato, and a little bacon gravy, if any was left. Mix and mold it into little balls, roll in raw egg and cracker crumbs, and fry in a spider the same as frying eggs; fry a light brown on both sides. Serve hot. Very appetizing.

SCRAPPLE

Scrapple is a most palatable dish. Take the head, heart and any lean scraps of pork, and boil until the flesh slips easily from the bones. Remove the fat, gristle and bones, then chop fine. Set the liquor in which the meat was boiled aside until cold, take the cake of fat from the surface and return to the fire. When it boils put in the chopped meat and season well with pepper and salt. Let it boil again, then thicken with corn meal as you would in making ordinary corn meal mush, by letting it slip through the fingers slowly to prevent lumps. Cook an hour, stirring constantly at first, afterwards putting back on the range in a position to boil gently. When done, pour into a long, square pan, not too deep, and mold. In cold weather this can be kept several weeks. Cut into slices when cold, and fried brown, as you do mush, is a cheap and delicious breakfast dish.

CORNED HAM

Take a medium-sized ham and place it to soak for ten or twelve hours. Then cut away the rusty part from underneath, wipe it dry, and cover it rather thickly over with a paste made of flour and water. Put it into an earthen dish, and set it in a moderately heated oven. When done, take off the crust carefully, and peel off the skin, put a frill of cut paper around the knuckle, and raspings of bread over the fat of the ham, or serve it glazed and garnished with cut vegetables. It will take about four or five hours to bake it.

Cooked in this way the flavor is much finer than when

boiled.

PICKLED PIGS' FEET

Take twelve pigs' feet, scrape and wash them clean, put them into a saucepan with enough hot (not boiling) water to cover them. When partly done, salt them. It requires four to five hours to boil them soft. Pack them in a stone crock, and pour over them spiced vinegar made hot. They will be ready to use in a day or two. If you wish them for breakfast, split them, make a batter of two eggs, a cup of milk, salt, a teaspoonful of butter, with flour enough to make a thick batter; dip each piece in this and fry in hot lard. Or, dip them in beaten egg and flour and fry. Souse is good eaten cold or warm.

BOILED HAM

First remove all dust and mold by wiping with a coarse cloth; soak it for an hour in cold water, then wash it thoroughly. Cut with a sharp knife the hardened surface from the base and butt of the ham. Place it over the fire in *cold* water, and let it come to a moderate boil, keeping it steadily at this point, allowing it to cook twenty minutes for every pound of meat. A ham weighing twelve pounds will require four hours to cook properly, as underdone ham is very unwholesome. When the ham is to be served hot, remove the skin by pealing it off, place it on a platter, the fat side up, and dot the surface with spots of black pepper. Stick in also some whole cloves.

If the ham is to be served cold, allow it to remain in the pot until the water in which it was cooked becomes cold. This makes it more juicy. Serve it in the same manner as when served hot.

BROILED HAM

Cut your ham into thin slices, which should be a little less than one quarter of an inch thick. Trim very closely the skin from the upper side of each slice, and also trim off the outer edge where the smoke has hardened the meat. If the ham is very salt lay it in *cold* water for one hour before cooking, then wipe with a dry cloth. Never soak ham in tepid or hot water, as it will toughen the meat.

Broil over a brisk fire, turning the slices constantly. It will require about five minutes, and should be served the last thing directly from the gridiron, placed on a warm platter, with a little butter and a sprinkle of pepper on the top of each slice. If ham or bacon is allowed to stand by the fire after it has been broiled or fried, it will speedily toughen, loosing all its grateful juices.

Cold boiled ham is very nice for broiling, and many prefer it to using the raw ham.

POTTED HAM

To two pounds of lean ham allow one pound of fat, two teaspoonfuls of powdered mace, half a nutmeg, grated, rather more than half a teaspoonful of cayenne.

Mode – Mince the ham, fat and lean together, in the above proportion, and pound it well in a mortar, seasoning it with cayenne pepper, pounded mace and nutmeg; put the mixture into a deep baking dish, and bake for half an hour; then press it well into a stone jar, fill up the jar with clarified lard, cover it closely, and paste over it a piece of thick paper. If well seasoned, it will keep a long time in winter, and will be found very convenient for sandwiches, etc.

BOLOGNA SAUSAGE (Cooked)

Two pounds of lean pork, two pounds of lean veal, two pounds of fresh lean beef, two pounds of fat salt pork, one pound of beef suet, ten tablespoonfuls of powdered sage, one ounce each of parsley, savory, marjoram and thyme mixed. Two teaspoonfuls of cayenne pepper, the same of black, one grated nutmeg, one teaspoonful of cloves, one minced onion, salt to taste. Chop or grind the meat and suet; season, and stuff into beef skins; tie these up, prick each in several places to allow the escape of steam; put into hot, not boiling, water, and heat gradually to the boiling point. Cook slowly for one hour; take out the skins and lay them to dry in the sun, upon clean sweet straw or hay. Rub the outside of the skins with oil or melted butter, and place in a cool, dry cellar. If you wish to keep them more than a week, rub ginger or pepper on the outside, then wash it off before using. This is eaten without further cooking. Cut in round slices and lay sliced lemons around the edge of the dish, as many like to squeeze a few drops upon the sausage before eating. These are very nice smoked like hams.

COUNTRY PORK SAUSAGES

Six pounds lean fresh pork, three pounds of chine fat, three tablespoonfuls of salt, two of black pepper, four tablespoonfuls of pounded and sifted sage, two of summer savory. Chop the lean and fat pork finely, mix the seasoning in with your hands, taste to see that it has the right flavor, then put them into cases, either the cleaned intestines of the hog, or make long, narrow bags of stout muslin, large enough to contain each enough sausage for a family dish. Fill these with the meat, dip in melted lard, and hang them in a cool, dry, dark place. Some prefer to pack the meat in jars, pouring melted lard over it, covering the top, to be taken out as wanted and made into small round cakes with the hands, then fried brown. Many like spices added to the seasoning – cloves, mace and nutmeg. This is a matter of taste.

Marion Harland.

TO FRY SAUSAGES

Put a small piece of lard or butter into the frying pan. Prick the sausages with a fork, lay them in the melted grease, keep moving them about, turning them frequently to prevent bursting; in ten or twelve minutes they will be sufficiently browned and cooked. Another sure way to prevent the cases from bursting is to cover them with cold water and let it come to the boiling point; turn off the water and fry them. Sausages are nicely cooked by putting them in a baking-pan them in the oven, turning them once or twice. In this way you avoid all smoke and disagreeable odor. A pound will cook brown in ten minutes in a hot oven.

HEAD CHEESE

Boil the forehead, ears and feet, and nice scraps trimmed from the hams of a fresh pig, until the meat will almost drop from the bones. Then separate the meat from the bones, put in a large chopping-bowl, and season with pepper, salt, sage and summer savory. Chop it rather coarsely; put it back in the same kettle it was boiled in, with just enough of the liquor in which it was boiled to prevent its burning; warm it through thoroughly, mixing it well together. Now pour it into a strong muslin bag, press the bag between two flat surfaces, with a heavy weight on top; when cold and solid it can be cut in slices. Good cold, or warmed up in vinegar.

Eat Like a President: Book I

FISH

In selecting fish, choose those only in which the eye is full and prominent, the flesh thick and firm, the scales bright and fins stiff. They should be thoroughly cleaned before cooking.

The usual modes of cooking fish are boiled, baked, broiled, fried and occasionally stewed. Steaming fish is much superior to boiling, but the ordinary conveniences in private houses do not admit of the possibility of enjoying this delicate way of cooking it. Large fish are generally boiled, medium-sized ones baked or boiled, the smaller kinds fried or broiled. Very large fish, such as cod, halibut, etc., are cut in steaks or slices for frying or broiling. The heads of some fish, as the cod, halibut, etc., are considered tidbits by many. Small fish, or pan fish, as they are usually called, are served without the heads, with the exception of brook trout and smelts; these are usually cooked whole, with the heads on. Bake fish slowly, basting often with butter and water. Salmon is considered the most nutritious of all fish. When boiling fish, by adding a little vinegar and salt to the water, it seasons and prevents the nutriment from being drawn out; the vinegar acting on the water hardens the water.

Fill the fish with a nicely prepared stuffing of rolled cracker or stale breadcrumbs, seasoned with butter, pepper, salt, sage and any other aromatic herbs fancied; sew up; wrap in a well-floured cloth, tied closely with twine, and boil or steam. The garnishes for boiled fish are: for turbot, fried smelts; for other boiled fish, parsley, sliced beets, lemon or sliced boiled egg. Do not use the knives, spoons, etc., that are used in cooking fish, for other food, as they will be apt to impart a fishy flavor.

Fish to be boiled should be put into *cold water* and set on the fire to cook very gently, or the outside will break before the inner part is done. Unless the fish are small, they should never be put into warm water; nor should water, either hot or cold, be poured *on* to the fish, as it is liable to break the skin; if it should be necessary to add a little water while the fish is cooking, it ought to be poured in gently at the side of the vessel.

Fish to be broiled should lie, after they are dressed, for two or three hours, with their inside well sprinkled with salt and pepper.

Salt fish should be soaked in water before boiling, according to the time it has been in salt. When it is hard and dry, it will require thirty-six hours soaking before it is dressed, and the water must be changed three or four times. When fish is not very salt, twenty-four hours, or even one night, will suffice.

When frying fish the fire must be hot enough to bring the fat to such a degree of heat as to sear the surface and make it impervious to the fat, and at the same time seal up the rich juices. As soon as the fish is browned by this sudden application of heat, the pan may be moved to a cooler place on the stove, that the process may be finished more slowly.

Fat in which fish has been fried is just as good to use again for the same purpose, but it should be kept by itself and not put to any other use.

TO FRY FISH

Most of the smaller fish (generally termed pan-fish) are usually fried. Clean well, cut off the head, and, if quite large, cut out the backbone, and slice the body crosswise into five or six pieces; season with salt and pepper. Dip in Indian meal or wheat flour, or in beaten egg, and roll in bread or fine cracker crumbs – trout and perch should not be dipped in meal; put into a thick bottomed iron frying pan, the flesh side down, with hot lard or drippings; fry slowly, turning when lightly browned. The following method may be deemed preferable: Dredge the pieces with flour; brush them over with beaten egg; roll in breadcrumbs, and fry in hot lard or drippings sufficient to cover, the same as frying crullers. If the fat is very hot, the fish will fry without absorbing it, and it will be palatably cooked. When browned on one side, turn it over in the fat and brown the other, draining when done. This is a particularly good way to fry slices of large fish. Serve with tomato sauce; garnish with slices of lemon.

PAN FISH

Place them in a thick-bottomed frying pan with heads all one way. Fill the spaces with smaller fish. When they are fried quite brown and ready to turn, put a dinner plate over them, drain off the fat; then invert the pan, and they will be left unbroken on the plate. Put the lard back into the pan, and when *hot* slip back the fish. When the other side is brown, drain, turn on a plate as before, and slip them on a warm platter, to be sent to the table. Leaving the heads on and the fish a crispy-brown, in perfect shape, improves the appearance if not the flavor. Garnish with slices of lemon.

Hotel Lafayette, Philadelphia.

STEAMED FISH

Secure the tail of the fish in its mouth, the body in a circle; pour over it half a pint of vinegar, seasoned with pepper and salt; let it stand an hour in a cool place; pour off the vinegar, and put it in a steamer over boiling water, and steam twenty minutes, or longer for large fish. When the meat easily separates from the bone it is done.

Drain well and serve on a very clean white napkin, neatly folded and placed on the platter; decorate the napkin around the fish with sprigs of curled parsley, or with fanciful beet cuttings, or alternately with both.

BOILED SALMON

The middle slice of salmon is the best. Sew up neatly in a mosquito-net bag, and boil a quarter of an hour to the pound in hot salted water. When done, unwrap with care, and lay upon a hot dish, taking care not to break it. Have ready a large cupful of drawn butter, very rich, in which has been stirred a tablespoonful of minced parsley and the juice of a lemon. Pour half upon the salmon and serve the rest in a boat. Garnish with parsley and sliced eggs.

BROILED SALMON

Cut slices from an inch to an inch and an half thick, dry them in a cloth, season with salt and pepper, dredge them in sifted flour, and broil on a gridiron rubbed with suet.

Another Mode – Cut the slices one inch thick, and season them with pepper and salt; butter a sheet of white paper, lay each slice on a separate piece, envelop them in it with their ends twisted; broil gently over a clear fire, and serve with anchovy or caper sauce. When higher seasoning is required, add a few chopped herbs and a little spice.

FRESH SALMON FRIED

Cut the slices three-quarters of an inch thick, dredge them with flour, or dip them in egg and crumbs; fry a light brown. This mode answers for all fish cut into steaks. Season well with salt and pepper.

SALMON AND CAPER SAUCE

Two slices of salmon, one-quarter pound butter, and one-half teaspoonful of chopped parsley, one shallot; salt and pepper to taste.

Lay the salmon in a baking dish, place pieces of butter over it, and add the other ingredients, rubbing a little of the seasoning into the fish; place it in the oven and baste it frequently; when done, take it out and drain for a minute or two; lay it in a dish, pour caper sauce over it and serve. Salmon dressed in this way, with tomato sauce, is very delicious.

BROILED SALT SALMON (Or Other Salt Fish)

Soak salmon in tepid or cold water twenty-four hours, changing water several times, or let stand under faucet of running water. If in a hurry, or desiring a very salt relish, it may do to soak a short time, having water warm, and changing, parboiling slightly. At the hour wanted, broil sharply. Season to suit taste, covering with butter. This recipe will answer for all kinds of salt fish.

PICKLED SALMON

Take a fine, fresh salmon, and, having cleaned it, cut it into large pieces, and boil it in salted water as if for eating. Then drain it, wrap it in a dry cloth, and set it in a cold place till next day. Then make the pickle, which must be in proportion to the quantity of fish. To one quart of the water in which the salmon was boiled, allow two quarts of the best vinegar, one ounce of whole black pepper, one nutmeg grated and a dozen blades of mace. Boil all these together in a kettle closely covered to prevent the flavor from evaporating. When the vinegar thus prepared is quite cold, pour it over the salmon, and put on the top a tablespoonful of sweet oil, which will make it keep the longer.

Cover it closely, put it in a dry, cool place, and it will be good for many months. This is the nicest way of preserving salmon, and is approved by all who have tried it.

SMOKED SALMON

Smoked salmon to be broiled should be put upon the gridiron first, with the flesh side to the fire.

Smoked salmon is very nice when shaved like smoked beef, and served with coffee or tea.

FRICASSEE SALMON

This way of cooking fresh salmon is a pleasant change

from the ordinary modes of cooking it. Cut one and one-half pounds of salmon into pieces one inch square; put the pieces in a stew pan with half a cupful of water, a little salt, a little white pepper, one clove, one blade of mace, three pieces of sugar, one shallot and a heaping teaspoonful of mustard mixed smoothly with half a teacupful of vinegar. Let this boil up once and add six tomatoes peeled and cut into tiny pieces, a few sprigs of parsley finely minced, and one wine-glassful of sherry. Let all simmer gently for three-quarters of an hour. Serve very hot, and garnish with dry toast cut in triangular pieces. This dish is good, very cold, for luncheon or breakfast.

SALMON CROQUETTES

One pound of cooked salmon (about one and a half pints when chopped), one cup of cream, two tablespoonfuls of butter, one tablespoonful of flour, three eggs, one pint of crumbs, pepper and salt; chop the salmon fine, mix the flour and butter together, let the cream come to a boil, and stir in the flour and butter, salmon and seasoning; boil one minute; stir in one well-beaten egg, and remove from the fire; when cold make into croquettes; dip in beaten egg, roll in crumbs and fry. Canned salmon can be used.

SALMON PATTIES

Cut cold, cooked salmon into dice. Heat about a pint of the dice in half a pint of cream. Season to taste with cayenne pepper and salt. Fill the shells and serve. Cold, cooked fish of any kind may be made into patties in this way. Use any fish sauce you choose – all are equally good.

FISH AND OYSTER PIE

Any remains of cold fish, such as cod or haddock, 2 dozen oysters, pepper and salt to taste, breadcrumbs, sufficient for the quantity of fish; ½ teaspoonful of grated nutmeg, 1 teaspoonful of finely chopped parsley.

Clear the fish from the bones, and put a layer of it in a pie-dish, which sprinkle with pepper and salt; then a layer of breadcrumbs, oysters, nutmeg and chopped parsley. Repeat this till the dish is quite full. You may form a covering either of breadcrumbs, which should be browned, or puff-paste, which should be cut off into long strips, and laid in cross-bars over the fish, with a line of the paste first laid round the edge. Before putting on the top, pour in some made melted butter, or a little thin white sauce, and the oyster-liquor, and bake.

Time – If of cooked fish, ¼ hour; if made of fresh fish and puff-paste, ¾ hour.

BROILED SHAD

Split and wash the shad and afterwards dry it in a cloth. Season it with salt and pepper. Have ready a bed of clear, bright coals. Grease your gridiron well, and as soon as it is hot, lay the shad upon it, the flesh side down; cover with a dripping-pan and broil it for about a quarter of an hour, or more, according to the thickness.

Butter it well and send it to the table. Covering it while broiling gives it a more delicious flavor.

BAKED SHAD

Many people are of the opinion that the very best method of cooking a shad is to bake it. Stuff it with breadcrumbs, salt, pepper, butter and parsley, and mix this up with the beaten yolk of egg; fill the fish with it, and sew it up or fasten a string around it. Pour over it a little water and some butter, and bake as you would a fowl. A shad will require from an hour to an hour and a quarter to bake. Garnish with slices of lemon, watercress, etc.

Dressing for Baked Shad – Boil up the gravy in which the shad was baked, put in a large tablespoonful of ketchup, a tablespoonful of brown flour which has been wet with cold water, the juice of a lemon, and a glass of sherry or Madeira wine. Serve in a sauceboat.

TO COOK A SHAD ROE

Drop into boiling water and cook gently for twenty minutes; then take from the fire and drain. Butter a tin plate and lay the drained roe upon it. Dredge well with salt and pepper and spread soft butter over it; then dredge thickly with flour. Cook in the oven for half an hour, basting frequently with salt, pepper, flour, butter and water.

TO COOK SHAD ROE (Another Way)

First partly boil them in a small covered pan, take out and season them with salt, a little pepper, dredge with flour and fry as any fish.

BOILED BASS

After thoroughly cleaning it place in a saucepan with enough water to cover it; add two tablespoonfuls of salt; set the saucepan over the fire, and when it has boiled about five minutes try to pull out one of the fins; if it loosens easily from the body carefully take the fish out of the water, lay it on a platter, surround it with half a dozen hard-boiled eggs, and serve it with a sauce.

BOILED BLUEFISH
Boiled the same as BASS.

BAKED BLUEFISH
Baked the same as BAKED SHAD.

BAKED PICKEREL
Carefully clean and wipe the fish, and lay in a dripping pan with enough hot water to prevent scorching. A perforated sheet of tin, fitting loosely, or several muffin rings may be used to keep it off the bottom. Lay it in a circle on its belly, head and tail touching, and tied, or as directed in note on fish; bake slowly, basting often with butter and water. When done, have ready a cup of sweet cream or rich milk to which a few spoons of hot water has been added; stir in two large spoons of melted butter and a little chopped parsley; heat all by setting the cup in boiling water; add the gravy from the dripping-pan, and let it boil up once; place the fish in a hot dish and pour over it the sauce. Or an egg sauce may be made with drawn butter; stir in the yolk of an egg quickly, and then a teaspoon of chopped parsley. It can be stuffed or not, just as you please.

FRIED EELS
After cleaning the eels well, cut them in pieces two inches long; wash them and wipe them dry; roll them in wheat flour or rolled cracker, and fry, as directed for other fish, in hot lard or beef dripping, salted. They should be

browned all over and thoroughly done.

Eels are sometimes dipped in batter and then fried, or into egg and breadcrumbs. Serve with crisped parsley.

SHEEPSHEAD WITH DRAWN BUTTER

Select a medium-sized fish, clean it thoroughly, and rub a little salt over it; wrap it in a cloth and put it in a steamer; place this over a pot of fast-boiling water and steam one hour; then lay it whole upon a hot side-dish, garnish with tufts of parsley and slices of lemon, and serve with drawn butter, prepared as follows: Take two ounces of butter and roll it into small balls, dredge these with flour; put one-fourth of them in a saucepan, and as they begin to melt, whisk them; add the remainder, one at a time, until thoroughly smooth; while stirring, add a tablespoonful of lemon juice, half a tablespoonful of chopped parsley; pour into a hot sauce boat and serve.

BAKED WHITE FISH

Thoroughly clean the fish; cut off the head or not, as preferred; cut out the backbone from the head to within two inches of the tail, and stuff with the following: Soak stale bread in water, squeeze dry; cut in pieces a large onion, fry in butter, chop fine; add the bread, two ounces of butter, salt, pepper and a little parsley or sage; heat through, and when taken off the fire, add the yolks of two well-beaten eggs; stuff the fish rather full, sew up with fine twine, and wrap with several coils of white tape. Rub the fish over slightly with butter; just cover the bottom of a baking pan with hot water, and place the fish in it, standing back upward, and bent in the form of an S. Serve with the following dressing: Reduce the yolks of two hard-boiled eggs to a smooth paste with two tablespoonfuls good salad oil; stir in half a teaspoon English mustard, and add pepper and vinegar to taste.

BAKED WHITE FISH (Bordeaux Sauce)

Clean and stuff the fish. Put it in a baking pan and add a liberal quantity of butter, previously rolled in flour, to the fish. Put in the pan half a pint of claret, and bake for an hour and a quarter. Remove the fish and strain the gravy; add to the latter a gill more of claret, a teaspoonful of brown flour and a pinch of cayenne, and serve with the fish.

BOILED WHITE FISH

The most delicate mode of cooking white fish. Prepare the fish as for broiling, laying it open; put it into a dripping pan with the back down; nearly cover with water; to one fish two tablespoonfuls of salt; cover tightly and simmer (not boil) one-half hour. Dress with gravy, a little butter and pepper, and garnish with hard-boiled eggs.

BOILED HALIBUT

The cut next to the tailpiece is the best to boil. Rub a little salt over it, soak it for fifteen minutes in vinegar and cold water, then wash it and scrape it until quite clean; tie it in a cloth and boil slowly over a moderate fire, allowing seven minutes' boiling to each pound of fish; when it is half-cooked, turn it over in the pot; serve with drawn butter or egg sauce.

Boiled halibut minced with boiled potatoes and a little butter and milk makes an excellent breakfast dish.

STEAMED HALIBUT

Select a three-pound piece of white halibut, cover it with a cloth and place it in a steamer; set the steamer over a pot of fast-boiling water and steam two hours; place it on a hot dish surrounded with a border of parsley and serve with egg sauce.

FRIED HALIBUT. No. 1

Select choice, firm slices from this large and delicate looking fish, and, after carefully washing and drying with a soft towel, with a sharp knife take off the skin. Beat up two eggs and roll out some brittle crackers upon the kneading board until they are as fine as dust. Dip each slice into the beaten egg, then into the cracker crumbs (after you have salted and peppered the fish), and place them in a hot frying pan half full of boiling lard, in which a little butter has been added to make the fish brown nicely; turn and brown both sides, remove from frying pan and drain. Serve hot.

FRIED HALIBUT. No. 2

First fry a few thin slices of salt pork until brown in an iron frying pan; then take it up on a hot platter and keep it warm until the halibut is fried. After washing and drying two pounds of sliced halibut, sprinkle it with salt and pepper, dredge it well with flour, put it into the hot pork drippings and fry brown on both sides; then serve the pork with the fish.

Halibut broiled in slices is a very good way of cooking it, broiled the same as Spanish mackerel.

BAKED HALIBUT

Take a nice piece of halibut weighing five or six pounds and lay it in salt water for two hours. Wipe it dry and score the outer skin. Set it in a dripping pan in a moderately hot oven and bake an hour, basting often with butter and water heated together in a saucepan or tin cup. When a fork will penetrate it easily, it is done. It should be a fine, brown color. Take the gravy in the dripping pan, add a little boiling water, should there not be enough, stir in a tablespoonful of walnut ketchup, a teaspoonful of Worcestershire sauce, the juice of a lemon, and thicken with brown flour, previously wet with cold water. Boil up once and put in a sauceboat.

FRIED BROOK TROUT

These delicate fish are usually fried, and form a delightful breakfast or supper dish. Clean, wash and dry the fish, split them to the tail, salt and pepper them, and flour them nicely. If you use lard instead of the fat of fried salt pork, put in a piece of butter to prevent their sticking, and which causes them to brown nicely. Let the fat be hot; fry quickly to a delicate brown. They should be sufficiently browned on one side before turning on the other. They are nice served with slices of fried pork, fried crisp. Lay them side by side on a heated platter, garnish and send hot to the table. They are often cooked and served with their heads on.

FRIED SMELTS

Fried with their heads on the same as brook trout. Many think that they make a much better appearance as a dish when cooked whole with the heads on, and nicely garnished for the table.

BAKED SMELTS

Wash and dry them thoroughly in a cloth, and arrange them nicely in a flat baking dish; the pan should be buttered, also the fish; season with salt and pepper, and cover with bread or cracker crumbs. Place a piece of butter over each. Bake for fifteen or twenty minutes. Garnish with fried parsley and cut lemon.

BAKED SALMON TROUT

This deliciously flavored game fish is baked precisely as shad or white fish, but should be accompanied with cream gravy to make it perfect. It should be baked slowly, basting often with butter and water. When done have ready in a saucepan a cup of cream, diluted with a few spoonfuls of hot water, for fear it might clot in heating, in which have been stirred cautiously two tablespoonfuls of melted butter, a scant tablespoonful of flour, and a little chopped parsley. Heat this in a vessel set within another of boiling water, add the gravy from the dripping-pan, boil up once to thicken, and when the trout is laid on a suitable hot dish, pour this sauce around it. Garnish with sprigs of parsley.

This same fish boiled, served with the same cream gravy (with the exception of the fish gravy), is the proper way to cook it.

BROILED SPANISH MACKEREL

Split the fish down the back, take out the backbone, wash it in cold water, dry it with a clean, dry cloth, sprinkle it lightly with salt and lay it on a buttered gridiron, over a clear fire, with the flesh side downward, until it begins to brown; then turn the other side. Have ready a mixture of two tablespoonfuls of butter melted, a tablespoonful of lemon juice, a teaspoonful of salt, some pepper. Dish up the fish hot from the gridiron on a hot dish, turn over the mixture and serve it while hot.

Broiled Spanish mackerel is excellent with other fish sauces. Boiled Spanish mackerel is also very fine with most of the fish sauces, more especially "Maître d'Hotel Sauce."

BOILED SALT MACKEREL

Wash and clean off all the brine and salt; put it to soak with the meat side down, in cold water over night; in the morning rinse it in one or two waters. Wrap each up in a cloth and put it into a kettle with considerable water, which should be cold; cook about thirty minutes. Take it carefully from the cloth, take out the backbones and pour over a little melted butter and cream; add a light sprinkle of pepper. Or make a cream sauce like the following:

Heat a small cup of milk to scalding. Stir into it a teaspoonful of cornstarch wet up with a little water. When this thickens, add two tablespoonfuls of butter, pepper, salt and chopped parsley, to taste. Beat an egg light, pour the sauce gradually over it, put the mixture again over the fire, and stir one minute, not more. Pour upon the fish, and serve it with some slices of lemon, or a few sprigs of parsley or watercress, on the dish as a garnish.

BAKED SALT MACKEREL.

When the mackerel have soaked over night, put them in a pan and pour on boiling water enough to cover. Let them stand a couple of minutes, then drain them off, and put them in the pan with a few lumps of butter; pour on a half teacupful of sweet cream, or rich milk, and a little pepper; set in the oven and let it bake a little until brown.

FRIED SALT MACKEREL

Select as many salt mackerel as required; wash and cleanse them well, then put them to soak all day in *cold* water, changing them every two hours; then put them into fresh water just before retiring. In the morning drain off the water, wipe them dry, roll them in flour, and fry in a little butter on a hot, thick-bottomed frying pan. Serve with a little melted butter poured over, and garnish with a little parsley.

BOILED FRESH MACKEREL

Fresh mackerel are cooked in water salted, and a little vinegar added; with this exception they can be served in the same way as the salt mackerel. Broiled ones are very nice with the same cream sauce, or you can substitute egg sauce.

FRESH STURGEON STEAK MARINADE

Take one slice of sturgeon two inches thick; let it stand in hot water five minutes; drain, put it in a bowl and add a gill of vinegar, two tablespoonfuls of melted butter, half a teaspoonful of salt, 1/2 teaspoonful of black pepper and the juice of half a lemon; let it stand six hours, turning it occasionally; drain and dry on a napkin; dip it in egg; roll in breadcrumbs and fry, or rather boil, in very hot fat. Beat up the yolks of two raw eggs, add a teaspoonful of French mustard, and by degrees, half of the marinade, to make a smooth sauce, which serve with the fish.

POTTED FRESH FISH

After the fish has laid in salt water six hours, take it out, and to every six pounds of fish take one-quarter cupful each of salt, black pepper and cinnamon, one-eighth cupful of allspice, and one teaspoonful of cloves.

Cut the fish in pieces and put into a half-gallon stone baking-jar, first a layer of fish, then the spices, flour, and then spread a thin layer of butter on, and continue so until the dish is full. Fill the jar with equal parts of vinegar and water, cover with tightly fitting lid, so that the steam cannot escape; bake five hours, remove from the oven, and when it is cold it is to be cut in slices and served. This is a tea or lunch dish.

FISH IN WHITE SAUCE

Flake up cold boiled halibut and set the plate into the steamer that the fish may heat without drying. Boil the bones and skin of the fish with a slice of onion and a *very* small piece of red pepper; a bit of this the size of a kernel of coffee will make the sauce quite as hot as most persons like it. Boil this stock down to half a pint; thicken with one teaspoonful of butter and one teaspoonful of flour, mixed together. Add one drop of extract of almond. Pour this sauce over your halibut and stick bits of parsley over it.

MAYONNAISE FISH

Take a pound or so of cold boiled fish (halibut, rock or cod), not chop, but cut, into pieces an inch in length. Mix in a bowl a dressing as follows: The yolks of four boiled eggs rubbed to a smooth paste with salad oil or butter; add to these salt, pepper, mustard, two teaspoonfuls of white sugar, and, lastly, six tablespoonfuls of vinegar. Beat the mixture until light, and just before pouring it over the fish, stir in lightly the frothed white of a raw egg. Serve the fish in a glass dish, with half the dressing stirred in with it. Spread the remainder over the top, and lay lettuce leaves (from the core of the head of lettuce) around the edges, to be eaten with it.

FISH CHOWDER (Rhode Island)

Fry five or six slices of fat pork crisp in the bottom of the pot you are to make your chowder in; take them out and chop them into small pieces, put them back into the bottom of the pot with their own gravy. (This is much better than having the slices whole.)

Cut four pounds of fresh cod or sea bass into pieces two inches square, and lay enough of these on the pork to cover it. Follow with a layer of chopped onions, a little parsley, summer savory and pepper, either black or cayenne. Then a layer of split Boston, or butter, or whole cream crackers, which have been soaked in warm water until moistened through, but not ready to break. Above this put a layer of pork and repeat the order given above – onions, seasoning (not too much), crackers and pork, until your materials are exhausted. Let the topmost layer be buttered crackers well soaked. Pour in enough cold water to barely cover all. Cover the pot, stew gently for an hour, watching that the water does not sink too low. Should it leave the upper layer exposed, replenish cautiously from the boiling teakettle. When the chowder is thoroughly done, take out with a perforated skimmer and put into a tureen. Thicken the gravy with a tablespoonful of flour and about the same quantity of butter; boil up and pour over the chowder. Serve sliced lemon, pickles and stewed tomatoes with it, that the guests may add if they like.

CODFISH BALLS

Take a pint bowl of codfish picked very fine, two pint bowls of whole raw peeled potatoes, sliced thickly; put them together in plenty of cold water and boil until the potatoes are thoroughly cooked; remove from the fire and drain off all the water. Mash them with the potato masher; add a piece of butter the size of an egg, one well-beaten egg, and three spoonfuls of cream or rich milk. Flour your hands and make into balls or cakes. Put an ounce each of butter and lard into a frying pan; when hot, put in the balls and fry a nice brown. Do not freshen the fish before boiling with the potatoes. Many cooks fry them in a quantity of lard similar to boiled doughnuts.

STEWED CODFISH (Salt)

Take a thick, white piece of salt codfish, lay it in cold water for a few minutes to soften it a little, enough to render it more easily to be picked up. Shred it in very small bits, put it over the fire in a stew pan with cold water; let it come to a boil, turn off this water carefully, and add a pint of milk to the fish, or more according to quantity. Set it over the fire again and let it boil slowly about three minutes, now add a good-sized piece of butter, a shake of pepper and a thickening of a tablespoonful of flour in enough cold milk to make a cream. Stew five minutes longer, and just before serving stir in two well-beaten eggs. The eggs are an addition that could be dispensed with, however, as it is very good without them. An excellent breakfast dish.

CODFISH A LA MODE

Pick up a teacupful of salt codfish very fine and freshen – the desiccated is nice to use; two cups mashed potatoes, one pint cream or milk, two well-beaten eggs, half a cup butter, salt and pepper; mix; bake in an earthen baking dish from twenty to twenty-five minutes; serve in the same dish, placed on a small platter, covered with a fine napkin.

BOILED FRESH COD

Sew up the piece of fish in thin cloth, fitted to shape; boil in salted water (boiling from the first), allowing about fifteen minutes to the pound. Carefully unwrap and pour over it warm oyster sauce. A whole one boiled the same.

Hotel Brighton.

BOILED SALT CODFISH (New England Style)

Cut the fish into square pieces, cover with cold water, set on the back part of the stove; when hot, pour off water and cover again with cold water; let it stand about four hours and simmer, not boil; put the fish on a platter, then cover with a drawn-butter gravy and serve. Many cooks prefer soaking the fish overnight.

BOILED CODFISH AND OYSTER SAUCE

Lay the fish in cold, salted water half an hour before it is time to cook it, then roll it in a clean cloth dredged with flour; sew up the edges in such a manner as to envelop the fish entirely, yet have but *one* thickness of cloth over any part. Put the fish into boiling water slightly salted; add a few whole cloves and peppers and a bit of lemon peel; pull gently on the fins, and when they come out easily the fish is done. Arrange neatly on a folded napkin, garnish and serve with oyster sauce. Take six oysters to every pound of fish and scald (blanch) them in a half-pint of hot oyster liquor; take out the oysters and add to the liquor, salt, pepper, a bit of mace and an ounce of butter; whip into it a gill of milk containing half of a teaspoonful of flour. Simmer a moment; add the oysters, and send to table in a sauceboat. Egg sauce is good with this fish.

BAKED CODFISH

If salt fish, soak, boil and pick the fish, the same as for fish-balls. Add an equal quantity of mashed potatoes, or cold, boiled, chopped potatoes, a large piece of butter, and warm milk enough to make it quite soft. Put it into a buttered dish, rub butter over the top, shake over a little sifted flour, and bake about thirty minutes, and until a rich brown. Make a sauce of drawn butter, with two hard-boiled eggs sliced, served in a gravy boat.

CODFISH STEAK (New England Style)

Select a medium-sized fresh codfish, cut it in steaks crosswise of the fish, about an inch and a half thick; sprinkle a little salt over them, and let them stand two hours. Cut into dice a pound of salt fat pork, fry out all the fat from them and remove the crisp bits of pork; put the codfish steaks in a pan of corn meal, dredge them with it, and when the pork fat is smoking hot, fry the steaks in it to a dark brown color on both sides. Squeeze over them a little lemon juice, add a dash of freshly ground pepper, and serve with hot, old-fashioned, well-buttered Johnny Cake.

SCALLOPED FISH

Pick any cold fresh fish, or salt codfish, left from the dinner, into fine bits, carefully removing all the bones.

Take a pint of milk in a suitable dish and place it in a saucepan of boiling water; put into it a few slices of onion cut very fine, a sprig of parsley minced fine, add a piece of butter as large as an egg, a pinch of salt, a sprinkle of white pepper, then stir in two tablespoonfuls of cornstarch, or flour, rubbed in a little cold milk; let all boil up and remove from the fire. Take a dish you wish to serve it in, butter the sides and bottom. Put first a layer of the minced fish, then a layer of the cream, then sprinkle over that some cracker or breadcrumbs, then a layer of fish again, and so on until the dish is full; spread cracker or breadcrumbs last on the top to prevent the milk from scorching.

This is a very good way to use up cold fish, making a nice breakfast dish, or a side dish for dinner.

POTTED FISH

Take out the backbone of the fish; for one weighing two pounds take a tablespoonful of allspice and cloves mixed; these spices should be put into little bags of not too thick muslin; put sufficient salt directly upon each fish; then roll in cloth, over which sprinkle a little cayenne pepper; put alternate layers of fish, spice and sage in an earthen jar; cover with the best cider vinegar; cover the jar closely with a plate, and over this, put a covering of dough, rolled out to twice the thickness of pie crust. Make the edges of paste, to adhere closely to the sides of the jar, so as to make it air tight. Put the jar into a pot of cold water and let it boil from three to five hours, according to quantity. Ready when cold.

FISH FRITTERS

Take a piece of salt codfish, pick it up very fine, put it into a saucepan, with plenty of *cold* water; bring it to a boil, turn off the water, and add another of cold water; let this boil with the fish about fifteen minutes, very slowly; strain off this water, making the fish quite dry, and set aside to cool. In the meantime, stir up a batter of a pint of milk, four eggs, a pinch of salt, one large teaspoonful of baking powder in flour, enough to make thicker than battercakes. Stir in the fish and fry like any fritters. Very fine accompaniment to a good breakfast.

Eat Like a President: Book I

SHELLFISH
And Other Seafood

BOILED LOBSTER

Put a handful of salt into a large kettle or pot of boiling water. When the water boils very hard put in the lobster, having first brushed it and tied the claws together with a bit of twine. Keep it boiling from twenty minutes to half an hour, in proportion to its size. If boiled too long the meat will be hard and stringy. When it is done take it out, lay it on its claws to drain, and then wipe it dry.

It is scarcely necessary to mention that the head of a lobster and what are called the ladyfingers are not to be eaten.

Very large lobsters are not the best, the meat being coarse and tough. The male is best for boiling; the flesh is firmer and the shell a brighter red. It may readily be distinguished from the female; the tail is narrower, and the two uppermost fins within the tail are stiff and hard. Those of the hen lobster are not so, and the tail is broader.

Hen lobsters are preferred for sauce or salad, on account of their coral. The head and small claws are never used.

They should be alive and freshly caught when put into the boiling kettle. After being cooked and cooled, split open the body and tail and crack the claws, to extract the meat. The sand pouch found near the throat should be removed. Care should be exercised that none of the feathery, tough, gill-like particles found under the body shell get mixed with the meat, as they are indigestible and have caused much trouble.

Serve on a platter. Lettuce and other concomitants of a salad should also be placed on the table or platter.

SCALLOPED LOBSTER

Butter a deep dish and cover the bottom with fine breadcrumbs; put on this a layer of chopped lobster, with pepper and salt; so on, alternately, until the dish is filled, having crumbs on top. Put on bits of butter, moisten with milk and bake about twenty minutes.

DEVILED LOBSTER

Take out all the meat from a boiled lobster, reserving the coral; season highly with mustard, cayenne, salt and some kind of table sauce; stew until well mixed and put it in a covered saucepan, with just enough hot water to keep from burning; rub the coral smooth, moistening with vinegar until it is thin enough to pour easily, then stir it into the saucepan. The dressing should be prepared before the meat is put on the fire, and which ought to boil but once before the coral is put in; stir in a heaping teaspoonful of butter, and when it boils again it is done and should be taken up at once, as too much cooking toughens the meat.

LOBSTER CROQUETTES

Take any of the lobster remaining from table and pound it until the dark, light meat and coral are well mixed; put with it not quite as much fine breadcrumbs; season with pepper, salt and a very little cayenne pepper; add a little melted butter, about two tablespoonfuls if the bread is rather dry; form into egg-shaped or round balls; roll them in egg, then in fine crumbs, and fry in boiling lard.

LOBSTER PATTIES

Cut some boiled lobster in small pieces; then take the small claws and the spawn, put them in a suitable dish, and jam them to a paste with a potato masher. Now add to them a ladleful of gravy or broth, with a few breadcrumbs; set it over the fire and boil; strain it through a strainer, or sieve, to the thickness of a cream, and put half of it to your lobsters, and save the other half to sauce them with after they are baked.

Put to the lobster the bigness of an egg of butter, a little pepper and salt; squeeze in a lemon, and warm these over the fire enough to melt the butter, set it to cool, and sheet your patty pan or a plate or dish with good puff paste, then put in your lobster, and cover it with a paste; bake it within three-quarters of an hour before you want it; when it is baked, cut up your cover, and warm up the other half of your sauce above mentioned, with a little butter, to the thickness of cream, and pour it over your patty, with a little squeezed lemon; cut your cover in two, and lay it on the top, two inches distant, so that what is under may be seen. You may bake crawfish, shrimps or prawns the same way; and they are all proper for plates or little dishes for a second course.

LOBSTER Á LA NEWBURG

Take one whole lobster, cut up in pieces about as large as a hickory nut. Put in the same pan with a piece of butter size of a walnut, season with salt and pepper to taste, and thicken with heavy cream sauce; add the yolk of one egg and two oz. of sherry wine.

Cream sauce for above is made as follows: 1 oz. butter, melted in saucepan; 2 oz. flour, mixed with butter, thin down to proper consistency with boiling cream.

Rector's Oyster House, Chicago.

CRABS (Soft Shell)

Crabs may be boiled as lobsters. They make a fine dish when stewed. Take out the meat from the shell, put it into a saucepan with butter, pepper, salt, a pinch of mace and a very little water; dredge with flour and let simmer five minutes over a slow fire. Serve hot; garnish the dish with the claws laid around it.

The usual way of cooking them is frying them in plenty of butter and lard mixed; prepare them the same as frying fish. The spongy substance from the sides should be taken off, also the sand bag. Fry a nice brown and garnish with parsley.

BAKED CRABS

Mix with the contents of a can of crabs, breadcrumbs or

pounded crackers. Pepper and salt the whole to taste; mince some cold ham; have the baking pan well buttered, place therein first a layer of the crab meat, prepared as above, then a layer of the minced ham, and so on, alternately until the pan is filled. Cover the top with breadcrumbs and bits of butter, and bake.

DEVILED CRABS

Half a dozen fresh crabs, boiled and minced, two ounces of butter, one small teaspoonful of mustard powder; cayenne pepper and salt to taste. Put the meat into a bowl and mix carefully with it an equal quantity of fine breadcrumbs. Work the butter to a light cream, mix the mustard well with it, then stir in very carefully, a handful at a time, the mixed crabs, a tablespoonful of cream and crumbs. Season to taste with cayenne pepper and salt; fill the crab shells with the mixture, sprinkle breadcrumbs over the tops, put three small pieces of butter upon the top of each, and brown them quickly in a hot oven. They will puff in baking and will be found very nice. Half the quantity can be made. A crab shell will hold the meat of two crabs.

CRAB CROQUETTES

Pick the meat of boiled crabs and chop it fine. Season to taste with pepper, salt and melted butter. Moisten it well with rich milk or cream, then stiffen it slightly with bread or cracker crumbs. Add two or three well-beaten eggs to bind the mixture. Form the croquettes, egg and bread, crumb them and fry them delicately in boiling lard. It is better to use a wire frying basket for croquettes of all kinds.

SCALLOPED CRABS

Put the crabs into a kettle of boiling water, and throw in a handful of salt. Boil from twenty minutes to half an hour. Take them from the water when done and pick out all the meat; be careful not to break the shell. To a pint of meat put a little salt and pepper; taste, and if not enough add more, a little at a time, till suited. Grate in a very little nutmeg and add one spoonful of cracker or breadcrumbs, two eggs well beaten, and two tablespoonfuls of butter (even full); stir all well together; wash the shells clean, and fill each shell full of the mixture; sprinkle crumbs over the top and moisten with the liquor; set in the oven till of a nice brown; a few minutes will do it. Send to the table hot, arranged on large dishes. They are eaten at breakfast or supper.

CRAB PIE

Procure the crabs alive, and put them in boiling water, along with some salt. Boil them for a quarter of an hour or twenty minutes, according to the size. When cold pick the meat from the claws and body. Chop all together, and mix it with crumbs of bread, pepper and salt, and a little butter. Put all this into the shell and brown in a hot oven. A crab shell will hold the meat of two crabs.

OYSTERS

Oysters must be fresh and fat to be good. They are in season from September to May.

The small ones, such as are sold by the quart, are good for pies, fritters, or stews; the largest of this sort are nice for frying or pickling for family use.

FRIED OYSTERS

Take large oysters from their own liquor into a thickly folded napkin to dry them; then make hot an ounce each of butter and lard in a thick-bottomed frying pan. Season the oysters with pepper and salt, then dip each one into egg and cracker crumbs rolled fine, until it will take up no more. Place them in the hot grease and fry them a delicate brown, turning them on both sides by sliding a broad-bladed knife under them. Serve them crisp and hot.

Boston Oyster House.

Some prefer to roll oysters in corn meal and others use flour, but they are much more crisp with egg and cracker crumbs.

OYSTERS FRIED IN BATTER

Ingredients – One-half pint of oysters, two eggs, one-half pint of milk, sufficient flour to make the batter; pepper and salt to taste; when liked, a little nutmeg; hot lard.

Scald the oysters in their own liquor, beard them, and lay them on a cloth to drain thoroughly. Break the eggs into a basin, mix the flour with them, add the milk gradually, with nutmeg and seasoning, and put the oysters in a batter. Make some lard hot in a deep frying pan; put in the oysters one at a time; when done, take them up with a sharp pointed skewer and dish them on a napkin. Fried oysters are frequently used for garnishing boiled fish, and then a few breadcrumbs should be added to the flour.

STEWED OYSTERS (in Milk or Cream)

Drain the liquor from two quarts of oysters; mix with it

a small teacupful of hot water, add a little salt and pepper and set it over the fire in a saucepan. Let it boil up once, put in the oysters, let them come to a boil, and when they "ruffle" add two tablespoonfuls of butter. The instant it is melted and well stirred in, put in a pint of boiling milk and take the saucepan from the fire. Serve with oyster or cream crackers. Serve while hot.

If thickening is preferred, stir in a little flour or two tablespoonfuls of cracker crumbs.

PLAIN OYSTER STEW

Same as milk or cream stew, using only oyster liquor and water instead of milk or cream, adding more butter after taking up.

OYSTER SOUP

For oyster soup, see SOUPS.

DRY OYSTER STEW

Take six to twelve large oysters and cook them in half a pint of their own liquor; season with butter and white pepper; cook for five minutes, stirring constantly. Serve in hot soup plates or bowls.

Fulton Market, New York.

BOSTON FRY

Prepare the oysters in egg batter and fine cracker meal; fry in butter over a slow fire for about ten minutes; cover the hollow of a hot platter with tomato sauce; place the oysters in it, but not covering; garnished with chopped parsley sprinkled over the oysters.

Hugo Ziemann and Fanny Lemira Gillette

Boston Oyster House.

BROILED OYSTERS

Dry a quart of oysters in a cloth, dip each in melted butter well peppered; then in beaten egg, or not, then in bread or cracker crumbs also peppered. Broil on a wire broiler over live coals three to five minutes. Dip over each a little melted butter. Serve hot.

OYSTER ROAST IN THE SHELL No. 1

Select the large ones, those usually termed "Saddle Rocks," formerly known as a distinct variety, but which are now but the large oysters selected from any beds; wash and wipe them, and place with the upper or deep shell down, to catch the juice, over or on live coals. When they open their shells, remove the shallow one, being careful to save all the juice in the other; place them, shells and all, on a hot platter, and send to the table hot to be seasoned by each person with butter and pepper to taste. If the oysters are fine, and they are just cooked enough and served hot, this is, *par excellence*, the style.

OYSTER ROAST No. 2

Put one quart of oysters in a basin with their own liquor and let them boil three or four minutes; season with a little salt, pepper and a heaping spoonful of butter. Serve on buttered toast.

STEAMED OYSTERS

Wash and drain a quart of counts or select oysters; put them in a shallow pan and place in a steamer over boiling water; cover and steam till they are plump, with the edges ruffled, but no longer. Place to a heated dish, with butter, pepper, and salt, and serve.

Baltimore Style

STEAMED OYSTERS IN THE SHELL

Wash and place them in an airtight vessel, laying them the upper shell downward, so that the liquor will not run out when they open. Place this dish or vessel over a pot of boiling water where they will get the steam. Boil them rapidly until the shells open, about fifteen to twenty minutes. Serve at once while hot, seasoned with butter, salt and pepper.

PAN OYSTERS No. 1

Cut some stale bread into thin slices, taking off all the crust, round the slices to fit patty-pans; toast, butter, place them in the pans and moisten with three or four teaspoonfuls of oyster liquor; place on the toast a layer of oysters, sprinkle with pepper, and put a small piece of butter on top of each pan; place all the pans in a baking-pan, and place in the oven, covering tightly. They will cook in seven or eight minutes if the oven is hot; or, cook till the beards are ruffled; remove the cover, sprinkle lightly with salt, replace, and cook one minute longer. Serve in patty pans. They are delicious.

New York Style.

PAN OYSTERS No. 2

Lay in a thin pie tin or dripping-pan, half a pint of large oysters, or more if required; have the pan large enough so that each oyster will lie flat on the bottom; put in over them a little oyster liquor, but not enough to float; place them carefully in a hot oven and just heat them through thoroughly – do not bake them – which will be in three to five minutes, according to fire; take them up and place on toast; first moistened with the hot juice from the pan. A very good substitute for oysters roasted in the shell, the slow cooking brings out the flavor.

French Restaurant, New Orleans, La.

OYSTER FRITTERS

Select plump, good-sized oysters; drain off the juice, and to a cup of this juice add a cup of milk, a little salt, four well-beaten eggs, and flour enough to make batter like griddle cakes. Envelope an oyster in a spoonful of this batter (some cut them in halves or chop them fine), then fry in butter and lard, mixed in a frying pan the same as we fry eggs, turning to fry brown on both sides. Send to the table very hot.

Delmonico.

Most cooks fry oyster fritters the same as crullers, in a quantity of hot lard, but this is not always convenient; either way they are excellent.

OYSTER PATTIES

Line patty-pans with thin pastry, pressing it well to the tin. Put a piece of bread or a ball of paper in each. Cover them with paste and brush them over with the white of an egg. Cut an inch square of thin pastry, place on the center of each, glaze this also with egg, and bake in a quick oven fifteen to twenty minutes. Remove the bread or paper when half cold.

Scald as many oysters as you require (allowing two for each patty, three if small) in their own liquor. Cut each in four and strain the liquor. Put two tablespoonfuls of butter and two of flour into a thick saucepan; stir them together over the fire till the flour smells cooked, and then pour half a pint of oyster liquor and half a pint of milk into the flour and butter. (If you have cream use it instead of milk.) Stir till it is a thick, smooth sauce. Put the oysters into it and let them boil once. Beat the yolks of two eggs. Remove the oysters for one minute from the fire, then stir the eggs into them till the sauce looks like thick custard.

Fill the patties with this oyster fricassee, taking care to make it hot by standing in boiling water before dinner on the day required, and to make the patty cases hot before you fill them.

FULTON MARKET ROAST

It is still known in New York from the place at which it was and is still served. Take nine large oysters out of the shell; wash, dry and roast over a charcoal fire, on a broiler. Two minutes after the shells open they will be done. Take them off quickly, saving the juice in a small shallow, tin pan; keep hot until all are done; butter them and sprinkle with pepper. This is served for one person when calling for a roast of this kind. It is often poured over a slice of toast.

SCALLOPED OYSTERS

Have ready about a pint of fine cracker crumbs. Butter a deep earthen dish; put a layer of the cracker crumbs on the bottom; wet this with some of the oyster liquor; next have a layer of oysters; sprinkle with salt and pepper, and lay small bits of butter upon them; then add another layer of cracker crumbs and oyster juice; then oysters, pepper, salt and butter, and so on, until the dish is full; the top layer to be cracker crumbs. Beat up an egg in a cup of milk and turn over all. Cover the dish and set it in the oven for thirty or forty-five minutes. When baked through, uncover the top, set on the upper grate and brown.

OYSTER POTPIE

Scald a quart can of oysters in their own liquor; when it boils, skim out the oysters and set them aside in a warm place. To the liquor add a pint of hot water; season well with salt and pepper, a generous piece of butter, thicken with flour and cold milk. Have ready nice light biscuit dough, rolled twice as thick as piecrust; cut out into inch squares, drop them into the boiling stew, cover closely, and cook forty minutes. When taken up, stir the oysters into the juice and serve all together in one dish. A nice side *entrée*.

Prince's Bay, S. I.

BOSTON OYSTER PIE

Having buttered the inside of a *deep* pie plate, line it with puff paste, or common pie crust, and prepare another sheet of paste for the lid; put a clean towel into the dish (folded so as to support the lid), set it into the oven and bake the paste well; when done, remove the lid and take out the towel. While the paste is baking, prepare the oysters. Having picked off carefully every bit of shell that may be found about them, drain the liquor into a pan and put the oysters into a stew pan with barely enough of the liquor to keep them from burning; season them with pepper, salt and butter; add a little sweet cream or milk, and one or two crackers rolled fine; let the oysters simmer, but *not boil*, as that will shrivel them. Remove the upper crust of pastry and fill the dish with the oysters and gravy. Replace the cover and serve hot.

Some prefer baking the upper crust on a pie plate, the same size as the pie, then slipping it off on top of the pie after the same pie is filled with the oysters.

MOCK OYSTERS

Grate the corn, while green and tender, with a coarse grater, into a deep dish. For two ears of corn, allow one egg; beat the whites and yolks separately, and add them to the corn, with one tablespoonful of wheat flour and one of butter, a teaspoonful of salt and pepper to taste. Drop spoonfuls of this batter into a frying pan with hot butter and lard mixed, and fry a light brown on both sides.

In taste, they have a singular resemblance to fried oysters. The corn *must* be *young*.

FRICASSEED OYSTERS

Take a slice of raw ham, which has been pickled, but not smoked, and soak in boiling water for half an hour; cut it in quite small pieces, and put in a saucepan with two-thirds of a pint of veal or chicken broth, well strained; the liquor from a quart of oysters, one small onion, minced fine, a little chopped parsley, sweet marjoram, and pepper; let them simmer for twenty minutes, and then boil rapidly for two or three minutes; skim well and add one scant tablespoon of cornstarch, mixed smoothly in one-third cup of milk; stir constantly, and when it boils add the oysters and one ounce of butter; after which, just let it come to a boil, and remove the oysters to a deep dish; beat one egg, and add to it gradually some of the hot broth, and, when cooked, stir it into the pan; season with salt, and pour the whole over the oysters. When placed upon the table, squeeze the juice of a lemon over it.

SMALL OYSTER PIES

For each pie take a tin plate half the size of an ordinary dinner plate; butter it, and cover the bottom with a puff paste, as for pies; lay on it five or six select oysters, or enough to cover the bottom; butter them and season with a little salt and plenty of pepper; spread over this an egg batter, and cover with a crust of the paste, making small openings in it with a fork. Bake in a hot oven fifteen to twenty minutes, or until the top is nicely browned.

Boston Oyster House.

STEWED CLAMS

Wash clean as many round clams as required; pile them in a large iron pot, with half a cupful of hot water in the bottom, and put over the fire; as soon as the shells open take out the clams, cut off the hard, uneatable "fringe" from each with strong, clean scissors, put them into a stew pan with the broth from the pot, and boil slowly till they are quite tender; pepper well and thicken the gravy with flour stirred into melted butter.

Or, you may get two dozen freshly opened *very* small clams. Boil a pint of milk, a dash of white pepper and a small pat of butter. Now add the clams. Let them come to a boil and serve. Longer boiling will make the clams almost indigestible.

ROAST CLAMS IN THE SHELL

Roast in a pan over a hot fire, or in a hot oven, or, at a "Clam Bake," on hot stones; when they open, empty the juice into a saucepan; add the clams, with butter, pepper and a very little salt.

Rye Beach.

CLAM FRITTERS

Take fifty small or twenty-five large sand clams from their shells; if large, cut each in two, lay them on a thickly-folded napkin; put a pint bowl of wheat flour into a basin, add to it three well-beaten eggs, half a pint of sweet milk and nearly as much of their own liquor; beat the batter until it is smooth and perfectly free from lumps, then stir in the clams.

Put plenty of lard or beef fat into a thick-bottomed frying pan, let it become boiling hot; put in the batter by the spoonful; let them fry gently; when one side is a delicate brown turn the other.

CLAM CHOWDER

The materials needed are fifty round clams (quahogs), a large bowl of salt pork cut up fine, the same of onions finely chopped, and the same (or more, if you desire) of potatoes cut into eighths or sixteenths of original size; wash the clams very thoroughly and put them in a pot with half a pint of water; when the shells are open they are done; then take them from the shells and chop fine, saving all the clam water for the chowder; fry out the pork very gently, and when the scraps are a good brown take them out and put in the chopped onions to fry; they should be fried in a frying pan, and the chowder kettle be made very clean before they are put in it, or the chowder will burn. (The chief secret in making chowder is to fry the onions so delicately that they will be missing in the chowder.)

Add a quart of hot water to the onions; put in the clams, clam-water and pork scraps. After it boils, add the potatoes, and when they are cooked, the chowder is finished. Just before it is taken up, thicken it with a cup of powdered crackers, and add a quart of fresh milk. If too rich, add more water. No seasoning is needed but good black pepper.

With the addition of six sliced tomatoes, or half a can of the canned ones, this is the best recipe of this kind, and is served in many of our best restaurants.

New Bedford Recipe

SCALLOPED CLAMS

Purchase a dozen large soft clams in the shell and three dozen opened clams. Ask the dealer to open the first dozen, care being used not to injure the shells, which are to be used in cooking the clams. Clean the shells well, and put two soft clams on each half shell; add to each a dash of white pepper, and half a teaspoonful of minced celery. Cut a slice of fat bacon into the smallest dice, add four of these to each shell, strew over the top a thin layer of cracker dust; place a piece of table butter on top, and bake in the oven until brown. They are delightful when properly prepared.

SCALLOPS

If bought in the shell boil them and take out the hearts, which is the only part used. Dip them in beaten egg and fry in the same manner as oysters.

Some prefer them stewed the same as oysters.

FROGS (Fried)

Frogs are usually fried, and are considered a great delicacy. Only the hind-legs and quarters are used. Clean them well, season, and fry in egg batter, or dip in beaten egg and fine cracker crumbs, the same as oysters.

FROGS (Stewed)

Wash and skin the quarters, parboil them about three minutes, drain them. Now put into a stew pan two ounces of butter. When it is melted, lay in the frogs, and fry about two minutes, stirring them to prevent burning; shake over them a tablespoonful of sifted flour and stir it into them; add a sprig of parsley, a pinch of powdered summer savory, a bay leaf, three slices of onion, salt and pepper, a cup of hot water and one of cream. Boil gently until done; remove the legs, strain and mix into the gravy the yolks of two eggs, well beaten to a cream; put the legs in a suitable dish, pour over the gravy and serve.

STEWED WATER TURTLES, OR TERRAPINS

Select the largest, thickest and fattest, the females being the best; they should be alive when brought from market. Wash and put them alive into boiling water, add a little salt, and boil them until thoroughly done, or from ten to fifteen minutes, after which take off the shell, extract the meat, and remove carefully the sand-bag and gall; also all the entrails; they are unfit to eat, and are no longer used in cooking terrapins for the best tables. Cut the meat into pieces, and put it into a stew pan with its eggs, and sufficient fresh butter to stew it well. Let it stew till quite hot throughout, keeping the pan carefully covered, that none of the flavor may escape, but shake it over the fire while stewing. In another pan make a sauce of beaten yolk of egg, highly flavored with Madeira or sherry, and powdered nutmeg and mace, a gill of currant jelly, a pinch of cayenne pepper, and salt to taste, enriched with a large lump of fresh butter. Stir this sauce well over the fire, and when it has almost come to a boil take it off. Send the terrapins to the table hot in a covered dish, and the sauce separately in a sauce tureen, to be used by those who like it, and omitted by those who prefer the genuine flavor of the terrapins when simply stewed with butter. This is now the usual mode of dressing terrapins in Maryland, Virginia, and many other parts of the South, and will be found superior to any other. If there are no eggs in the terrapin, "egg balls" may be substituted. (See recipe.)

STEWED TERRAPIN

Plunge the terrapins alive into boiling water, and let them remain until the sides and lower shell begin to crack – this will take less than an hour; then remove them and let them get cold; take off the shell and outer skin, being careful to save all the blood possible in opening them. If there are eggs in them put them aside in a dish; take all the inside out, and be very careful not to break the gall, which must be immediately removed or it will make the rest bitter. It lies within the liver. Then cut up the liver and all the rest of the terrapin into small pieces, adding the blood and juice that have flowed out in cutting up; add half a pint of water; sprinkle a little flour over them as you place them in the stew pan; let them stew slowly ten minutes, adding salt, black and cayenne pepper, and a very small blade of mace; then add a gill of the best brandy and half a pint of the very best sherry wine; let it simmer over a slow fire very gently. About ten minutes or so, before you are ready to dish them, add half a pint of rich cream, and half a pound of sweet butter, with flour, to prevent boiling; two or three minutes before taking them off the fire peel the eggs carefully and throw them in whole. If there should be no eggs use the yolks of hens' eggs, hard-boiled. This recipe is for four terrapins.

STEWED TERRAPIN (with Cream)

Place in a saucepan, two heaping tablespoonfuls of butter and one of dry flour; stir it over the fire until it bubbles; then gradually stir in a pint of cream, a teaspoonful of salt, a quarter of a teaspoonful of white pepper, the same of grated nutmeg, and a very small pinch of cayenne. Next, put in a pint of terrapin meat and stir all until it is scalding hot. Move the saucepan to the back part of the stove or range, where the contents will keep hot but not boil; then stir in four well-beaten yolks of eggs; do not allow the terrapin to boil after adding the eggs, but pour it immediately into a tureen containing a gill of good Madeira and a tablespoonful of lemon juice. Serve hot.

Eat Like a President: Book I

PASTA

MACARONI Á LA ITALIENNE
Divide a quarter of a pound of macaroni into four-inch pieces. Simmer fifteen minutes in plenty of boiling water, salted. Drain.

Put the macaroni into a saucepan and turn over it a strong soup stock, enough to prevent burning. Strew over it an ounce of grated cheese; when the cheese is melted, dish. Put alternate layers of macaroni and cheese, then turn over the soup stock and bake half an hour.

MACARONI AND CHEESE
Break half a pound of macaroni into pieces an inch or two long; cook it in boiling water, enough to cover it well; put in a good teaspoonful of salt; let it boil about twenty minutes.

Drain it well and then put a layer in the bottom of a well-buttered pudding-dish; upon this some grated cheese and small pieces of butter, a bit of salt, then more macaroni, and so on, filling the dish; sprinkle the top layer with a thick layer of cracker crumbs.

Pour over the whole a teacupful of cream or milk. Set it in the oven and bake half an hour. It should be nicely browned on top. Serve in the same dish in which it was baked with a clean napkin pinned around it.

TIMBALE OF MACARONI

Break in very short lengths small macaroni (vermicelli, spaghetti, tagliarini). Let it be rather overdone; dress it with butter and grated cheese; then work into it one or two eggs, according to quantity.

Butter and breadcrumb a plain mold, and when the macaroni is nearly cold fill the mold with it, pressing it well down and leaving a hollow in the center, into which place a well-flavored mince of meat, poultry or game.

Then fill up the mold with more macaroni, pressed well down. Bake in a moderately heated oven, turn out and serve.

MACARONI Á LA CRÊME

Boil one-quarter of a pound of macaroni in plenty of hot water, salted, until tender; put half a pint of milk in a double boiler, and when it boils stir into it a mixture of two tablespoonfuls of butter and one of flour.

Add two tablespoonfuls of cream, a little white and cayenne pepper; salt to taste, and from one-quarter to one-half a pound of grated cheese, according to taste.

Drain and dish the macaroni; pour the boiling sauce over it and serve immediately.

MACARONI AND TOMATO SAUCE

Divide half a pound of macaroni into four-inch pieces, put it into boiling salted water enough to cover it; boil from fifteen to twenty minutes then drain.

Arrange it neatly on a hot dish and pour tomato sauce over it, and serve immediately while hot. See SAUCES for tomato sauce.

Eat Like a President: Book I

POULTRY AND GAME FOWL

Preparations

In choosing poultry, select those that are fresh and fat, and the surest way to determine whether they are young is to try the skin under the leg or wing. If it is easily broken, it is young; or, turn the wing backwards, if the joint yields readily, it is tender. When poultry is young the skin is thin and tender, the legs smooth, the feet moist and limber, and the eyes full and bright. The body should be thick and the breast fat.

Old turkeys have long hairs, and the flesh is purplish where it shows under the skin on the legs and back. About March they deteriorate in quality.

Young ducks and geese are plump, with light, semi-transparent fat, soft breast bone, tender flesh, leg-joints which will break by the weight of the bird, fresh-colored and brittle beaks, and windpipes that break when pressed between the thumb and forefinger. They are best in fall and winter.

Young pigeons have light red flesh upon the breast, and full, fresh-colored legs; when the legs are thin and the breast very dark the birds are old.

Fine game birds are always heavy for their size; the flesh of the breast is firm and plump and the skin clear; and if a few feathers be plucked from the inside of the leg and around the vent, the flesh of freshly-killed birds will be fat and fresh-colored; if it is dark and discolored, the game has been hung a long time. The wings of good ducks, geese, pheasants and woodcock are tender to the touch; the tips of the long wing feathers of partridges are pointed in young birds and round in old ones. Quail, snipe and small birds should have full, tender breasts.

Poultry should never be cooked until six or eight hours after it has been killed, but it should be picked and drawn as soon as possible. Plunge it in a pot of scalding hot water; then pluck off the feathers, taking care not to tear the skin; when it is picked clean, roll up a piece of white paper, set fire to it and singe off all the hairs. The head, neck and feet should be cut off, and the ends of the legs skewered to the body, and a string tied tightly around the body. When roasting a chicken or small fowl there is danger of the legs browning or becoming too hard to be eaten. To avoid this, take strips of cloth, dip them into a little melted lard, or even just rub them over with lard, and wind them around the legs. Remove them in time to allow the legs to brown delicately.

Fowls, and also various kinds of game, when bought at our city markets, require a more thorough cleansing than those sold in country places, where as a general thing the meat is wholly dressed. In large cities they lay for some length of time with the intestines undrawn, until the flavor of them diffuses itself all through the meat, rendering it distasteful. In this case, it is safe, after taking out the intestines, to rinse out in several waters, and in next to the last water, add a teaspoonful of baking soda, say to a quart of water. This process neutralizes all sourness, and helps to destroy all unpleasant taste in the meat.

Poultry may be baked so that its wings and legs are soft and tender, by being placed in a deep roasting pan with close cover, thereby retaining the aroma and essences by absorption while confined. These pans are a recent innovation, and are made double with a small opening in the top for giving vent to the accumulation of steam and gases when required. Roast meats of any kind can also be cooked in the same manner, and it is a great improvement on the old plan.

ROAST TURKEY

Select a young turkey; remove all the feathers carefully, singe it over a burning newspaper on the top of the stove; then "draw" it nicely, being very careful not to break any of the internal organs; remove the crop carefully; cut off the head, and tie the neck close to the body by drawing the skin over it. Now rinse the inside of the turkey out with several waters, and in the next to the last, mix a teaspoonful of baking soda; oftentimes the inside of a fowl is very sour, especially if it is not freshly killed. Soda, being cleansing, acts as a corrective, and destroys that unpleasant taste which we frequently experience in the dressing when fowls have been killed for some time.

Now, after washing, wipe the turkey dry, inside and out, with a clean cloth, rub the inside with some salt, then stuff the breast and body with "Dressing for Fowls" (see below). Then sew up the turkey with a strong thread, tie the legs and wings to the body, rub it over with a little soft butter, sprinkle over some salt and pepper, dredge with a little flour; place it in a dripping-pan, pour in a cup of boiling water, and set in the oven. Baste the turkey often, turning it around occasionally so that every part will be uniformly baked.

When pierced with a fork and the liquid runs out perfectly clear, the bird is done. If any part is likely to scorch, pin over it a piece of buttered white paper. A fifteen-pound turkey requires between three and four hours to bake. Serve with cranberry sauce.

Gravy for Turkey – When you put the turkey in to roast, put the neck, heart, liver and gizzard into a stew pan with a pint of water; boil until they become quite tender; take them out of the water, chop the heart and gizzard, mash the liver and throw away the neck; return the chopped heart, gizzard and liver to the liquor in which they were stewed; set it to one side, and when the turkey is done it should be added to the gravy that dripped from the turkey, having first skimmed off the fat from the surface of the dripping-pan; set it all over the fire, boil three minutes and thicken with flour. It will not need brown flour to color the gravy. The garnishes for turkey or chicken are fried oysters, thin slices of ham, slices of lemon, fried sausages, or force meatballs, also parsley.

DRESSING OR STUFFING FOR FOWL

For an eight or ten pound turkey, cut the brown crust from slices or pieces of stale bread until you have as much as the inside of a pound loaf; put it into a suitable dish and pour tepid water (not warm, for that makes it heavy) over it; let it stand one minute, as it soaks very quickly. Now take up a handful at a time and squeeze it hard and dry with both hands, placing it, as you go along, in another dish; this process makes it very light.

When all is pressed dry, toss it all up lightly through your fingers; now add pepper, salt – about a teaspoonful – also a teaspoonful of powdered summer savory, the same amount of sage, or the green herb minced fine; add half a cup of melted butter, and a beaten egg, or not. Work thoroughly all together, and it is ready for dressing either fowls, fish or meats.

Some considers a little chopped sausage in turkey dressing an improvement, when well incorporated with the other ingredients.

For geese and ducks the stuffing may be made the same as for turkey, with the addition of a few slices of onion chopped fine.

OYSTER DRESSING OR STUFFING

This is made with the same ingredients as the above, with the exception of half a can of oysters drained and slightly chopped and added to the rest. This is used mostly with boiled turkey and chicken, and the remainder of the can of oysters used to make an oyster sauce to be poured over the turkey when served; served generally in a separate dish, to be dipped out as a person desires.

These recipes were obtained from an old colored cook, who was famous for his fine dressing for fowls, fish and meats, and his advice was, *always* soak stale bread in *cold* liquid, either milk or water, when *used* for stuffings or for puddings, as they were much lighter. Hot liquid makes them heavy.

BOILED TURKEY

Prepare as you would for baking or roasting; fill with an oyster stuffing, made as the above. Tie the legs and wings close to the body, place in salted boiling water with the breast downward; skim it often and boil about two hours, but not till the skin breaks. Serve with oyster or celery sauce. Boil a nicely pickled piece of salt pork, and serve at table a thin slice to each plate. Some prefer bacon or ham instead of pork.

Some roll the turkey in a cloth dipped in flour. If the liquor is to be used afterwards for soup, the cloth imparts an unpleasant flavor. The liquor can be saved and made into a nice soup for the next day's dinner, by adding the same seasoning as for chicken soup.

TURKEY SCALLOP

Pick the meat from the bones of cold turkey and chop it fine. Put a layer of breadcrumbs on the bottom of a buttered dish, moisten them with a little milk, then put in a layer of turkey with some of the filling, and cut small pieces of butter over the top; sprinkle with pepper and salt; then another layer of breadcrumbs, and so on until the dish is nearly full; add a little hot water to the gravy left from the turkey and pour over it; then take two eggs, two tablespoonfuls of milk, one of melted butter, a little salt and cracker crumbs as much as will make it thick enough to spread on with a knife; put bits of butter over it, and cover with a plate. Bake three-quarters of an hour. Ten minutes before serving, remove the plate and let it brown.

TURKEY HASHED

Cut the remnants of turkey from a previous dinner into pieces of equal size. Boil the bones in a quart of water, until the quart is reduced to a pint; then take out the bones, and to the liquor in which they were boiled add turkey gravy, if you have any, or white stock, or a small piece of butter with salt and pepper; let the liquor thus prepared boil up once; then put in the pieces of turkey, dredge in a little flour, give it one boil-up, and serve in a hot dish.

TURKEY WARMED OVER

Pieces of cold turkey or chicken may be warmed up with a little butter in a frying pan; place it on a warm platter, surround it with pieces of small thick slices of bread or biscuit halved, first dipping them in hot salted water; then place the platter in a warm oven with the door open. Have already made the following gravy to pour over all:

Into the frying pan put a large spoonful of butter, one or two cupfuls of milk, and any gravy that may be left over. Bring it to a boil; then add sufficient flour, wet in a little cold milk or water, to make it the consistency of cream. Season with salt, pepper and add a little of the dark meat chopped *very* fine. Let the sauce cook a few moments, then pour over the biscuit and fowl. This will be found a really nice dish.

BONED TURKEY

Clean the fowl as usual. With a sharp and pointed knife, begin at the extremity of the wing, and pass the knife down close to the bone, cutting all the flesh from the bone, and preserving the skin whole; run the knife down each side of the breast bone and up the legs, keeping close to the bone; then split the back half way up, and draw out the bones; fill the places whence the bones were taken with a stuffing, restoring the fowl to its natural form, and sew up all the incisions made in the skin. Lard with two or three rows of slips of fat bacon on the top, basting often with salt and water, and a little butter. Some like a glass of port wine in the gravy.

This is a difficult dish to attempt by any but skillful hands. Carve across in slices, and serve with tomato sauce.

ROAST GOOSE

The goose should not be more than eight months old, and the fatter the more tender and juicy the meat. Stuff with the following mixture: Three pints of breadcrumbs, six ounces of butter, or part butter and part salt pork, one teaspoonful each of sage, black pepper and salt, one chopped onion. Do not stuff very full, and stitch openings firmly together to keep flavor in and fat out. Place in a baking pan with a little water, and baste frequently with salt and water (some add vinegar); turn often so that the sides and back may be nicely browned. Bake two hours or more; when done take from the pan, pour off the fat, and to the brown gravy left add the chopped giblets which have previously been stewed until tender, together with the water they were boiled in; thicken with a little flour and butter rubbed together, bring to a boil and serve, English style.

ROAST CHICKEN

Pick and draw them, wash out well in two or three waters, adding a little soda to the last but one to sweeten it, if there is doubt as to its being fresh. Dry it well with a clean cloth, and fill the crop and body with a stuffing the same as "Dressing for Fowls."

Lay it in a dripping-pan; put a pint of hot water and a piece of butter in the dripping-pan, add to it a small tablespoonful of salt, and a small teaspoonful of pepper; baste frequently, and let it roast quickly, without scorching; when nearly done, put a piece of butter the size of a large egg to the water in the pan; when it melts, baste with it, dredge a little flour over, baste again, and let it finish; half an hour will roast a full grown chicken, if the fire is right. When done, take it up.

Having stewed the necks, gizzards, livers and hearts in a very little water, strain it and mix it hot with the gravy that has dripped from the fowls, and which must be first skimmed. Thicken it with a little browned flour, add to it the livers, hearts and gizzards chopped small. Or, put the giblets in the pan with the chicken and let them roast. Send the fowls to the table with the gravy in a boat. Cranberry sauce should accompany them, or any tart sauce.

BOILED CHICKEN

Clean, wash and stuff, as for roasting. Baste a floured cloth around each and put into a pot with enough boiling water to cover them well. The hot water cooks the skin at once and prevents the escape of the juice. The broth will not be so rich as if the fowls are put on in cold water, but this is a proof that the meat will be more nutritious and better flavored. Stew very slowly, for the first half hour especially. Boil an hour or more, guiding yourself by size and toughness. Serve with egg, bread or oyster sauce. (See SAUCES.)

STEAMED CHICKEN

Rub the chicken on the inside with pepper and half a teaspoonful of salt; place in a steamer in a kettle that will keep it as near the water as possible, cover and steam an hour and a half; when done, keep hot while dressing is prepared, then cut up, arrange on the platter, and serve with the dressing over it.

The dressing is made as follows: Boil one pint of gravy from the kettle without the fat, add cayenne pepper and half a teaspoonful of salt; stir a tablespoonful of flour into a quarter of a pint of cream until smooth and add to the gravy. Cornstarch may be used instead of the flour, and some cooks add nutmeg or celery salt.

FRICASSEE CHICKEN

Cut up two young chickens, put them in a stew pan with just enough cold water to cover them. Cover closely and let them heat very slowly; then stew them over an hour, or until tender. If they are old chickens they will require long, slow boiling, often from three to four hours. When tender, season with salt and pepper, a piece of butter as large as an egg, and a little celery, if liked. Stir up two tablespoonfuls of flour in a little water or milk and add to the stew, also two well-beaten yolks of eggs; let all boil up one minute; arrange the chicken on a warm platter, pour some of the gravy over it and send the rest to the table in a boat. The egg should be added to a little of the cooled gravy before putting with the hot gravy.

STEWED WHOLE SPRING CHICKEN

Dress a full-grown spring chicken the same as for roasting, seasoning it with salt and pepper inside and out; then fill the body with oysters; place it in a tin pail with a close-fitting cover. Set the pail in a pot of fast-boiling water and cook until the chicken is tender. Dish up the chicken on a warm dish, then pour the gravy into a saucepan, put into it a tablespoonful of butter, half a cupful of cream or rich milk, three hard-boiled eggs chopped fine, some minced herbs and a tablespoonful of flour. Let all boil up and then pour it over the chicken. Serve hot.

PICKLED CHICKEN

Boil four chickens till tender enough for meat to fall from bones; put meat in a stone jar and pour over it three pints of cold, good cider vinegar and a pint and a half of the water in which the chickens were boiled; add spices if preferred, and it will be ready for use in two days. This is a popular Sunday evening dish; it is good for luncheon at any time.

RISSOLES OF CHICKEN

Mince up finely the remains of a cold chicken together with half the quantity of lean, cold ham. Mix them well, adding enough white sauce to moisten them. Now have light paste rolled out until about a quarter of an inch or a little more in thickness. Cut the paste into pieces, one inch by two in size, and lay a little of the mixture upon the centers of half of the pieces and cover them with the other halves, pressing the edges neatly together and forming them into little rolls. Have your frying pan ready with plenty of boiling hot lard, or other frying medium, and fry until they become a golden-brown color. A minute or two will be sufficient for this. Then drain them well and serve immediately on a napkin.

CHICKEN PATTIES

Mince up fine cold chicken, either roasted or boiled. Season it with pepper and salt, and a little minced parsley and onion. Moisten it with chicken gravy or cream sauce, fill scalloped shells that are lined with pastry with the mixture, and sprinkle breadcrumbs over the tops. Put two or three tiny pieces of butter over each, and bake brown in a hot oven.

BROILED CHICKEN

After dressing and washing the chickens as previously directed, split them open through the backbone; frog them by cutting the cords under the wings and laying the wings out flat; cut the sinews under the second joint of the leg and turn the leg down; press down the breast-bone without breaking it.

Season the chicken with salt and pepper, lay it upon the gridiron with the inside first to the fire; put the gridiron over a slow fire, and place a tin sheet and weight upon the chicken, to keep it flat; let it broil ten minutes, then turn and proceed in the same manner with the other side.

The chicken should be perfectly cooked, but not scorched. A broiled chicken brought to the table with its wings and legs burnt, and its breast half cooked, is very disagreeable. To avoid this, the chicken must be closely watched while broiling, and the fire must be arranged so that the heat shall be equally dispensed. When the fire is too hot under any one part of the chicken, put a little ash on the fire under that part, that the heat may be reduced.

Dish a broiled chicken on a hot plate, putting a large lump of butter and a tablespoonful of hot water upon the plate, and turning the chicken two or three times that it may absorb as much of the butter as possible. Garnish with parsley. Serve with poached eggs on a separate dish. It takes from thirty to forty minutes to broil a chicken well.

CHICKEN PIE

Prepare the chicken as for fricassee. When the chicken is stewed tender, seasoned, and the gravy thickened, take it from the fire; take out the largest bones, scrape the meat from the neck and backbone, throw the bones away; line the sides of a four or six quart pudding-dish with a rich baking powder or soda biscuit dough, a quarter of an inch thick; put in part of the chicken, a few lumps of butter, pepper and salt, if needed, some cold boiled eggs cut in slices. Add the rest of the chicken and season as before; a few new potatoes in their season might be added. Pour over the gravy, being sure to have enough to fill the dish, and cover with a crust a quarter of an inch thick, made with a hole in the center the size of a teacup.

Brush over the top with beaten white of egg and bake

for half to three-quarters of an hour. Garnish the top with small bright celery leaves, neatly arranged in a circle.

FRIED CHICKEN

Wash and cut up a young chicken, wipe it dry, season with salt and pepper, dredge it with flour, or dip each piece in beaten egg and then in cracker crumbs. Have in a frying pan one ounce each of butter and sweet lard made boiling hot. Lay in the chicken and fry brown on both sides. Take up, drain it and set aside in a covered dish. Stir into the gravy left, if not too much, a large tablespoonful of flour, make it smooth, add a cup of cream or milk, season with salt and pepper, boil up and pour over the chicken. Some like chopped parsley added to the gravy. Serve hot.

If the chicken is old, put into a stew pan with a little water and simmer gently till tender; season with salt and pepper, dip in flour or cracker crumb and egg, and fry as above. Use the broth the chicken was cooked in to make the gravy, instead of the cream or milk, or use an equal quantity of both.

FRIED CHICKEN Á LA ITALIENNE

Make common batter; mix into it a cupful of chopped tomatoes, one onion chopped, some minced parsley, salt and pepper. Cut up young, tender chickens, dry them well and dip each piece in the batter; then fry brown in plenty of butter in a thick-bottomed frying pan. Serve with tomato sauce.

CHICKEN CROQUETTES No. 1

Put a cup of cream or milk in a saucepan, set it over the

fire, and when it boils add a lump of butter as large as an egg, in which has been mixed a tablespoonful of flour. Let it boil up thick; remove from the fire, and when cool mix into it a teaspoonful of salt, half a teaspoonful of pepper, a bit of minced onion or parsley, one cup of fine breadcrumbs, and a pint of finely-chopped cooked chicken, either roasted or boiled. Lastly, beat up two eggs and work in with the whole. Flour your hands and make into small, round, flat cakes; dip in egg and breadcrumbs and fry like fish cakes in butter and good sweet lard mixed, or like fried cakes in plenty of hot lard. Take them up with a skimmer and lay them on brown paper to free them from the grease. Serve hot.

CHICKEN CROQUETTES No. 2

Take any kind of fresh meat or fowl, chop very fine, add an equal quantity of smoothly mashed potatoes, mix, and season with butter, salt, black pepper, a little prepared mustard, and a little cayenne pepper; make into cakes, dip in egg and breadcrumbs and fry a light brown. A nice relish for tea.

TO FRY CROQUETTES

Beat up two eggs in a deep bowl; roll enough crackers until you have a cupful of crumbs, or the same of fine stale breadcrumbs; spread the crumbs on a large plate or pie tin. Have over the fire a kettle containing two or three inches of boiling lard. As fast as the croquettes are formed, roll them in the crumbs, then dip them in the beaten egg, then again roll them in crumbs; drop them in the smoking hot fat and fry them a light golden brown.

PRESSED CHICKEN

Clean and cut up your chickens. Stew in just enough water to cover them. When nearly cooked, season them well with salt and pepper. Let them stew down until the water is nearly all boiled out, and the meat drops easily from the bones. Remove the bones and gristle; chop the meat rather coarsely, then turn it back into the stew-kettle, where the broth was left (after skimming off all fat), and let it heat through again. Turn it into a square bread pan, placing a platter on the top, and a heavy weight on the platter. This, if properly prepared, will turn out like a mold of jelly and may be sliced in smooth, even slices. The success of this depends upon not having too much water; it will not jelly if too weak, or if the water is allowed to boil away entirely while cooking. A good way to cook old fowls.

CHICKEN LUNCH FOR TRAVELING

Cut a young chicken down the back; wash and wipe dry; season with salt and pepper; put in a dripping-pan and bake in a moderate oven three-quarters of an hour. This is much better for traveling lunch than when seasoned with butter.

All kinds of poultry and meat can be cooked quicker by adding to the water in which they are boiled a little vinegar or a piece of lemon. By the use of a little acid there will be a considerable saving of fuel, as well as shortening of time. Its action is beneficial on old tough meats, rendering them quite tender and easy of digestion. Tainted meats and fowls will lose their bad taste and odor if cooked in this way, and if not used too freely no taste of it will be acquired.

POTTED CHICKEN

Strip the meat from the bones of a cold roast fowl; to every pound of meat allow a quarter of a pound of butter, salt and cayenne pepper to taste; one teaspoonful of pounded mace, half a small nutmeg. Cut the meat into small pieces, pound it well with the butter, sprinkle in the spices gradually and keep pounding until reduced to a perfectly smooth paste. Pack it into small jars and cover with clarified butter, about a quarter of an inch in thickness. Two or three slices of ham minced and pounded with the above will be an improvement. Keep in a dry place. A luncheon or breakfast dish.

Old fowls can be made very tender by putting into them, while boiling, a piece of soda as large as a bean.

SCALLOPED CHICKEN

Divide a fowl into joints and boil till the meat leaves the bone readily. Take out the bones and chop the meat as small as dice. Thicken the water in which the fowl was boiled with flour and season to taste with butter and salt. Fill a deep dish with alternate layers of breadcrumbs and chicken and slices of cooked potatoes, having crumbs on top. Pour the gravy over the top and add a few bits of butter and bake till nicely browned. There should be gravy enough to moisten the dish. Serve with a garnish of parsley. Tiny new potatoes are nice in place of sliced ones when in season.

BREADED CHICKEN

Prepare young chickens as for fricassee by cutting them into pieces. Dip each piece in beaten egg, then in grated breadcrumbs or rolled cracker; season them with pepper and salt and a little minced parsley. Place them in a baking pan and put on the top of each piece a lump of butter, add half of a cupful of hot water; bake slowly, basting often. When sufficiently cooked take up on a warm platter. Into the pan pour a cup of cream or rich milk, a cupful of breadcrumbs. Stir it well until cooked, then pour it over the chicken. Serve while hot.

BROILED CHICKEN ON TOAST

Broil the usual way and when thoroughly done take it up in a square tin or dripping-pan, butter it well, season with pepper and salt and set it in the oven for a few minutes. Lay slices of moistened buttered toast on a platter; take the chicken up over it, add to the gravy in the pan part of a cupful of cream, if you have it; if not, use milk. Thicken with a little flour and pour over the chicken.

This is considered most excellent.

CURRY CHICKEN.

Cut up a chicken weighing from a pound and a half to two pounds, as for fricassee, wash it well, and put it into a stew pan with sufficient water to cover it; boil it, closely covered, until tender; add a large teaspoonful of salt, and cook a few minutes longer; then remove from the fire, take out the chicken, pour the liquor into a bowl, and set it one side. Now cut up into the stew pan two small onions, and fry them with a piece of butter as large as an egg; as soon as the onions are brown, skim them out and put in the chicken; fry for three or four minutes; next sprinkle over two teaspoonfuls of Curry Powder. Now pour over the liquor in which the chicken was stewed, stir all well together, and stew for five minutes longer, then stir into this a tablespoonful of sifted flour made thin with a little water; lastly, stir in a beaten yolk of egg, and it is done.

Serve with hot boiled rice laid around on the edge of a platter, and the chicken curry in the center.

This makes a handsome side dish, and a fine relish accompanying a full dinner of roast beef or any roast.

All first-class grocers and druggists keep this "India Curry Powder," put up in bottles. Beef, veal, mutton, duck, pigeons, partridges, rabbits or fresh fish may be substituted for the chicken, if preferred, and sent to the table with or without a dish of rice.

To Boil Rice or Curry – Pick over the rice, a cupful. Wash it thoroughly in two or three cold waters; then leave it about twenty minutes in cold water. Put into a stew pan two quarts of water with a teaspoonful of salt in it; and when it boils, sprinkle in the rice. Boil it briskly for twenty minutes, keeping the pan covered. Take it from the fire, and drain off the water. Afterwards set the saucepan on the back of the stove, with the lid off, to allow the rice to dry and the grains to separate.

Rice, if properly boiled, should be soft and white, and every grain stand alone. Serve it hot in a separate dish or served as above, laid around the chicken curry.

CHICKEN POTPIE No. 1

Cut and joint a large chicken, cover with cold water, and let it boil gently until tender. Season with salt and pepper, and thicken the gravy with two tablespoonfuls of flour, mixed smooth with a piece of butter the size of an egg. Have ready nice light bread-dough, cut with the top of a wineglass about a half an inch thick; let them stand half an hour and rise, then drop these into the boiling gravy. Put the cover on the pot closely, wrap a cloth around it, in order that no steam shall escape; and by no means allow the pot to cease boiling. Boil three-quarters of an hour.

CHICKEN POTPIE No. 2

This style of potpie was made more in our grandmother's day than now, as most cooks consider that cooking crust so long destroys its spongy lightness, and renders it too hard and dry.

Take a pair of fine fowls, cut them up, wash the pieces, and season with pepper only. Make a light biscuit dough, and plenty of it, as it is always much liked by the eaters of potpie. Roll out the dough not very thin, and cut most of it into long squares. Butter the sides of a pot, and line them with dough nearly to the top. Lay slices of cold ham at the bottom of the pot, and then the pieces of fowl, interspersed all through with squares of dough and potatoes, pared and quartered. Pour in a quart of water. Cover the whole with a lid of dough, having a slit in the center, through which the gravy will bubble up. Boil it steadily for two hours. Half an hour before you take it up, put in through the hole in the center of the crust some bits of butter rolled in flour, to thicken the gravy. When done, put the pie on a large dish, and pour the gravy over it.

You may intersperse it all through with cold ham.

A potpie may be made of ducks, rabbits, squirrels or venison. Also of beefsteak. A beefsteak, or some pork steaks (the lean only), greatly improve a chicken potpie. If you use no ham, season with salt.

CHICKEN STEWED WITH BISCUIT

Take chickens, and make a fricassee; just before you are ready to dish it up, have ready two baking-tins of rich soda or baking-powder biscuits; take them from the oven hot, split them apart by breaking them with your hands, lay them on a large meat platter, covering it, then pour the hot chicken stew over all. Send to the table hot. This is a much better way than boiling this kind of biscuit in the stew, as you are more sure of its being always light.

CHICKEN DRESSED AS TERRAPIN

Select young chickens, clean and cut them into pieces; put them into a stew pan with just *enough* water to cook them. When tender stir into it half of a cup of butter and one beaten egg. Season it with salt and pepper, a teaspoonful of powdered thyme; add two hard-boiled eggs coarsely minced and a small glass of wine. Boil up once and serve with jelly.

CHICKEN ROLY-POLY

One quart of flour, two teaspoonfuls of cream tartar mixed with the flour, one teaspoonful of soda dissolved in a teacupful of milk; a teaspoonful of salt; do not use shortening of any kind, but roll out the mixture half an inch thick, and on it lay minced chicken, veal or mutton. The meat must be seasoned with pepper and salt and be free from gristle. Roll the crust over and over, and put it on a buttered plate and place in a steamer for half an hour. Serve for breakfast or lunch, giving a slice to each person with gravy served with it.

CHICKEN TURNOVERS

Chop cold roast chicken very fine. Put it into a saucepan, place it over the fire, and moisten it with a little water and gravy, or a piece of butter. Season with salt and pepper; add a small tablespoonful of sifted flour dissolved in a little water; heat all through and remove from the fire to become cool. When cooled roll out some plain pie-crust quite thin, cut out in rounds as large as a saucer; wet the edge with cold water and put a large spoonful of the minced meat on one-half of the round; fold the other half over and pinch the edges well together, then fry them in hot drippings or fat a nice brown. They may also be cooked in a moderate oven.

CHICKEN PUDDING

Cut up two young chickens into good-sized pieces; put them in a saucepan with just enough water to cover them well. When boiled quite tender, season with salt and pepper; let them simmer ten or fifteen minutes longer; then take the chicken from the broth and remove all the large bones. Place the meat in a well-buttered pudding dish, season again, if necessary, adding a few bits of butter. Pour over this the following batter:

Eight eggs beaten light and mixed with one quart of milk, three tablespoonfuls of melted butter, a teaspoonful of salt and two large teaspoonfuls of baking powder, added to enough sifted flour to make a batter like griddle-cakes.

Bake one hour in a *moderate* oven.

Make a gravy of the broth that remained from the cooking of the chicken, adding a tablespoonful of flour stirred into a third of a cup of melted butter; let it boil up, putting in more water if necessary. Serve hot in a gravy boat with the pudding.

CHICKEN AND MACARONI

Boil a chicken until very tender, take out all the bones, and pick up the meat quite fine. Boil half a pound of macaroni until tender, first breaking it up to pieces an inch long. Butter a deep pudding dish, put on the bottom a layer of the cooked macaroni, then a layer of the minced chicken, bits of butter, pepper and salt, then some of the chicken liquor, over this put another layer of macaroni, and so on, until, the dish is filled. Pour a cup of cream over the whole, and bake half an hour. Serve on a platter.

ROAST DUCK (Tame)

Pick, draw, clean thoroughly, and wipe dry. Cut the neck close to the back, beat the breast-bone flat with a rolling pin, tie the wings and legs securely, and stuff with the following:

Three pints breadcrumbs, six ounces butter, or part butter and salt pork, two chopped onions and one teaspoonful each of sage, black pepper and salt. Do not stuff very full, and sew up the openings firmly to keep the flavor in and the fat out. If not fat enough, it should be larded with salt pork, or tie a slice upon the breast. Place in a baking pan, with a little water, and baste frequently with salt and water – some add onion, and some vinegar; turn often, so that the sides and back may all be nicely browned. When nearly done, baste with butter and a little flour. These directions will apply to tame geese as well as ducks. Young ducks should roast from twenty-five to thirty minutes, and full-grown ones for an hour or more, with frequent basting.

Some prefer them underdone and served very hot; but, as a rule, thorough cooking will prove more palatable. Make a gravy out of the necks and gizzards by putting them in a quart of cold water that must be reduced to a pint by boiling. The giblets, when done, may be chopped fine and added to the juice. The preferred seasonings are one tablespoonful of Madeira or sherry, a blade of mace, one small onion, and a little cayenne pepper; strain through a hair sieve; pour a little over the ducks and serve the remainder in a boat. Served with jellies or any tart sauce.

BRAISED DUCK

Prepare a pair of fine young ducks, the same as for roasting, place them in a stew pan together with two or three slices of bacon, a carrot, an onion stuck with two cloves, and a little thyme and parsley. Season with pepper, and cover the whole with a broth, adding to the broth a gill of white wine. Place the pan over a gentle fire and allow the ducks to simmer until done, basting them frequently. When done remove them from the pan, and place them where they will keep hot. A turnip should then be cut up and fried in some butter. When nicely browned, drain the pieces and cook them until tender in the liquor in which the ducks were braised. Now strain and thicken the gravy, and after dishing up the ducks, pour it over them, garnishing with the pieces of turnip.

Palmer House, Chicago.

STEWED DUCK

Prepare them by cutting them up the same as chicken for fricassee. Lay two or three very thin slices of salt pork upon the bottom of a stew pan; lay the pieces of duck upon the pork. Let them stew slowly for an hour, closely covered. Then season with salt and pepper, half a teaspoonful of powdered sage, or some green sage minced fine; one chopped onion. Stew another half hour until the duck is tender. Stir up a large tablespoonful of brown flour in a little water and add it to the stew. Let it boil up, and serve all together in one dish, accompanied with green peas.

Palmer House, Chicago.

DUCK PIE

Cut all the meat from cold roast ducks; put the bones and stuffing into cold water; cover them and let boil; put the meat into a deep dish; pour on enough of the stock made from the bones to moisten; cover with pastry slit in the center with a knife, and bake a light brown.

WARMED-UP DUCK

A nice dish for breakfast, and very relishing, can be made from the remains of a roast of duck. Cut the meat from the bones, pick out all the little tidbits in the recesses, lay them in a frying pan, and cover with water and the cold gravy left from the roast; add a piece of butter; let all boil up once and if not quite thick enough, stir in a little dissolved flour. Serve hot.

WILD DUCKS

Most wild ducks are apt to have the flavor of fish, and when in the hands of inexperienced cooks are sometimes unpalatable on this account. Before roasting them, parboil them with a small peeled carrot put within each duck. This absorbs the unpleasant taste. An onion will have the same effect, but unless you use onions in the stuffing the carrot is preferable. Roast the same as tame duck. Or put into the duck a whole onion peeled, plenty of salt and pepper and a glass of claret, bake in a hot oven twenty minutes. Serve hot with the gravy it yields in cooking and a dish of currant jelly.

ROAST DUCK (Wild)

Wild duck should not be dressed too soon after being killed. If the weather is cold it will be better for being kept several days. Bake in a hot oven, letting it remain for five or ten minutes without basting to keep in the gravy, then baste frequently with butter and water. If over-done it loses flavor, thirty to forty minutes in the right kind of an oven being sufficient. Serve on a very hot dish, and send to table as hot as possible with a cut lemon and the following sauce:

Put in a tiny saucepan a tablespoonful each of Worcestershire sauce and mushroom ketchup, a little salt and cayenne pepper and the juice of half a lemon. Mix well, make it hot, remove from the fire and stir in a teaspoonful of made mustard. Pour into a hot gravy boat.

California Style, Lick House.

CANVASBACK DUCK

The epicurean taste declares that this special kind of bird requires no spices or flavors to make it perfect, as the meat partakes of the flavor of the food that the bird feeds upon, being mostly wild celery; and the delicious flavor is best preserved when roasted quickly with a hot fire. After dressing the duck in the usual way by plucking, singeing, drawing, wipe it with a wet towel, truss the head under the wing; place it in a dripping-pan, put it in the oven, basting often, and roast it half an hour. It is generally preferred a little underdone. Place it when done on a hot dish, season well with salt and pepper, pour over it the gravy it has yielded in baking and serve it immediately while hot.

Delmonico.

ROAST PIGEONS

Pigeons lose their flavor by being kept more than a day after they are killed. They may be prepared and roasted or broiled the same as chickens; they will require from twenty to thirty minutes' cooking. Make a gravy of the giblets or not, season it with pepper and salt, and add a little flour and butter.

STEWED PIGEONS

Clean and stuff with onion dressing, thyme, etc., – do not sew up; take five or more slices of corned pork, let it fry a while in a pot so that the fat comes out and it begins to brown a little; then lay the pigeons all around in the fat, leaving the pork still in; add hot water enough to partially cover them; cover tightly and boil an hour or so until tender; then turn off some of the liquid, and keep turning them so they will brown nicely; then heat and add the liquor poured off; add extra thyme, pepper, and keep turning until the pigeons and gravy are nicely browned. Thicken with a little flour, and serve with the gravy poured over them; garnish with parsley.

PIGEON PIE

Take half a dozen pigeons; stuff each one with a

dressing the same as for turkey; loosen the joints with a knife, but do not separate them.

Put them in a stew pan with water enough to cover them, let them cook until nearly tender, then season them with salt and pepper and butter. Thicken the gravy with flour, remove and cool.

Butter a pudding dish, line the sides with a rich crust. Have ready some hard-boiled eggs cut in slices. Put in a layer of egg and birds and gravy until the dish is full. Cover with a crust and bake.

BROILED PIGEONS OR SQUABS

Split them down the back and broil the same as chicken; seasoning well with salt, pepper and plenty of butter. Broil slices of salt pork, very thin; place a slice over each bird and serve.

SQUAB POTPIE

Cut into dice three ounces of salt pork; divide six wild squabs into pieces at the joints; remove the skin. Cut up four potatoes into small squares, and prepare a dozen small dough balls.

Put into a yellow, deep baking dish the pork, potatoes and squabs, and then the balls of dough, season with salt, white pepper, a dash of mace or nutmeg; add hot water enough to cover the ingredients, cover with a "short" piecrust and bake in a moderate oven three-quarters of an hour.

Palmer House, Chicago.

ROASTED WOODCOCK

Skin the head and neck of the bird, pluck the feathers,

and truss it by bringing the beak of the bird under the wing, and fastening the pinion to the thigh; twist the legs at the knuckles and press the feet upon the thigh. Put a piece of bread under each bird to catch the drippings, baste with butter, dredge with flour, and roast fifteen or twenty minutes with a sharp fire. When done, cut the bread in diamond shape, each piece large enough to stand one bird upon, place them aslant on your dish, and serve with gravy enough to moisten the bread; serve some in the dish and some in the tureen; garnish with slices of lemon. Roast from twenty to twenty-five minutes.

SNIPE

Snipe are similar to woodcock, and may be served in the same manner; they will require less time to roast.

REED BIRDS

Pick and draw them very carefully, salt and dredge with flour, and roast with a quick fire ten or fifteen minutes. Serve on toast with butter and pepper. You can put in each one an oyster dipped in butter and then in breadcrumbs before roasting. They are also very nice broiled.

ROAST QUAIL

Rinse well and steam over boiling water until tender, then dredge with flour, and smother in butter; season with salt and pepper and roast inside the stove; thicken the gravy; serve with green grape jelly, and garnish with parsley.

TO ROAST PARTRIDGES, PHEASANTS, QUAIL, OR GROUSE

Carefully cut out all the shot, wash thoroughly but quickly, using soda in the water; rinse again, and dry with a clean cloth. Stuff them and sew them up. Skewer the legs and wings to the body, larder the breast with very thin slices of fat salt pork, place them in the oven, and baste with butter and water before taking up, having seasoned them with salt and pepper; or you can leave out the pork and use only butter, or cook them without stuffing. Make a gravy of the drippings thickened with browned flour. Boil up and serve in a boat.

These are all very fine broiled, first splitting down the back, placing on the gridiron the inside down, cover with a baking tin, and broil slowly at first. Serve with cream gravy.

GAME PIE

Clean well, inside and out, a dozen small birds, quail, snipe, woodcock, etc., and split them in half; put them in a saucepan with about two quarts of water; when it boils, skim off all scum that rises; then add salt and pepper, a bunch of minced parsley, one onion chopped fine, and three whole cloves. Cut up half a pound of salt pork into dice, and let all boil until tender, using care that there be enough water to cover the birds. Thicken this with two tablespoonfuls of browned flour and let it boil up. Stir in a piece of butter as large as an egg; remove from the fire and let it cool. Have ready a pint of potatoes cut as small as dice, and a rich crust made. Line the sides of a buttered pudding dish with the crust; lay in the birds, then some of the potatoes, then birds and so on, until the dish is full. Pour over the gravy, put on the top crust, with a slit cut in the center, and bake. The top can be ornamented with pastry leaves in a wreath about the edge, with any fancy design placed in the center across the slit.

Eat Like a President: Book I

WILD GAME

ROAST HARE OR RABBIT

A very close relationship exists between the hare and the rabbit, the chief difference being in the smaller size and shorter legs and ears of the latter. The manner of dressing and preparing each for the table is, therefore, pretty nearly the same. To prepare them for roasting, first skin, wash well in cold water and rinse thoroughly in lukewarm water. If a little musty from being emptied before they were hung up, and afterward neglected, rub the insides with vinegar and afterward remove all taint of the acid by a thorough washing in lukewarm water. After being well wiped with a soft cloth put in a dressing as usual, sew the animal up, truss it, and roast for half or three-quarters of an hour, until well browned, basting it constantly with butter and dredging with flour, just before taking up.

To make a gravy, after the rabbits are roasted, pour nearly all the fat out of the pan, but do not pour the bottom or brown part of the drippings; put the pan over the fire, stir into it a heaping tablespoonful of flour, and stir until the flour browns. Then stir in a pint of boiling water. Season the gravy with salt and pepper; let it boil for a moment. Send hot to the table in a tureen with the hot rabbits. Serve with currant jelly.

FRICASSEE RABBIT

Clean two young rabbits, cut into joints, and soak in salt and water half an hour. Put into a saucepan with a pint of cold water, a bunch of sweet herbs, an onion finely minced, a pinch of mace, half a nutmeg, a pinch of pepper and half a pound of salt pork cut in small thin slices. Cover and stew until tender. Take out the rabbits and set in a dish where they will keep warm. Add to the gravy a cup of cream (or milk), two well-beaten eggs, stirred in a little at a time, a tablespoonful of butter, and a thickening made of a tablespoonful of flour and a little milk. Boil up once; remove the saucepan from the fire, squeeze in the juice of a lemon, stirring all the while, and pour over the rabbits. Do not cook the head or neck.

FRIED RABBIT

After the rabbit has been thoroughly cleaned and washed, put it into boiling water, and let it boil ten minutes; drain it, and when cold, cut it into joints, dip into beaten egg, and then in fine breadcrumbs; season with salt and pepper. When all are ready, fry them in butter and sweet lard, mix over a moderate fire until brown on both sides. Take them out, thicken the gravy with a spoonful of flour, turn in a cup of milk or cream; let all boil up, and turn over the rabbits. Serve hot with onion sauce. (See SAUCES.) Garnish with sliced lemon.

RABBIT PIE

This pie can be made the same as "Game Pie" excepting you scatter through it four hard-boiled eggs cut in slices. Cover with puff paste, cut a slit in the middle, and bake one hour, laying paper over the top should it brown too fast.

BROILED RABBITS

After skinning and cleaning the rabbits, wipe them dry, split them down the back lengthwise, pound them flat, then wrap them in letter paper well buttered, place them on a buttered gridiron, and broil over a clear, brisk fire, turning them often. When sufficiently cooked, remove the papers, lay them on a very hot platter, season with salt, pepper and plenty of butter, turning them over and over to soak up the butter. Cover and keep hot in a warming oven until served.

SQUIRREL

They are cooked similar to rabbits, are excellent when broiled or made into a stew, and, in fact, are very good in all the different styles of cooking similar to rabbit.

There are many species common to this country; among them the black, red, gray and fox. Gophers and chipmunks may also be classed as another but smaller variety.

ROAST HAUNCH OF VENISON

To prepare a haunch of venison for roasting, wash it slightly in tepid water and dry it thoroughly by rubbing it with a clean, soft cloth. Lay over the fat side a large sheet of thickly-buttered paper, and next a paste of flour and water about three-quarters of an inch thick; cover this again with two or three sheets of stout paper, secure the whole well with twine, and put down to roast, with a little water, in the dripping-pan. Let the fire be clear and strong; baste the paper immediately with butter or clarified drippings, and roast the joint from three to four hours, according to its weight and quality. Doe venison will require half an hour less time than buck venison. About twenty minutes before the joint is done remove the paste and paper, baste the meat in every part with butter, and dredge it very lightly with flour; let it take a pale brown color, and serve hot with unflavored gravy made with a thickening in a tureen and good currant jelly. Venison is much better when the deer has been killed in the autumn, when wild berries are plentiful, and it has had abundant opportunities to fatten upon this and other fresh food.

Windsor Hotel, Montreal.

BROILED VENISON STEAK

Venison steaks should be broiled over a clear fire, turning often. It requires more cooking than beef. When sufficiently done, season with salt and pepper, pour over two tablespoonfuls of currant jelly melted with a piece of butter. Serve hot on hot plates.

Delicious steaks, corresponding to the shape of muttonchops, are cut from the loin.

BAKED SADDLE OF VENISON

Wash the saddle carefully; see that no hairs are left dried on to the outside. Use a saddle of venison of about ten pounds. Cut some salt pork in strips about two inches long and an eighth of an inch thick, with which lard the saddle with two rows on each side. In a large dripping-pan cut two carrots, one onion and some salt pork in thin slices; add two bay-leaves, two cloves, four kernels of allspice, half a lemon sliced, and season with salt and pepper; place the saddle of venison in the pan, with a quart of good stock boiling hot and a small piece of butter, and let it boil about fifteen minutes on top of the stove; then put it in a hot oven and bake, basting well every five minutes, until it is medium rare, so that the blood runs when cut; serve with jelly or a wine sauce. If the venison is desired well done, cook much longer, and use a cream sauce with it, or stir cream into the venison gravy. (For cream sauce see SAUCES.)

Venison should never be roasted unless very fat. The shoulder is a roasting piece and may be done without the paper or paste.

In ordering the saddle request the butcher to cut the ribs off pretty close, as the only part that is of much account is the tenderloin and thick meat that lies along the backbone up to the neck. The ribs which extend from this have very little meat on them, but are always sold with the saddle. When neatly cut off they leave the saddle in a better shape, and the ribs can be put into your stockpot to boil for soup.

Windsor Hotel, Montreal.

VENISON PIE OR PASTRY

The neck, breast and shoulder are the parts used for a venison pie or pastry. Cut the meat into pieces (fat and lean together) and put the bones and trimmings into the stew pan with pepper and salt, and water or veal broth enough to cover it. Simmer it till you have drawn out a good gravy.

Then strain it.

In the meantime make a good rich paste, and roll it rather thick. Cover the bottom and sides of a deep dish with one sheet of it, and put in your meat, having seasoned it with pepper, salt, nutmeg and mace.

Pour in the gravy which you have prepared from the trimmings, and a glass of port wine. Lay on the top some bits of butter rolled in flour. Cover the pie with a thick lid of paste and ornament it handsomely with leaves and flowers formed with a tin cutter. Bake two or more hours according to the size. Just before it is done, pull it forward in the oven, and brush it over with beaten egg; push it back and let it slightly brown.

Windsor Hotel, Montreal.

VENISON HASHED

Cut the meat in nice small slices, and put the trimmings and bones into a saucepan with barely water enough to cover them.

Let them stew for an hour. Then strain the liquid into a stew pan; add to it some bits of butter, rolled in flour, and whatever gravy was left of the venison the day before. Stir in some currant jelly, and give it a boil up. Then put in the meat, and keep it over the fire just long enough to warm it through; but do not allow it to boil, as it has been once cooked already.

FRIED VENISON STEAK

Cut a breast of venison into steaks; make a quarter of a pound of butter hot in a pan; rub the steaks over with a mixture of a little salt and pepper; dip them in wheat flour, or rolled crackers, and fry a rich brown; when both sides are done, take them up on a dish, and put a tin cover over; dredge a heaping teaspoonful of flour into the butter in the pan, stir it with a spoon until it is brown, without burning; put to it a small teacupful of boiling water, with a tablespoonful of currant jelly dissolved into it; stir it for a few minutes, then strain it over the meat and serve.

A glass of wine, with a tablespoonful of white sugar dissolved in it, may be used for the gravy, instead of the jelly and water. Venison may be boiled, and served with boiled vegetables, pickled beets, etc., and sauce.

SAUCES AND DRESSINGS

DRAWN BUTTER

Melted butter is the foundation of most of the common sauces. Have a covered saucepan for this purpose. One lined with porcelain will be best. Take a quarter of a pound of the best fresh butter, cut it up, and mix with it about one tablespoonful of flour. When it is thoroughly mixed, put it into the saucepan, and add to it half a teacupful of hot water. Cover the saucepan and set it in a large tin pan of boiling water. Shake it round continually (always moving it the same way) till it is entirely melted and begins to simmer. Then let it rest till it boils up.

- If you set it on too hot a fire it will be oily.
- If the butter and flour are not well mixed, it will be lumpy.
- If you put in too much water, it will be thin and poor. All these defects are to be carefully avoided.

In melting butter for sweet or pudding sauce, you may use milk instead of water.

TARTARE SAUCE

The raw yolks of two eggs, half a teacupful of pure olive oil, three tablespoonfuls of vinegar, one of made mustard, one teaspoonful of sugar, a quarter of a teaspoonful of pepper, one teaspoonful of salt, one of onion juice, one tablespoonful of chopped capers, one of chopped cucumber pickle. Put together the same as mayonnaise dressing, adding the chopped ingredients the last thing.

This sauce is good for fried or boiled fish, boiled tongue, fish salad, and may be used with fried and broiled meats.

WHITE SAUCE

Mix two tablespoonfuls of sifted flour with half a teacup of warm butter. Place over the fire a saucepan containing a pint of sweet milk and a half teaspoon of salt, and a dash of white pepper; when it reaches the boiling point, add the butter and flour, stirring briskly until it thickens and becomes like cream. Have ready three cold hard-boiled eggs, sliced and chopped, add them to the sauce; let them heat through thoroughly, and serve in a boat. If you have plenty of cream, use it and omit the butter. By omitting the eggs, you have the same as "White Sauce."

OYSTER SAUCE

Take a pint of oysters and heat them in their own liquor long enough to come to a boil, or until they begin to ruffle. Skim out the oysters into a warm dish, put into the liquor a teacup of milk or cream, two tablespoonfuls of cold butter, a pinch of cayenne and salt; thicken with a tablespoonful of flour stirred to a paste, boil up and then add the oysters.

Oyster sauce is used for fish, boiled turkey, chicken and

boiled white meats of most kinds.

LOBSTER SAUCE

Put the coral and spawn of a boiled lobster into a mortar with a tablespoonful of butter; pound it to a smooth mass, then rub it through a sieve; melt nearly a quarter of a pound of sweet butter, with a wine-glass of water or vinegar; add a teaspoonful of made mustard, stir in the coral and spawn, and a little salt and pepper; stir it until it is smooth and serve. Some of the meat of the lobster may be chopped fine and stirred into it.

SAUCE FOR SALMON AND OTHER FISH

One cupful of milk heated to a boil and thickened with a tablespoonful of cornstarch previously wet up with cold water, the liquor from the salmon, one great spoonful of butter, one raw egg beaten light, the juice of half a lemon, mace and cayenne pepper to taste. Add the egg to thickened milk when you have stirred in the butter and liquor; take from the fire, season and let it stand in hot water three minutes, covered. Lastly put in lemon juice and turn out immediately. Pour it all over and around the salmon.

SAUCE FOR BOILED COD

To one gill of boiling water add as much milk; stir into this while boiling two tablespoonfuls of butter gradually, one tablespoonful of flour wet up with cold water; as it thickens, the chopped yolk of one boiled egg, and one raw egg beaten light. Take directly from the fire, season with pepper, salt, a little chopped parsley and the juice of one lemon, and set covered in boiling water (but not over fire) five minutes, stirring occasionally. Pour part of the sauce over fish when dished; the rest in a boat. Serve mashed potatoes with it.

FISH SAUCE No. 1

Make a pint of drawn butter, add one tablespoonful of pepper sauce or Worcestershire sauce, a little salt and six hard-boiled eggs chopped fine. Pour over boiled fish and garnish with sliced lemon. Very nice.

FISH SAUCE No. 2

Half a cupful of melted butter, half a cupful of vinegar, two tablespoonfuls of tomato ketchup, salt, and a tablespoonful of made mustard. Boil ten minutes.

CELERY SAUCE

Mix two tablespoonfuls of flour with half a teacupful of butter; have ready a pint of boiling milk; stir the flour and butter into the milk; take three heads of celery, cut into small bits, and boil for a few minutes in water, which strain off; put the celery into the melted butter, and keep it stirred over the fire for five or ten minutes. This is very nice with boiled fowl or turkey. Another way to make celery sauce is: Boil a head of celery until quite tender, then put it through a sieve; put the yolk of an egg in a basin, and beat it well with the strained juice of a lemon; add the celery and a couple of spoonfuls of liquor in which the turkey was boiled; salt and pepper to taste.

CAPER SAUCE

Chop the capers a very little, unless quite small; make

half a pint of drawn butter, to which add the capers, with a large spoonful of the juice from the bottle in which they are sold; let it just simmer and serve in a tureen. Nasturtiums much resemble capers in taste, though larger, and may be used, and, in fact, are preferred by many. They are grown on a climbing vine, and are cultivated for their blossom and for pickling. When used as capers they should be chopped more. If neither capers nor nasturtiums are at hand, some pickles chopped up form a very good substitute in the sauce.

BREAD SAUCE

One cup of stale breadcrumbs, one onion, two ounces of butter, pepper and salt, a little mace. Cut the onion fine, and boil it in milk till quite soft; then strain the milk on to the stale breadcrumbs, and let it stand an hour. Put it in a saucepan with the boiled onion, pepper, salt and mace. Give it a boil, and serve in sauce tureen. This sauce can also be used for grouse, and is very nice. Roast partridges are nice served with breadcrumbs, fried brown in butter, with cranberry or currant jelly laid beside them in the platter.

TOMATO SAUCE

Take a quart can of tomatoes, put it over the fire in a stew pan, put in one slice of onion and two cloves, a little pepper and salt; boil about twenty minutes; then remove from the fire and strain it through a sieve. Now melt in another pan an ounce of butter, and as it melts, sprinkle in a tablespoonful of flour; stir it until it browns and froths a little. Mix the tomato pulp with it, and it is ready for the table.

Excellent for mutton, chops, roast beef, etc.

ONION SAUCE

Work together until light a heaping tablespoonful of flour and half a cupful of butter, and gradually add two cups of boiling milk; stir constantly until it come to a boil; then stir into that four tender boiled onions that have been chopped fine. Salt and pepper to taste. Serve with boiled veal, poultry of mutton.

CHILI SAUCE

Boil together two-dozen ripe tomatoes, three small green peppers, or a half teaspoonful of cayenne pepper, one onion cut fine, half a cup of sugar. Boil until thick; then add two cups of vinegar; then strain the whole, set back on the fire and add a tablespoonful of salt, and a teaspoonful each of ginger, allspice, cloves and cinnamon; boil all five minutes, remove and seal in glass bottles. This is very nice.

MINT SAUCE

Take fresh young spearmint leaves stripped from the stems; wash and drain them, or dry on a cloth. Chop very fine, put in a gravy boat, and to three tablespoonfuls of mint put two of white sugar; mix and let it stand a few minutes, then pour over it six tablespoonfuls of good cider or white-wine vinegar. The sauce should be made some time before it is to be used, so that the flavor of the mint may be well extracted. Fine with roast lamb.

SHARP BROWN SAUCE

Put in a saucepan one tablespoonful of chopped onion, three tablespoonfuls of good cider vinegar, six tablespoonfuls of water, three of tomato ketchup, a little pepper and salt, half a cup of melted butter, in which stir a tablespoonful of sifted flour; put all together and boil until it thickens. This is most excellent with boiled meats, fish and poultry.

BECHAMEL SAUCE

Put three tablespoonfuls of butter in a saucepan; add three tablespoonfuls of sifted flour, quarter of a teaspoonful of nutmeg, ten peppercorns, a teaspoonful of salt; beat all well together; then add to this three slices of onion, two slices of carrot, two sprigs of parsley, two of thyme, a bay leaf and half a dozen mushrooms cut up. Moisten the whole with a pint of stock or water and a cup of sweet cream. Set it on the stove and cook slowly for half-an-hour, watching closely that it does not burn; then strain through a sieve. Most excellent with roast veal, meats and fish.

St. Charles Hotel, New Orleans.

MAITRE D'HOTEL SAUCE

Make a teacupful of drawn butter; add to it the juice of a lemon, two tablespoonfuls of minced onion, three tablespoonfuls of chopped parsley, a teaspoonful of powdered thyme or summer savory, a pinch of cayenne and salt. Simmer over the fire and stir well. Excellent with all kinds of fish.

WINE SAUCE FOR GAME

Half a glass of currant jelly, half a glass of port wine, half a glass of water, a tablespoonful of cold butter, a teaspoonful of salt, the juice of half a lemon, a pinch of cayenne pepper and three cloves. Simmer all together a few minutes, adding the wine after it is strained. A few spoonfuls of the gravy from the game may be added to it. This sauce is especially nice with venison.

Taber House, Denver.

HOLLANDAISE SAUCE

Half a teacupful of butter, the juice of half a lemon, the yolk of two eggs, a speck of cayenne pepper, half a cupful of boiling water, half a teaspoonful of salt; beat the butter to a cream, add the yolks of eggs one by one; then the lemon juice, pepper and salt, beating all thoroughly; place the bowl in which is the mixture in a saucepan of boiling water; beat with an egg-beater until it begins to thicken which will be in about a minute; then add the boiling water, beating all the time; stir until it begins to thicken like soft custard; stir a few minutes after taking from the fire; be careful not to cook it too long.

This is very nice with baked fish.

CURRANT JELLY SAUCE

Three tablespoonfuls of butter, one onion, one bay leaf, one sprig of celery, two tablespoonfuls of vinegar, half a cupful of currant jelly, one tablespoonful of flour, one pint of stock, salt, pepper. Cook the butter and onion until the latter begins to color. Add the flour and herbs. Stir until brown; add the stock, and simmer twenty minutes. Strain and skim off all the fat. Add the jelly and stir over the fire until it is melted. Serve with game.

BROWN SAUCE

Delicious sauce for meats is made in this way: Slice a large onion and fry in butter till it is brown; then cover the onion with rich brown gravy, which is left from roast beef; add mustard, salt and pepper, and if you choose a tablespoonful of Worcestershire sauce; let this boil up, and if too thick, thin it with a little stock or gravy, or even a little hot water with butter. Pour this when done through a fine sieve. Of course a larger quantity can be prepared at once than is mentioned here.

MUSHROOM SAUCE

Wash a pint of small button mushrooms, remove the stems and outside skins, stew them slowly in veal gravy or milk or cream, adding an onion, and seasoning with pepper, salt and a little butter rolled in flour. Their flavor will be heightened by salting a few the night before, to extract the juice. In dressing mushrooms only those of a dull pearl color on the outside and the under part tinged with pale pink should be selected. If there is a poisonous one among them, the onion in the sauce will turn black. In such a case throw the whole away. Used for poultry, beef or fish.

APPLESAUCE

When you wish to serve apple sauce with meat prepare it in this way: Cook the apples until they are very tender, then stir them thoroughly so there will be no lumps at all; add the sugar and a little gelatin dissolved in warm water, a tablespoonful in a pint of sauce; pour the sauce into bowls, and when cold it will be stiff like jelly, and can be turned out on a plate.

Cranberry sauce can be treated in the same way. Many

prefer this to plain stewing.

Apples cooked in the following way look very pretty on a tea table, and are appreciated by the palate. Select firm, round greenings; pare neatly and cut in halves; place in a shallow stew pan with sufficient boiling water to cover them, and a cupful of sugar to every six apples. Each half should cook on the bottom of the pan, and be removed from the others so as not to injure its shape. Stew slowly until the pieces are very tender; remove to a dish carefully; boil the syrup half an hour longer; pour it over the apples and eat cold. A few pieces of lemon boiled in the syrup add to the flavor.

These sauces are a fine accompaniment to roast pork or roast goose.

CIDER APPLESAUCE

Boil four quarts of new cider until it is reduced to two quarts; then put into it enough pared and quartered apples to fill the kettle; let the whole stew over a moderate fire four hours; add cinnamon if liked. This sauce is very fine with almost any kind of meat.

OLD-FASHIONED APPLESAUCE

Pare and chop a dozen medium-sized apples, put them in a deep pudding-dish; sprinkle over them a heaping cupful of sugar and one of water. Place them in the oven and bake slowly two hours or more, or until they are a deep red brown; quite as nice as preserves.

CRANBERRY SAUCE

One quart of cranberries, two cupfuls of sugar and a

pint of water. Wash the cranberries, then put them on the fire with the water, but in a covered saucepan. Let them simmer until each cranberry bursts open; then remove the cover of the saucepan, add the sugar and let them all boil twenty minutes without the cover. The cranberries must never be stirred from the time they are placed on the fire. This is an unfailing recipe for a most delicious preparation of cranberries. Very fine with turkey and game.

APPLE OMELET

Apple omelet, to be served with broiled sparerib or roast pork, is very delicate. Take nine large, tart apples, four, eggs, one cup of sugar, one tablespoonful of butter; add cinnamon or other spices to suit your taste; stew the apples till they are very soft; mash them so that there will be no lumps; add the butter and sugar while they are still warm; but let them cool before putting in the beaten eggs; bake this till it is brown.

You may put it all in a shallow pudding-dish or in two tin plates to bake. Very good.

FLAVORED VINEGARS

Almost all the flavorings used for meats and salads may be prepared in vinegar with little trouble and expense, and will be found useful to impart an acid to flavors when lemons are not at hand.

Tarragon, sweet basil, burnet, green mint, sage, thyme, sweet marjoram, etc., may be prepared by putting three ounces of either of these herbs, when in blossom, into one gallon of sharp vinegar, let stand ten days, strain off clear, and bottle for use.

Celery and cayenne may be prepared, using three ounces of the seed as above.

CUCUMBER VINEGAR

Ingredients – Ten large cucumbers, or twelve smaller ones, one quart of vinegar, two onions, two shallots, one tablespoonful of salt, two tablespoonfuls of pepper, a quarter of a teaspoonful of cayenne.

Mode – Pare and slice the cucumbers, put them in a stone jar, or wide-mouthed bottle, with the vinegar; slice the onions and shallots, and add them, with all the other ingredients, to the cucumbers. Let it stand four or five days; boil it all up, and when cold, strain the liquor through a piece of muslin, and store it away in small bottles well sealed. This vinegar is a very nice addition to gravies, hashes, etc., as well as a great improvement to salads, or to eat with cold meat.

CURRY POWDER

To make curry powder, take one ounce of ginger, one ounce of mustard, one ounce of pepper, three ounces of coriander seed, three ounces of turmeric, half an ounce of cardamoms, one-quarter ounce of cayenne pepper, one-quarter ounce of cinnamon, and one-quarter ounce of cumin seed. Pound all these ingredients very fine in a mortar; sift them and cork tight in a bottle.

This can be had ready prepared at most druggists, and it is much less trouble to purchase it than to make it at home.

CURRY SAUCE

One tablespoonful of butter, one of flour, one

teaspoonful of curry powder, one large slice of onion, one large cupful of stock, salt and pepper to taste. Cut the onion fine, and fry brown in the butter. Add the flour and curry powder. Stir for one minute, add the stock and season with the salt and pepper. Simmer five minutes; then strain and serve. This sauce can be served with a broil or *sauté* of meat or fish.

TO BROWN BUTTER

Put a lump of butter into a hot frying pan and toss it about until it browns. Stir brown flour into it until it is smooth and begins to boil. Use it for coloring gravies, and sauces for meats.

TO BROWN FLOUR

Spread flour upon a tin pie-plate, set it upon the stove or in a *very* hot oven, and stir continually, after it begins to color, until it is brown all through. Keep it always on hand; put away in glass jars covered closely. It is excellent for coloring and thickening many dishes.

TO MAKE MUSTARD

Boil some vinegar; take four spoonfuls of mustard, half of a teaspoonful of sugar, a half teaspoonful of salt, a tablespoonful of melted butter; mix well.

FRENCH MUSTARD

Three tablespoonfuls of mustard, one tablespoonful of granulated sugar, well worked together, then beat in an egg until it is smooth; add one teacupful of vinegar, a little at a time, working it all smooth; then set on the stove and cook three or four minutes, stirring all the time; when cool, add one tablespoonful of the best olive oil, taking care to get it all thoroughly worked in and smooth. You will find this very nice.

Mrs. D. Riegel.

KITCHEN PEPPER

Mix one ounce of ground ginger, half an ounce each of black pepper, ground cinnamon, nutmeg and allspice, one teaspoonful of ground cloves, and six ounces of salt. Keep in a tightly corked bottle.

The Caterer.

PREPARED COCOANUT (For Pies, Puddings, etc.)

To prepare cocoanut for future use, first cut a hole through the meat at one of the holes in the end, draw off the milk, then loosen the meat by pounding the nut well on all sides. Crack the nut and take out the meat, and place the pieces of meat in a cool open oven over night, or for a few hours, to dry; then grate it. If there is more grated than is needed for present use, sprinkle it with sugar, and spread out in a cool dry place. When dry enough put away in dry cans or bottles. Will keep for weeks.

SPICES

Ginger is the root of a shrub first known in Asia, and now cultivated in the West Indies and Sierra Leone. The stem grows three or four feet high and dies every year. There are two varieties of ginger – the white and black – caused by taking more or less care in selecting and preparing the roots, which are always dug in winter, when the stems are withered. The white is the best.

Cinnamon is the inner bark of a beautiful tree, a native of Ceylon that grows from twenty to thirty feet in height and lives to be centuries old.

Cloves – Native to the Molucca Islands, and so called from resemblance to a nail (*clavis*). The East Indians call them "changkek" from the Chinese "techengkia" (fragrant nails). They grow on a straight, smooth-barked tree, about forty feet high. Cloves are not fruits, but blossoms, gathered before they are quite unfolded.

Allspice – A berry so called because it combines the flavor of several spices – grows abundantly on the allspice or bayberry tree; native of South America and the West Indies. A single tree has been known to produce one hundred and fifty pounds of berries. They are purple when ripe.

Black pepper is made by grinding the dried berry of a climbing vine, native to the East Indies. White pepper is obtained from the same berries, freed from their husk or rind. Red or cayenne pepper is obtained by grinding the scarlet pod or seed-vessel of a tropical plant that is now cultivated in all parts of the world.

Nutmeg is the kernel of a small, smooth, pear-shaped fruit that grows on a tree in the Molucca Islands, and other parts of the East. The trees commence bearing in the seventh year, and continue fruitful until they are seventy or eighty years old. Around the nutmeg or kernel is a bright, brown shell. This shell has a soft, scarlet covering, which, when flattened out and dried, is known as mace. The best nutmegs are solid, and emit oil when pricked with a pin.

HERBS FOR WINTER

To prepare herbs for winter use, such as sage, summer savory, thyme, mint or any of the sweet herbs, they should be gathered fresh in their season, or procure them from the market. Examine them well, throwing out all poor sprigs; then wash and shake them; tie into small bundles, and tie over the bundles a piece of netting or old lace (to keep off the dust); hang up in a warm, dry place, the leaves downward. In a few days the herb will be thoroughly dry and brittle. Or you may place them in a cool oven and let them remain in it until perfectly dry.

Then pick off all the leaves and the tender tops of the stems; put them in a clean, large-mouthed bottle that is perfectly dry.

When wanted for use, rub fine, and sift through a sieve. It is much better to put them in bottles as soon as dried, as long exposure to the air causes them to lose strength and flavor.

MEATS AND THEIR ACCOMPANIMENTS

- With roast beef: tomato sauce, grated horseradish, mustard, cranberry sauce, pickles.
- With roast pork: applesauce, cranberry sauce.
- With roast veal: tomato sauce, mushroom sauce, onion sauce and cranberry sauce. Horseradish and lemons are good.
- With roast mutton: currant jelly, caper sauce.
- With boiled mutton: onion sauce, caper sauce.
- With boiled fowls: bread sauce, onion sauce, lemon sauce, cranberry sauce, and jellies. Also cream sauce.

With roast lamb: mint sauce.
- With roast turkey: cranberry sauce, currant jelly. With boiled turkey: oyster sauce.
- With venison or wild ducks: cranberry sauce, currant jelly, or currant jelly warmed with port wine.
- With roast goose: applesauce, cranberry sauce, grape or currant jelly.
- With boiled fresh mackerel: stewed gooseberries.
- With boiled blue fish: white cream sauce, lemon sauce.
- With broiled shad: mushroom sauce, parsley or egg sauce.
- With fresh salmon: green peas, cream sauce.

Pickles are good with all roast meats, and in fact are suitable accompaniments to all kinds of meats in general.

Spinach is the proper accompaniment to veal; green peas to lamb. Lemon juice makes a very grateful addition to nearly all the insipid members of the fish kingdom. Slices of lemon cut into very small dice and stirred into drawn butter and allowed to come to the boiling point, served with fowls, is a fine accompaniment.

VEGETABLES APPROPRIATE TO DIFFERENT DISHES.

Potatoes are good with all meats. With fowls they are nicest mashed. Sweet potatoes are most appropriate with roast meats, as also are onions, winter squash, cucumbers and asparagus. Carrots, parsnips, turnips, greens and cabbage are generally eaten with boiled meat, and corn, beets, peas and beans are appropriate to either boiled or roasted meat. Mashed turnip is good with roast pork and with boiled meats. Tomatoes are good with almost every kind of meats, especially with roasts.

WARM DISHES FOR BREAKFAST

The following of hot breakfast dishes may be of assistance in knowing what to provide for the comfortable meal called breakfast.

Broiled beefsteak, broiled chops, broiled chicken, broiled fish, broiled quail on toast, fried pork tenderloins, fried pig's feet, fried oysters, fried clams, fried liver and bacon, fried chops, fried pork, ham and eggs fried, veal cutlets breaded, sausages, fricasseed tripe, fricasseed kidneys, turkey or chicken hash, corn beef hash, beef croquettes, codfish balls, creamed codfish, stewed meats on toast, poached eggs on toast, omelets, eggs boiled plain, and eggs cooked in any of the various styles.

VEGETABLES FOR BREAKFAST

Potatoes in any of the various modes of cooking, also stewed tomatoes, stewed corn, raw radishes, cucumbers sliced, tomatoes sliced raw, watercress, lettuce.

To be included with the breakfast dishes: oatmeal mush, cracked wheat, hominy or corn meal mush, these with cream, milk and sugar or syrup.

Then numberless varieties of bread can be selected, in form of rolls, fritters, muffins, waffles, corn-cakes, griddle-cakes, etc., etc.

For beverages, coffee, chocolate and cocoa, or tea if one prefers it; these are all suitable for the breakfast table.

When obtainable always have a vase of choice flowers on the breakfast table; also some fresh fruit, if convenient.

Eat Like a President: Book I

SALADS

Everything in the make-up of a salad should be of the freshest material, the vegetables crisp and fresh, the oil or butter the very best, meats, fowl and fish well cooked, pure cider or white wine vinegar – in fact, every ingredient first class, to insure success.

The vegetables used in salad are: Beet-root, onions, potatoes, cabbage, lettuce, celery, cucumbers, lentils, haricots, winter cress, peas, French beans, radish, cauliflower – all these may be used judiciously in salad, if properly seasoned, according to the following directions.

Chervil is a delicious salad herb, invariably found in all salads prepared by a French *gourmet*. No man can be a true epicure who is unfamiliar with this excellent herb. It may be procured from the vegetable stands at Fulton and Washington markets the year round.

Its leaves resemble parsley, but are more divided, and a few of them added to a breakfast salad give a delightful flavor.

Chervil Vinegar – A few drops of this vinegar added to fish sauces or salads is excellent, and well repays the little trouble taken in its preparation. Half fill a bottle with fresh or dry chervil leaves; fill the bottle with good vinegar and heat it gently by placing it in warm water, which bring to boiling point; remove from the fire; when cool cork, and in two weeks it will be ready for use.

MAYONNAISE DRESSING

Put the yolks of four fresh raw eggs, with two hard-boiled ones, into a cold bowl. Rub these as smooth as possible before introducing the oil; a good measure of oil is a tablespoonful to each yolk of raw egg.

All the art consists in introducing the oil by degrees, a few drops at a time. You can never make a good salad without taking plenty of time. When the oil is well mixed, and assumes the appearance of jelly, put in two heaping teaspoonfuls of dry table salt, one of pepper and one of made mustard. Never put in salt and pepper before this stage of the process, because the salt and pepper would coagulate the albumen of the eggs, and you could not get the dressing smooth. Two tablespoonfuls of vinegar added gradually.

The *Mayonnaise* should be the thickness of thick cream when finished, but if it looks like curdling when mixing it, set in the refrigerator for about forty minutes or an hour, then mix it again. It is a good idea to place it in a pan of cracked ice while mixing.

For lobster salad, use the *coral*, mashed and pressed through a sieve, then add to the above.

Salad dressing should be kept in a separate bowl in a cold, place, and not mixed with the salad until the moment it is to be served, or it may lose its crispness and freshness.

DRESSING FOR COLD SLAW (Cabbage Salad)

Beat up two eggs with two tablespoonfuls of sugar, add a piece of butter the size of half an egg, a teaspoonful of mustard, a little pepper, and lastly a teacup of vinegar. Put all of these ingredients into a dish over the fire and cook like a soft custard. Some think it improved by adding half a cupful of thick sweet cream to this dressing; in that case use less vinegar. Either way is very fine.

SALAD CREAM DRESSING No. 1

One cup fresh cream, one spoonful fine flour, the whites of two eggs beaten stiff, three spoonfuls of vinegar, two spoonfuls of salad oil or soft butter, two spoonfuls of powdered sugar, one teaspoonful salt, one-half teaspoonful pepper, one teaspoonful of made mustard. Heat cream almost to boiling; stir in the flour, previously wet with cold milk; boil two minutes, stirring all the time; add sugar and take from fire. When half cold, beat in whipped whites of egg; set aside to cool. When quite cold, whip in the oil or butter, pepper, mustard and salt; if the salad is ready, add vinegar and pour at once over it.

CREAM DRESSING No. 2

Two tablespoonfuls of whipped sweet cream, two of sugar and four of vinegar; beat well and pour over the cabbage, previously cut very fine and seasoned with salt.

FRENCH SALAD DRESSING

Mix one-half teaspoon of pepper with one of salt; add three tablespoonfuls of olive oil and one even tablespoonful of onion scraped fine; then one tablespoonful of vinegar;

when well mixed, pour the mixture over your salad and stir all till well mingled.

The merit of a salad is that it should be cool, fresh and crisp. For vegetables use only the delicate white stalks of celery, the small heartleaves of lettuce; or tenderest stalks and leaves of the white cabbage. Keep the vegetable portion crisp and fresh until the time for serving, when add the meat. For chicken and fish salads use the "Mayonnaise dressing." For simple vegetable salads the French dressing is most appropriate, using onion rather than garlic.

MIXED SUMMER SALAD

Three heads of lettuce, two teaspoonfuls of green mustard leaves, a handful of water cresses, five tender radishes, one cucumber, three hard-boiled eggs, two teaspoonfuls of white sugar, one teaspoonful of salt, one teaspoonful of pepper, one teaspoonful of made mustard, one teacupful of vinegar, half a teacupful of oil.

Mix all well together, and serve with a lump of ice in the middle.

"Common Sense in the Household."

CHICKEN SALAD

Boil the fowls tender and remove all the fat, gristle and skin; mince the meat in small pieces, but do not hash it. To one chicken put twice and a half its weight in celery, cut in pieces of about one-quarter of an inch; mix thoroughly and set it in a cool place – the ice chest.

In the meantime prepare a "Mayonnaise dressing," and when ready for the table pour this dressing over the chicken and celery, tossing and mixing it thoroughly. Set it in a cool place until ready to serve. Garnish with celery tips, or cold hard-boiled eggs, lettuce leaves, from the heart, cold boiled beets or capers, olives.

Crisp cabbage is a good substitute for celery; when celery is not to be had use celery vinegar in the dressing. Turkey makes a fine salad.

LOBSTER SALAD No. 1

Prepare a sauce with the *coral* of a fine, new lobster, boiled fresh for about half an hour. Pound and rub it smooth, and mix very gradually with a dressing made from the yolks of two hard-boiled eggs, a tablespoonful of made mustard, three of salad oil, two of vinegar, one of white powdered sugar, a small teaspoonful of salt, as much black pepper, a pinch of cayenne and yolks of two fresh eggs. Next fill your salad bowl with some shred lettuce, the better part of two leaving the small curled center to garnish your dish with. Mingle with this the flesh of your lobster, torn, broken or cut into bits seasoned with salt and pepper and a small portion of the dressing. Pour over the whole the rest of the dressing; put your lettuce-hearts down the center and arrange upon the sides slices of hard-boiled eggs.

LOBSTER SALAD No. 2

Using canned lobsters, take a can, skim off all the oil on the surface, and chop the meat up coarsely on a flat dish. Prepare the same way six heads of celery; mix a teaspoonful of mustard into a smooth paste with a little vinegar; add yolks of two fresh eggs; a tablespoonful of butter, creamed, a small teaspoonful of salt, the same of pepper, a quarter of a teaspoonful of cayenne pepper, a gill of vinegar, and the mashed yolks of two hard-boiled eggs. Mix a small portion of the dressing with the celery and meat, and turn the remainder over all. Garnish with the green tops of celery and a hard-boiled egg, cut into thin rings.

FISH SALAD

Take a fresh white fish or trout, boil and chop it, but not too fine; put with the same quantity of chopped cabbage, celery or lettuce; season the same as chicken salad. Garnish with the tender leaves of the heart of lettuce.

OYSTER SALAD

Drain the liquor from a quart of fresh oysters. Put them in hot vinegar enough to cover them placed over the fire; let them remain until *plump*, but not cooked; then drop them immediately in cold water, drain off, and mix with them two pickled cucumbers cut fine, also a quart of celery cut in dice pieces, some seasoning of salt and pepper. Mix all well together, tossing up with a silver fork. Pour over the whole a "Mayonnaise dressing." Garnish with celery tips and slices of hard-boiled eggs arranged tastefully.

DUTCH SALAD

Wash, split and bone a dozen anchovies, and roll each one up; wash, split and bone one herring, and cut it up into small pieces; cut up into dice an equal quantity of Bologna or Lyons sausage, or of smoked ham and sausages; also, an equal quantity of the breast of cold roast fowl, or veal; add likewise, always in the same quantity, and cut into dice, beet-roots, pickled cucumbers, cold boiled potatoes cut in larger dice, and in quantity according to taste, but at least thrice as much potato as anything else; add a tablespoonful of capers, the yolks and whites of some hard-boiled eggs, minced separately, and a dozen stoned olives.

Mix all the ingredients well together, reserving the olives and anchovies to ornament the top of the bowl; beat up together oil and Tarragon vinegar with white pepper and French mustard to taste; pour this over the salad and serve.

HAM SALAD

Take cold boiled ham, fat and lean together, chop it until it is thoroughly mixed and the pieces are about the size of peas; then add to this an equal quantity of celery cut fine, if celery is out of season, lettuce may be substituted. Line a dish thickly with lettuce leaves and fill with the chopped ham and celery. Make a dressing the same as for cold slaw and turn over the whole. Very fine.

CRAB SALAD

Boil three dozen hard-shell crabs twenty-five minutes; drain and let them cool gradually; remove the upper shell and the tail, break the remainder apart and pick out the meat carefully. The large claws should not be forgotten, for they contain a dainty morsel, and the creamy fat attached to the upper shell should not be overlooked. Line a salad bowl with the small white leaves of two heads of lettuce, add the crab meat, pour over it a "Mayonnaise" garnish with crab claws, hard-boiled eggs and little mounds of cress leaves, which may be mixed with the salad when served.

COLE SLAW

Select the finest head of bleached cabbage – that is to

say one of the finest and most compact of the more delicate varieties; cut up enough into shreds to fill a large vegetable dish or salad bowl – that to be regulated by the size of the cabbage and the quantity required; shave very fine and after that chop up, the more thoroughly the better. Put this into a dish in which it is to be served, after seasoning it well with salt and pepper. Turn over it a dressing made as for cold slaw; mix it well and garnish with slices of hard-boiled eggs.

COLE SLAW (plain)

Slice cabbage very fine; season with salt, pepper and a little sugar; pour over vinegar and mix thoroughly. It is nice served in the center of a platter with fried oysters around it.

SLAW (hot)

Cut the cabbage as for cold slaw; put it into a stew pan and set it on the top of the stove for half an hour, or till hot all through; do not let it boil. Then make a dressing the same as for cold slaw, and, while hot, pour it over the hot cabbage. Stir it until well mixed and the cabbage looks coddled. Serve immediately.

TOMATO SALAD

Peel and slice twelve good, sound, fresh tomatoes; the slices about a quarter of an inch thick. Set them on the ice or in a refrigerator while you make the dressing. Make the same as "Mayonnaise," or you may use "Cream dressing." Take one head of the broad-leaved variety of lettuce, wash, and arrange them neatly around the sides of a salad bowl. Place the cold, sliced tomatoes in the center. Pour over the dressing and serve.

ENDIVE

This ought to be nicely blanched and crisp, and is the most wholesome of all salads. Take two, cut away the root, remove the dark green leaves, and pick off all the rest; wash and drain well, add a few chives. Dress with "Mayonnaise dressing."

Endive is extensively cultivated for the adulteration of coffee; is also a fine relish, and has broad leaves. Endive is of the same nature as chicory, the leaves being curly.

CELERY SALAD

Prepare the dressing the same as for tomato salad; cut the celery into bits half an inch long, and season. Serve at once before the vinegar injures the crispness of the vegetables.

LETTUCE SALAD

Take the yolks of three hard-boiled eggs, and salt and mustard to taste; mash it fine; make a paste by adding a dessertspoonful of olive oil or melted butter (use butter always when it is difficult to get *fresh* oil); mix thoroughly, and then dilute by adding *gradually* a teacupful of vinegar, and pour over the lettuce. Garnish by *slicing* another egg and laying over the lettuce. This is sufficient for a moderate-sized dish of lettuce.

POTATO SALAD (hot)

Pare six or eight large potatoes, and boil till done, and slice thin while hot; peel and cut up three large onions into small bits and mix with the potatoes; cut up some breakfast bacon into small bits, sufficient to fill a teacup and fry it a light brown; remove the meat, and into the grease stir three tablespoonfuls of vinegar, making a sour gravy, which with the bacon pour over the potato and onion; mix lightly. To be eaten when hot.

POTATO SALAD, COLD

Chop cold boiled potatoes fine, with enough raw onions to season nicely; make a dressing as for lettuce salad, and pour over it.

BEAN SALAD

String young beans; break into half-inch pieces or leave whole; wash and cook soft in salt water; drain well; add finely chopped onions, pepper, salt and vinegar; when cool, add olive oil or melted butter.

TO DRESS CUCUMBERS RAW

They should be as fresh from the vine as possible, few vegetables being more unwholesome when long gathered. As soon as they are brought in lay them in cold water. Just before they are to go to the table take them out, pare them and slice them into a pan of fresh cold water. When they are all sliced, transfer them to a deep dish; season them with a little salt and black pepper, and pour over them some of the best vinegar. You may mix with them a small quantity of sliced onions, not to be eaten, but to communicate a slight flavor of onion to the vinegar.

CELERY UNDRESSED

Celery is sometimes sent to the table without dressing.

Scrape the outside stalks, and cut off the green tops and the roots; lay it in cold water until near the time to serve, then change the water, in which let it stand three or four minutes; split the stalks in three, with a sharp knife, being careful not to break them, and serve in goblet-shaped salad glasses. To crisp celery, let it lie in ice water two hours before serving; to fringe the stalks, stick several coarse needles into a cork, and draw the stalk half way from the top through the needles several times and lay in the refrigerator to curl and crisp.

RADISHES

All the varieties are generally served in the same manner, by scraping and placing on the table in glasses containing some cold water to keep them fresh looking.

PEPPERGRASS AND CRESS

These are used mostly as an appetizer, served simply with salt. Cresses are occasionally used in making salad.

HORSE-RADISH

Horse-radish is an agreeable relish, and has a particularly fresh taste in the spring; is scraped fine or grated, and set on the table in a small covered cup; much that is bottled and sold as horse-radish is adulterated with grated turnip.

LETTUCE

Wash each leaf separately, breaking them from the head; crisp in ice water and serve the leaves whole, to be prepared at table, providing hard-boiled eggs cut in halves or slices, oil and other ingredients, to be mixed at table to individual taste.

Eat Like a President: Book I

KETCHUPS

TOMATO KETCHUP No. 1

Put into two quarts of tomato pulp (or two cans of canned tomatoes) one onion, cut fine, two tablespoonfuls of salt and three tablespoonfuls of brown sugar. Boil until quite thick; then take from the fire and strain it through a sieve, working it until it is all through but the seeds. Put it back on the stove, and add two tablespoonfuls of mustard, one of allspice, one of black pepper and one of cinnamon, one teaspoonful of ground cloves, half a teaspoonful of cayenne pepper, one grated nutmeg, one pint of good vinegar; boil it until it will just run from the mouth of a bottle. It should be watched, stirred often, that it does not burn. If sealed tight while *hot*, in large-mouthed bottles, it will keep good for years.

TOMATO KETCHUP. No. 2.

Cook one gallon of choice ripe tomatoes; strain them, and cook again until they become quite thick. About fifteen minutes before taking up put into them a small level teaspoonful of cayenne pepper, one tablespoonful of mustard seed, half a tablespoonful of whole cloves, one tablespoonful of whole allspice, all tied in a thin muslin bag. At the same time, add one heaping tablespoonful of sugar, and one teacupful of best vinegar and salt to suit the taste. Seal up air-tight, either in bottles or jugs. This is a valuable Southern recipe.

GREEN TOMATO KETCHUP

One peck of green tomatoes and two large onions sliced. Place them in layers, sprinkling salt between; let them stand twenty-four hours and then drain them. Add a quarter of a pound of mustard seed, one ounce allspice, one ounce cloves, one ounce ground mustard, one ounce ground ginger, two tablespoonfuls black pepper, two teaspoonfuls celery seed, a quarter of a pound of brown sugar. Put all in preserving-pan, cover with vinegar and boil two hours; then strain through a sieve and bottle for use.

WALNUT KETCHUP

One hundred walnuts, six ounces of shallots, one head of garlic, half a pound of salt, two quarts of vinegar, two ounces of anchovies, two ounces of pepper, a quarter of an ounce of mace, half an ounce of cloves; beat in a large mortar a hundred green walnuts until they are thoroughly broken; then put them into a jar with six ounces of shallots cut into pieces, a head of garlic, two quarts of vinegar and the half pound of salt; let them stand for a fortnight, stirring them twice a day. Strain off the liquor, put into a stew pan with the anchovies, whole pepper, half an ounce of cloves and a quarter of an ounce of mace; boil it half an hour, skimming it well. Strain it off, and, when cold, pour it clear from any sediment into small bottles, cork it down closely and store it in a dry place. The sediment can be used for flavoring sauces.

OYSTER KETCHUP

One pint of oyster meats, one teacupful of sherry, a tablespoonful of salt, a teaspoonful of cayenne pepper, the same of powdered mace, a gill of cider vinegar.

Procure the oysters very fresh and open sufficient to fill a pint measure; save the liquor and scald the oysters in it with the sherry; strain the oysters and chop them fine with the salt, cayenne and mace, until reduced to a pulp; then add it to the liquor in which they were scalded; boil it again five minutes and skim well; rub the whole through a sieve, and, when cold, bottle and cork closely. The corks should be sealed.

MUSHROOM KETCHUP

Use the larger kind known as umbrellas or "flaps." They must be very fresh and not gathered in very wet weather, or the ketchup will be less apt to keep. Wash and cut them in two to four pieces, and place them in a wide, flat jar or crock in layers, sprinkling each layer with salt, and let them stand for twenty-four hours; take them out and press out the juice, when bottle and cork; put the mushrooms back again, and in another twenty-four hours press them again; bottle and cork; repeat this for the third time, and then mix together all the juice extracted; add to it pepper, allspice, one or more cloves according to quantity, pounded together; boil the whole, and skim as long as any scum rises; bottle when cool; put in each bottle two cloves and a pepper-corn. Cork and seal, put in a dry place, and it will keep for years.

GOOSEBERRY KETCHUP

Ten pounds of fruit gathered just before ripening, five pounds of sugar, one quart of vinegar, two tablespoonfuls each of ground black pepper, allspice and cinnamon. Boil the fruit in vinegar until reduced to a pulp, then add sugar and the other seasoning. Seal it hot.

Grape ketchup is made in the same manner.

CUCUMBER KETCHUP

Take cucumbers suitable for the table; peel and grate them, salt a little, and put in a bag to drain over night; in the morning season to taste with salt, pepper and vinegar, put in small jars and seal tight for fall or winter use.

CURRANT KETCHUP

Four pounds of currants, two pounds of sugar, one pint of vinegar, one teaspoonful of cloves, a tablespoonful of cinnamon, pepper and allspice. Boil in a porcelain saucepan until thoroughly cooked. Strain through a sieve all but the skins; boil down until just thick enough to run freely from the mouth of a bottle when cold. Cork and set aside.

APPLE KETCHUP

Peel and quarter a dozen sound, tart apples; stew them until soft in as little water as possible, then pass them through a sieve. To a quart of the sifted apple, add a teacupful of sugar, one teaspoonful of pepper, one of cloves, one of mustard, two of cinnamon, and two medium-sized onions, chopped *very* fine. Stir all together, adding a tablespoonful of salt and a pint of vinegar. Place over the fire and boil one hour, and bottle while hot; seal very tight. It should be about as thick as tomato ketchup, so that it will just run from the bottle.

CELERY VINEGAR

A quart of fresh celery, chopped fine, or a quarter of a pound of celery seed; one quart of best vinegar; one tablespoonful of salt, and one of white sugar. Put the celery or seed into a jar, heat the vinegar, sugar and salt; pour it boiling hot over the celery, let it cool, cover it tightly and set away. In two weeks strain and bottle.

SPICED VINEGAR

Take one quart of cider vinegar, put into it half an ounce of celery seed, one-third of an ounce of dried mint, one-third of an ounce of dried parsley, one garlic, three small onions, three whole cloves, a teaspoonful of whole peppercorns, a teaspoonful of grated nutmeg, salt to taste and a tablespoonful of sugar; add a tablespoonful of good brandy. Put all into a jar, and cover it well; let it stand for three weeks, then strain and bottle it well. Useful for flavoring salad and other dishes.

Eat Like a President: Book I

PICKLES

Preparations

Pickles should never be put into vessels of brass, copper or tin, as the action of the acid on such metals often results in poisoning the pickles. Porcelain or granite-ware is the best for such purposes.

Vinegar that is used for pickling should be the best cider or white-wine, and should never be boiled more than five or six minutes, as it reduces its strength. In putting away pickles, use stone or glass jars; the glazing on common earthenware is rendered injurious by the action of the vinegar. When the jar is nearly filled with the pickles, the vinegar should completely cover them, and if there is any appearance of their not doing well, turn off the vinegar, cover with fresh vinegar and spices. Alum in small quantities is useful in making them firm and crisp. In using ground spices, tie them up in muslin bags.

To green pickles, put green grapevine leaves or green cabbage leaves between them when heating. Another way is to heat them in strong ginger tea. Pickles should be kept closely covered, put into glass jars and sealed tightly.

Turmeric is India saffron, and is used very much in pickling as a coloring.

A piece of horse radish put into a jar of pickles will keep the vinegar from losing its strength, and the pickles will keep sound much longer, especially tomato pickles.

CUCUMBER PICKLES

Select the medium, small-sized cucumbers. For one bushel make a brine that will bear up an egg; heat it boiling hot and pour it over the cucumbers; let them stand twenty-four hours, then wipe them dry; heat some vinegar boiling hot and pour over them, standing again twenty-four hours. Now change the vinegar, putting on fresh vinegar, adding one quart of brown sugar, a pint of white mustard seed, a small handful of whole cloves, the same of cinnamon sticks, a piece of alum the size of an egg, half a cup of celery seed; heat it all boiling hot and pour over the cucumbers.

SLICED CUCUMBER PICKLE

Take one gallon of medium-sized cucumbers, put them into a jar or pail. Put into enough *boiling* water to cover them a small handful of salt, turn it over them and cover closely; repeat this three mornings, and the fourth morning scald enough cider vinegar to cover them, putting into it a piece of alum as large as a walnut, a teacup of horse-radish root cut up fine; then tie up in a small muslin bag, one teaspoonful of mustard, one of ground cloves, and one of cinnamon. Slice up the cucumbers half of an inch thick, place them in glass jars and pour the scalding vinegar over them.

Seal tight and they will keep good a year or more.

Mrs. Lydia C. Wright, South Vernon, Vermont.

CUCUMBER PICKLES (For Winter Use)

A good way to put down cucumbers, a few at a time:

When gathered from the vines, wash, and put in a firkin or half barrel layers or cucumbers and rock-salt alternately, enough salt to make sufficient brine to cover them, no water; cover with a cloth; keep them under the brine with a heavy board; take off the cloth, and rinse it every time you put in fresh cucumbers, as a scum will rise and settle upon it. Use plenty of salt and it will keep a year. To prepare pickles for use, soak in hot water, and keep in a warm place until they are fresh enough, then pour spiced vinegar over them and let them stand over night, then pour that off and put on fresh.

GREEN TOMATO PICKLES (Sweet)

One peck of green tomatoes, sliced the day before you are ready for pickling, sprinkling them through and through with salt, not *too* heavily; in the morning drain off the liquor that will drain from them. Have a dozen good-sized onions rather coarsely sliced; take a suitable kettle and put in a layer of the sliced tomatoes, then of onions, and between each layer sprinkle the following spices: Six *red* peppers chopped coarsely, one cup of sugar, one tablespoonful of ground allspice, one tablespoonful of ground cinnamon, a teaspoonful of cloves, one tablespoonful of mustard. Turn over three pints of good vinegar, or enough to completely cover them; boil until tender. This is a choice recipe.

If the flavor of onions is objectionable, the pickle is equally as good without them.

GREEN TOMATO PICKLES (Sour)

Wash and slice, without peeling, one peck of sound green tomatoes, put them into a jar in layers with a slight sprinkling of salt between. This may be done over night; in the morning drain off the liquor that has accumulated. Have two dozen medium-sized onions peeled and sliced, also six red peppers chopped fine. Make some spiced vinegar by boiling for half an hour a quart of cider vinegar with whole spices in it. Now take a porcelain kettle and place in it some of the sliced tomatoes, then some of the sliced onions; shake in some black pepper and some of the chopped red peppers; pour over some of the spiced vinegar; then repeat with the tomatoes, onions, etc., until the kettle is full; cover with cold, pure cider vinegar and cook until tender, but not too soft. Turn into a jar well covered and set in a cool place.

PICKLED MUSHROOMS

Sufficient vinegar to cover the mushrooms; to each quart of mushrooms two blades pounded mace, one ounce ground pepper, salt to taste. Choose some nice young button mushrooms for pickling and rub off the skin with a piece of flannel and salt, and cut off the stalks; if very large, take out the red inside, and reject the black ones, as they are too old. Put them in a stew pan, sprinkle salt over them, with pounded mace and pepper in the above proportion; shake them well over a clear fire until the liquor flows and keep them there until it is all dried up again; then add as much vinegar as will cover them; just let it simmer for one minute and store it away in stone jars for use. When cold tie down with bladder and keep in a dry place; they will remain good for a length of time, and are generally considered excellent for flavoring stews and other dishes.

PICKLED CABBAGE (Purple)

Cut a sound cabbage into quarters, spread it on a large flat platter or dish and sprinkle thickly with salt; set it in a cool place for twenty-four hours; then drain off the brine, wipe it dry and lay it in the sun two hours, and cover with cold vinegar for twelve hours. Prepare a pickle by seasoning enough vinegar to cover the cabbage with equal quantities of mace, allspice, cinnamon and black pepper, a cup of sugar to every gallon of vinegar, and a teaspoonful of celery seed to every pint. Pack the cabbage in a stone jar; boil the vinegar and spices five minutes and pour on hot. Cover and set away in a cool, dry place. It will be good in a month. A few slices of beetroot improves the color.

PICKLED WHITE CABBAGE

This recipe recommends itself as of a delightful flavor yet easily made, and a convenient substitute for the old-fashioned, tedious method of pickling the same vegetable. Take a peck of quartered cabbage, put a layer of cabbage and one of salt, let it remain over night; in the morning squeeze them and put them on the fire, with four chopped onions covered with vinegar; boil for half an hour, then add one ounce of turmeric, one gill of black pepper, one gill of celery seed, a few cloves, one tablespoonful of allspice, a few pieces of ginger, half an ounce of mace, and two pounds of brown sugar. Let it boil half-an-hour longer, and when cold it is fit for use. Four tablespoonfuls of made mustard should be added with the other ingredients.

PICKLED CAULIFLOWER

Break the heads into small pieces and boil ten or fifteen minutes in salt and water; remove from the water and drain carefully. When cold, place in a jar, and pour over it hot vinegar, in which has been scalded a liberal supply of whole cloves, pepper, allspice and white mustard. Tie the spices in a bag, and, on removing the vinegar from the fire, stir into each quart of it two teaspoonfuls of French mustard, and half a cup of white sugar. Cover tightly and be sure to have the vinegar cover the pickle.

PICKLED GREEN PEPPERS

Take two dozen large, green, bell peppers, extract the seeds by cutting a slit in the side (so as to leave them whole). Make a strong brine and pour over them; let them stand twenty-four hours. Take them out of the brine, and soak them in water for a day and a night; now turn off this water and scald some vinegar, in which put a small piece of alum, and pour over them, letting them stand three days. Prepare a stuffing of two hard heads of white cabbage, chopped fine, seasoned slightly with salt and a cup of white mustard seed; mix it well and stuff the peppers hard and full; stitch up, place them in a stone jar, and pour over spiced vinegar scalding hot. Cover tightly.

GREEN PEPPER MANGOES

Select firm, sound, green peppers, and add a few red ones as they are ornamental and look well upon the table. With a sharp knife remove the top, take out the seed, soak over night in salt water, then fill with chopped cabbage and green tomatoes, seasoned with salt, mustard seed and ground cloves. Sew on the top. Boil vinegar sufficient to cover them, with a cup of brown sugar, and pour over the mangoes. Do this three mornings, then seal.

CHOWCHOW (Superior English Recipe)

This excellent pickle is seldom made at home, as we can get the imported article so much better than it can be made from the usual recipes. This we vouch for being as near the genuine article as can be made: One quart of young, tiny cucumbers, not over two inches long, two quarts of *very* small white onions, two quarts of tender string beans, each one cut in halves, three quarts of green tomatoes, sliced and chopped very coarsely, two fresh heads of cauliflower, cut into small pieces, or two heads of white, hard cabbage.

After preparing these articles, put them in a stone jar, mix them together, sprinkling salt between them sparingly. Let them stand twenty-four hours, then drain off *all* the brine that has accumulated. Now put these vegetables in a preserving kettle over the fire, sprinkling through them an ounce of turmeric for coloring, six red peppers, chopped coarsely, four tablespoonfuls of mustard seed, two of celery seed, two of whole allspice, two of whole cloves, a coffee cup of sugar, and two-thirds of a teacup of best ground mixed mustard. Pour on enough of the best cider vinegar to cover the whole well; cover tightly and simmer all well until it is cooked all through and seems tender, watching and stirring it often. Put in bottles or glass jars. It grows better as it grows older, especially if sealed when hot.

PICKLED ONIONS

Peel small onions until they are white. Scald them in salt and water until tender, then take them up, put them into wide-mouthed bottles, and pour over them hot spiced vinegar; when cold cork them close. Keep in a dry, dark place. A tablespoonful of sweet oil may be put in the bottles before the cork. The best sort of onions for pickling are the small white buttons.

PICKLED MANGOES

Let the mangoes, or young musk-melons, lie in salt water, strong enough to bear an egg, for two weeks; then soak them in pure water for two days, changing the water two or three times; then remove the seeds and put the mangoes in a kettle, first a layer of grape leaves, then mangoes, and so on until all are in, covering the top with leaves; add a lump of alum the size of a hickory nut; pour vinegar over them and boil them ten or fifteen minutes; remove the leaves and let the pickles stand in this vinegar for a week; then stuff them with the following mixture: One pound of ginger soaked in brine for a day or two, and cut in slices, one ounce of black pepper, one of mace, one of allspice, one of turmeric, half a pound of garlic, soaked for a day or two in brine and then dried; one pint grated horseradish, one of black mustard seed and one of white mustard seed; bruise all the spices and mix with a teacup of pure olive oil; to each mango add one teaspoonful of brown sugar; cut one solid head of cabbage fine; add one pint of small onions, a few small cucumbers and green tomatoes; lay them in brine a day and a night, then drain them well and add the imperfect mangoes chopped fine and the spices; mix thoroughly, stuff the mangoes and tie them; put them in a stone jar and pour over them the best cider vinegar; set them in a bright, dry place until they are canned. In a month add three pounds of brown sugar; if this is not sufficient, add more until agreeable to taste. This is for four dozen mangoes.

PICKLE OF RIPE CUCUMBERS

This is a French recipe and is the most excellent of all the high-flavored condiments; it is made by *sun-drying* thirty *old*, full grown cucumbers, which have first been pared and split, had the seeds taken out, been salted and let stand twenty-four hours. The sun should be permitted to *dry*, not simply drain them. When they are moderately dry, wash them with vinegar and place them in layers in a jar, alternating them with a layer of horseradish, mustard seed, garlic and onions for each layer of cucumbers. Boil in one quart of vinegar, one ounce of race ginger, half an ounce of allspice and the same of turmeric; when cool pour this over the cucumbers, tie up tightly and set away. This pickle requires several months to mature it, but is delicious when old, keeps admirably, and only a little is needed as a relish.

PICKLED OYSTERS

One gallon of oysters; wash them well in their own liquor; carefully clear away the particles of shell, then put them into a kettle, strain the liquor over them, add salt to your taste, let them just come to the boiling point, or until the edges curl up; then skim them out and lay in a dish to cool; put a sprig of mace and a little cold pepper and allow the liquor to boil some time, skimming it now and then so long as any skum rises. Pour it into a pan and let it cool. When perfectly cool, add a half pint of strong vinegar, place the oysters in a jar and pour the liquor over them.

RIPE CUCUMBER PICKLES (Sweet)

Pare and seed ripe cucumbers. Slice each cucumber lengthwise into four pieces, or cut it into fancy shapes, as preferred. Let them stand twenty-four hours covered with cold vinegar. Drain them; then put them into fresh vinegar, with two pounds of sugar and one ounce of cassia buds to one quart of vinegar, and a tablespoonful of salt. Boil all together twenty minutes. Cover them closely in a jar.

PICCALILLI

One peck of green tomatoes; eight large onions chopped fine, with one cup of salt well stirred in. Let it stand over night; in the morning drain off all the liquor. Now take two quarts of water and one of vinegar, boil all together twenty minutes. Drain all through a sieve or colander. Put it back into the kettle again; turn over it two quarts of vinegar, one pound of sugar, half a pound of white mustard seed, two tablespoonfuls of ground pepper, two of cinnamon, one of cloves, two of ginger, one of allspice, and half a teaspoonful of cayenne pepper. Boil all together fifteen minutes or until tender. Stir it often to prevent scorching. Seal in glass jars.

A most delicious accompaniment for any kind of meat or fish.

Mrs. St. Johns.

PICKLED EGGS

Pickled eggs are very easily prepared and most excellent as an accompaniment for cold meats. Boil quite hard three dozen eggs, drop in cold water and remove the shells, and pack them when entirely cold in a wide-mouthed jar, large enough to let them in or out without breaking. Take as much vinegar as you think will cover them entirely and boil it in white pepper, allspice, a little root ginger; pack them in stone or wide-mouthed glass jars, occasionally putting in a tablespoonful of white and black mustard seed mixed, a small piece of race ginger, garlic, if liked, horseradish ungrated, whole cloves, and a very little allspice. Slice two of three green peppers, and add in very small quantities. They will be fit for use in eight or ten days.

AN ORNAMENTAL PICKLE

Boil fresh eggs half an hour, then put them in cold water. Boil red beets until tender, peel and cut in dice form, and cover with vinegar, spiced; shell the eggs and drop into the pickle jar.

EAST INDIA PICKLE

Lay in strong brine for two weeks, or until convenient to use them, small cucumbers, very small common white onions, snap beans, gherkins, hard white cabbage quartered, plums, peaches, pears, lemons, green tomatoes and anything else you may wish. When ready, take them out of the brine and simmer in pure water until tender enough to stick a straw through – if still too salt, soak in clear water; drain thoroughly and lay them in vinegar in which is dissolved one ounce of turmeric to the gallon. For five gallons of pickle, take two ounces of mace, two of cloves, two of cinnamon, two of allspice, two of celery seed, a quarter of a pound of white race ginger, cracked fine, half a pound of white mustard seed, half a pint of small red peppers, quarter of a pound of grated horse-radish, half a pint of flour mustard, two ounces of turmeric, half a pint of garlic, if you like; soak in two gallons of cider vinegar for two weeks, stirring daily. After the pickles have lain in the turmeric vinegar for a week, take them out and put in jars or casks, one layer of pickle and one of spice out of the vinegar, till all is used. If the turmeric vinegar is still good and strong, add it and the spiced vinegar. If the turmeric vinegar be much diluted do not use it, but add enough fresh to the spiced to cover the pickles; put it on the fire with a pound of brown sugar to each gallon; when boiling, pour over the pickle. Repeat this two or three times as your taste may direct.

MIXED PICKLES

Scald in salt water until tender cauliflower heads, small onions, peppers, cucumbers cut in dice, nasturtiums and green beans; then drain until dry and pack into wide-mouthed bottles. Boil in each pint of cider vinegar one tablespoonful of sugar, half a teaspoonful of salt and two tablespoonfuls of mustard; pour over the pickle and seal carefully. Other spices may be added if liked.

BLUEBERRY PICKLES

For blueberry pickles, old jars which have lost their covers, or whose edges have been broken so that the covers will not fit tightly, serve an excellent purpose as these pickles *must not* be kept airtight.

Pick over your berries, using only sound ones; fill your jars or wide-mouthed bottles to within an inch of the top, then pour in molasses enough to settle down into *all* the spaces; this cannot be done in a moment, as molasses does not *run* very freely. Only lazy people will feel obliged to stand by and watch its progress. As it settles, pour in more until the berries are covered. Then tie over the top a piece of cotton cloth to keep the flies and other insects out and set away in the preserve closet. Cheap molasses is good enough, and your pickles will soon be "sharp." Wild grapes may be pickled in the same manner.

PICKLED BUTTERNUTS AND WALNUTS

These nuts are in the best state for pickling when the outside shell can be penetrated by the head of a pin. Scald them and rub off the outside skin, put them in a strong brine for six days, changing the water every other day, keeping them closely covered from the air. Then drain and wipe them (piercing each nut through in several places with a large needle) and prepare the pickle as follows: For a hundred large nuts, take of black pepper and ginger root each an ounce; and of cloves, mace and nutmeg, each a half ounce. Pound all the spices to powder and mix them well together, adding two large spoonfuls of mustard seed. Put the nuts into jars (having first stuck each of them through in several places with a large needle), strewing the powdered seasoning between every layer of nuts. Boil for five minutes a gallon of the very best cider vinegar and pour it boiling hot upon the nuts. Secure the jars closely with corks. You may begin to eat the nuts in a fortnight.

WATERMELON PICKLE

Ten pounds of watermelon rind boiled in pure water until tender; drain the water off, and make a syrup of two pounds of white sugar, one quart of vinegar, half an ounce of cloves, one ounce of cinnamon. The syrup to be poured over the rind boiling hot three days in succession.

SWEET PICKLE FOR FRUIT

Most of the recipes for making a sweet pickle for fruit, such as cling-stone peaches, damsons, plums, cherries, apricots, etc., are so similar, that we give that which is most successfully used.

To every quart of fruit, allow a cup of white sugar and a large pint of good cider vinegar, adding half an ounce of *stick* cinnamon, one tablespoonful of *whole* cloves, the same of whole allspice. Let it come to a boil, and pour it hot over the fruit; repeat this two or three days in succession; then seal hot in glass jars if you wish to keep it for a long time.

The *fruit*, not the liquor, is to be eaten, and used the same as any pickle. Some confound this with "Spiced Fruit," which is not treated the same, one being a pickle, the other a spiced preserve boiled down thick.

Damsons and plums should be pricked with a needle, and peaches washed with a weak lye, and then rubbed with a coarse cloth to remove the fur.

PEAR PICKLE

Select small, sound ones, remove the blossom end, stick them with a fork, allow to each quart of pears one pint of cider vinegar and one cup of sugar, put in a teaspoonful allspice, cinnamon and cloves to boil with the vinegar; then add the pears and boil, and seal in jars.

SPICED CURRANTS

Seven pounds of fruit, four pounds of sugar, one pint of good cider vinegar, one tablespoonful of ground cinnamon, one teaspoonful of cloves. Put into a kettle and boil until the fruit is soft; then skim out the fruit, putting it on dishes until the syrup is boiled down thick. Turn the fruit back into the syrup again, so as to heat it all through; then seal it hot in glass jars, and set it in a cool, dark place.

Any tart fruit may be put up in this way, and is considered a very good embellishment for cold meats.

SPICED PLUMS

Seven pounds of plums, one pint of *cider* vinegar, four pounds of sugar, two tablespoonfuls of broken cinnamon bark, half as much of whole cloves and the same of broken nutmeg; place these in a muslin bag and simmer them in a little vinegar and water for half an hour; then add it all to the vinegar and sugar, and bring to a boil; add the plums and boil carefully until they are cooked tender. Before cooking the plums they should be pierced with a darning needle several times; this will prevent the skins bursting while cooking.

SPICED GRAPES

Take the pulp from the grapes, preserving the skins. Boil the pulp and rub through a colander to get out the seeds; then add the skins to the strained pulp and boil with the sugar, vinegar and spices. To every seven pounds of grapes use four and one-half pounds of sugar, one pint of good vinegar. Spice quite highly with ground cloves and allspice, with a little cinnamon.

PICKLED CHERRIES

Select sound, large cherries, as large as you can get them; to every quart of cherries allow a large cupful of vinegar, two tablespoonfuls of sugar, a dozen whole cloves, and half a dozen blades of mace; put the vinegar and sugar on to heat with the spices; boil five minutes, turn out into a covered stoneware vessel; cover and let it get perfectly cold; pack the cherries into jars, and pour the vinegar over them when cold; cork tightly and set away; they are fit for use almost immediately.

Eat Like a President: Book I

VEGETABLES

Vegetables of all kinds should be thoroughly picked over, throwing out all decayed or unripe parts, then well washed in several waters. Most vegetables, when peeled, are better when laid in cold water a short time before cooking. When partly cooked a little salt should be thrown into the water in which they are boiled, and they should cook steadily after they are put on, not allowed to stop boiling or simmering until they are thoroughly done. Every sort of culinary vegetable is much better when freshly gathered and cooked as soon as possible, and, when done, thoroughly drained, and served immediately while hot.

Onions, cabbage, carrots and turnips should be cooked in a great deal of water, boiled only long enough to sufficiently cook them, and immediately drained. Longer boiling makes them insipid in taste, and with *too little* water they turn a dark color.

Potatoes rank first in importance in the vegetable line, and consequently should be properly served. It requires some little intelligence to cook even so simple and common a dish as boiled potatoes. In the first place, all defective or green ones should be cast out; a bad one will flavor a whole dish. If they are not uniform in size, they should be made so by cutting after they are peeled. The best part of a potato, or the most nutritious, is next to the skin, therefore they should be pared very thinly, if at all; then, if old, the cores should be cut out, thrown into *cold* water salted a little, and boiled until soft enough for a fork to pierce through easily; drain immediately, and replace the kettle on the fire with the cover partly removed, until they are completely dried. New potatoes should be put into boiling water, and when partly done salted a little. They should be prepared just in time for cooking by scraping off the thin outside skin. They require about twenty minutes to boil.

TO BOIL NEW POTATOES

Do not have the potatoes dug long before they are dressed, as they are never good when they have been out of the ground for some time. Well wash them, rub off the skins with a coarse cloth, and put them in *boiling* water salted. Let them boil until tender; try them with a fork, and when done pour the water away from them; let them stand by the side of the fire with the lid of the saucepan partly removed, and when the potatoes are thoroughly dry, put them in a hot vegetable dish, with a piece of butter the size of a walnut; pile the potatoes over this and serve. If the potatoes are too old to have the skins rubbed off; boil them in their jackets; drain, peel and serve them as above, with a piece of butter placed in the midst of them. They require twenty to thirty minutes to cook. Serve them hot and plain, or with melted butter over them.

MASHED POTATOES

Take the quantity needed, pare off the skins and lay them in cold water half an hour; then put them into a saucepan with a little salt; cover with water and boil them until done. Drain off the water and mash them fine with a potato masher. Have ready a piece of butter the size of an egg, melted in half a cup of boiling hot milk and a good pinch of salt; mix it well with the mashed potatoes until they are a smooth paste, taking care that they are not too wet. Put them into a vegetable dish, heaping them up and smooth over the top, put a small piece of butter on the top in the center, and have dots of pepper here and there on the surface as large as a half dime.

Some prefer using a heavy fork or wire beater, instead of a potato masher, beating the potatoes quite light and heaping them up in the dish without smoothing over the top.

BROWNED POTATOES

Mash them the same as the above, put them into a dish that they are to be served in, smooth over the top and brush over with the yolk of an egg, or spread on a bountiful supply of butter and dust well with flour. Set in the oven to brown; it will brown in fifteen minutes with a quick fire.

MASHED POTATOES (warmed over)

To two cupfuls of cold mashed potatoes add a half cupful of milk, a pinch of salt, a tablespoonful of butter, two tablespoonfuls of flour and two eggs beaten to a froth. Mix the whole until thoroughly light; then put into a pudding or vegetable dish, spread a little butter over the top and bake a golden brown. The quality depends upon very thoroughly beating the eggs before adding them, so that the potato will remain light and porous after baking, similar to sponge cake.

POTATO PUFFS

Prepare the potatoes as directed for mashed potato. While *hot*, shape in balls about the size of an egg. Have a tin sheet well buttered, and place the balls on it. As soon as all are done, brush over with beaten egg. Brown in the oven. When done, slip a knife under them and slide them upon a hot platter. Garnish with parsley and serve immediately.

POTATOES Á LA CRÊME

Heat a cupful of milk; stir in a heaping tablespoonful of butter cut up in as much flour. Stir until smooth and thick; pepper and salt, and add two cupfuls of cold boiled potatoes, sliced, and a little very finely chopped parsley. Shake over the fire until the potatoes are hot all through, and pour into a deep dish.

NEW POTATOES AND CREAM

Wash and rub new potatoes with a coarse cloth or scrubbing-brush; drop into boiling water and boil briskly until done, and no more; press a potato against the side of the kettle with a fork; if done, it will yield to a gentle pressure; in a saucepan have ready some butter and cream, hot, but not boiling, a little green parsley, pepper and salt; drain the potatoes, add the mixture, put over hot water for a minute or two, and serve.

SARATOGA CHIPS

Peel good-sized potatoes, and slice them as evenly as possible. Drop them into ice water; have a kettle of very hot lard, as for cakes; put a few at a time into a towel and shake, to dry the moisture out of them, and then drop them into the boiling lard. Stir them occasionally, and when of a light brown take them out with a skimmer, and they will be crisp and not greasy. Sprinkle salt over them while hot.

FRIED RAW POTATOES

Peel half a dozen medium-sized potatoes very evenly, cut them in slices as thin as an egg-shell, and be sure to cut them from the *breadth*, not the length, of the potato. Put a tablespoonful each of butter and sweet lard into the frying pan, and as soon as it boils add the sliced potatoes, sprinkling over them salt and pepper to season them. Cover them with a tight-fitting lid, and let the steam partly cook them; then remove it, and let them fry a bright gold color, shaking and turning them carefully, so as to brown equally. Serve very hot.

Fried, cold cooked potatoes may be fried by the same recipe, only slice them a little thicker.

Remark – Boiled or steamed potatoes chopped up or sliced while they are yet warm never fry so successfully as when cold.

SCALLOPED POTATOES (Kentucky Style)

Peel and slice raw potatoes thin, the same as for frying. Butter an earthen dish, put in a layer of potatoes, and season with salt, pepper, butter, a bit of onion chopped fine, if liked; sprinkle a little flour. Now put another layer of potatoes and the seasoning. Continue in this way till the dish is filled. Just before putting into the oven, pour a quart of hot milk over. Bake three-quarters of an hour.

Cold boiled potatoes may be cooked the same. It requires less time to bake them; they are delicious either way. If the onion is disliked it can be omitted.

STEAMED POTATOES

This mode of cooking potatoes is now much in vogue, particularly where they are wanted on a large scale, it being so very convenient. Pare the potatoes, throw them into cold water as they are peeled, then put them in a steamer. Place the steamer over a saucepan of boiling water, and steam the potatoes from twenty to forty minutes, according to the size and sort. When the fork goes easily through them, they are done; then take them up, dish and serve very quickly.

POTATO SNOW

Choose some mealy potatoes that will boil exceedingly white; pare them and cook them well, but not so as to be watery; drain them, and mash and season them well. Put in the saucepan in which they were dressed, so as to keep them as hot as possible; then press them through a wire sieve into the dish in which they are to be served; strew a little fine salt upon them previous to sending them to table. French cooks also add a small quantity of pounded loaf sugar while they are being mashed.

HASTY COOKED POTATOES

Wash and peel some potatoes; cut them into slices of about a quarter of an inch in thickness; throw them into *boiling* salted water, and, if of good quality, they will be done in about ten minutes.

Strain off the water, put the potatoes into a hot dish, chop them slightly, add pepper, salt, and a few small pieces of fresh butter, and serve without loss of time.

FAVORITE WARMED POTATOES

The potatoes should be boiled *whole with the skins on* in plenty of water, well *salted*, and are much better for being boiled the day before needed. Care should be taken that they are not over cooked. Strip off the skins (not pare them with a knife) and slice them nearly a quarter of an inch thick. Place them in a chopping-bowl and sprinkle over them sufficient salt and pepper to season them well; chop them all one way, then turn the chopping-bowl half way around and chop across them, cutting them into little square pieces the shape of dice. About twenty-five minutes before serving time, place on the stove a saucepan (or any suitable dish) containing a piece of butter the size of an egg; when it begins to melt and run over the bottom of the dish, put in a cup of rich sweet milk. When this boils up put in the chopped potatoes; there should be about a quart of them; stir them a little so that they become moistened through with the milk; then cover and place them on the back of the stove, or in a moderate oven, where they will heat through gradually. When heated through, stir carefully from the bottom with a spoon and cover tightly again. Keep hot until ready to serve. Baked potatoes are very good warmed in this manner.

CRISP POTATOES

Cut cold raw potatoes into shavings, cubes, or any small

shape; throw them, a few at a time, into boiling fat and toss them about with a knife until they are a uniform light brown; drain and season with salt and pepper. Fat is never hot enough while bubbling – when it is ready it is still and smoking, but should never burn.

LYONNAISE POTATOES

Take eight or ten good-sized cold boiled potatoes, slice them end-wise, then crosswise, making them like dice in small squares. When you are ready to cook them, heat some butter or good drippings in a frying pan; fry in it one small onion (chopped fine) until it begins to change color and look yellow. Now put in your potatoes, sprinkle well with salt and pepper, stir well and cook about five minutes, taking care that you do not break them. *They must not brown.* Just before taking up stir in a tablespoonful of minced parsley. Drain dry by shaking in a heated colander. Serve *very hot*.

Delmonico

POTATO FILLETS

Pare and slice the potatoes thin; cut them if you like in small fillets about a quarter of an inch square, and as long as the potato will admit; keep them in cold water until wanted, then drop them into boiling lard; when nearly done, take them out with a skimmer and drain them, boil up the lard again, drop the potatoes back and fry till done; this operation causes the fillets to swell up and puff.

POTATO CROQUETTES No. 1

Wash, peel and put four large potatoes in cold water,

with a pinch of salt, and set them over a brisk fire; when they are done pour off all the water and mash them.

Take another saucepan, and put in it ten tablespoonfuls of milk and a lump of butter half the size of an egg; put it over a brisk fire; as soon as the milk comes to a boil, pour the potatoes into it, and stir them very fast with a wooden spoon; when thoroughly mixed, take them from the fire and put them on a dish.

Take a tablespoonful and roll it in a clean towel, making it oval in shape; dip it in a well-beaten egg, and then in breadcrumbs, and drop it in hot drippings or lard.

Proceed in this manner till all the potato is used, four potatoes making six croquettes.

Fry them a light brown all over, turning them gently as may be necessary. When they are done, lay them on brown paper or a hair sieve, to drain off all fat; then serve on a napkin.

POTATO CROQUETTES No. 2

Take two cups of cold mashed potatoes, season with a pinch of salt, pepper and a tablespoonful of butter. Beat up the whites of two eggs, and work all together thoroughly; make it into small balls slightly flattened, dip them in the beaten yolks of the eggs, then roll either in flour or cracker crumbs; fry the same as fish-balls.

Delmonico's.

POTATOES Á LA DELMONICO

Cut the potatoes with a vegetable cutter into small balls about the size of a marble; put them into a stew pan with plenty of butter and a good sprinkling of salt; keep the saucepan covered, and shake occasionally until they are quite done, which will be in about an hour.

FRIED POTATOES WITH EGGS

Slice cold boiled potatoes and fry in good butter until brown; beat up one or two eggs, and stir into them just as you dish them for the table; do not leave them a moment on the fire after the eggs are in, for if they harden they are not half so nice; one egg is enough for three or four persons, unless they are very fond of potatoes; if they are, have plenty and put in two.

BAKED POTATOES

Potatoes are either baked in their jackets or peeled; in either case they should not be exposed to a fierce heat, which is wasteful, inasmuch as thereby a great deal of vegetable is scorched and rendered uneatable. They should be frequently turned while being baked and kept from touching each other in the oven or dish. When done in their skins, be particular to wash and brush them before baking them. If convenient, they may be baked in wood-ashes, or in a Dutch oven in front of the fire. When pared they should be baked in a dish and fat of some kind added to prevent their outsides from becoming burnt; they are ordinarily baked thus as an accessory to baked meat.

Never serve potatoes, boiled or baked whole, in a closely covered dish. They become sodden and clammy. Cover with a folded napkin that allows the steam to escape, or absorbs the moisture. They should be served promptly when done and require about three-quarters of an hour to one hour to bake them, if of a good size.

BROWNED POTATOES WITH A ROAST No. 1

About three-quarters of an hour before taking up your roasts, peel middling-sized potatoes, boil them until partly done, then arrange them in the roasting-pan around the roast, basting them with the drippings at the same time you do the meat, browning them evenly. Serve hot with the meat. Many cooks partly boil the potatoes before putting around the roast. New potatoes are very good cooked around a roast.

BROWNED POTATOES WITH A ROAST No. 2

Peel, cook and mash the required quantity, adding while hot a little chopped onion, pepper and salt; form it into small oval balls and dredge them with flour; then place around the meat about twenty minutes before it is taken from the oven. When nicely browned, drain dry and serve hot with the meat.

SWEET POTATOES

Boiled, steamed and baked the same as Irish potatoes; generally cooked with their jackets on. Cold sweet potatoes may be cut in slices across or lengthwise, and fried as common potatoes; or may be cut in half and served cold.

Boiled sweet potatoes are very nice. Boil until partly done, peel them and bake brown, basting them with butter or beef drippings several times. Served hot. They should be a nice brown.

BAKED SWEET POTATOES

Wash and scrape them, split them lengthwise. Steam or boil them until nearly done. Drain, and put them in a baking dish, placing over them lumps of butter, pepper and salt; sprinkle thickly with sugar, and bake in the oven to a nice brown.

Hubbard squash is nice cooked in the same manner.

ONIONS BOILED

The white silver-skins are the best species. To boil them peel off the outside, cut off the ends, put them into cold water, and into a stew pan and let them scald two minutes; then turn off that water, pour on cold water salted a little, and boil slowly till tender, which will be in thirty or forty minutes, according to their size; when done drain them quite dry, pour a little melted butter over them, sprinkle them with pepper and salt and serve hot.

An excellent way to peel onions so as not to affect the eyes is to take a pan *full* of water and hold and peel them under the water.

ONIONS STEWED

Cook the same as boiled onions, and, when quite done, turn off all the water; add a teacupful of milk, a piece of butter the size of an egg, pepper and salt to taste, a tablespoonful of flour stirred to a cream; let all boil up once and serve in a vegetable dish hot.

ONIONS BAKED

Use the large Spanish onion, as best for this purpose; wash them clean, but do not peel, and put into a saucepan with slightly salted water; boil an hour, replacing the water with more boiling hot as it evaporates; turn off the water and lay the onions on a cloth to dry them well; roll each one in a piece of buttered tissue paper, twisting it at the top to keep it on, and bake in a slow oven about an hour, or until tender all through; peel them; place in a deep dish and brown slightly, basting well with butter for fifteen minutes; season with salt and pepper and pour some melted butter over them.

FRIED ONIONS

Peel, slice and fry them brown in equal quantities of butter and lard or nice drippings; cover until partly soft, remove the cover and brown them; salt and pepper.

SCALLOPED ONIONS

Take eight or ten onions of good size, slice them and boil until tender. Lay them in a baking dish, put in breadcrumbs, butter in small bits, pepper and salt, between each layer until the dish is full, putting breadcrumbs last; add milk or cream until full. Bake twenty minutes or half an hour.

A little onion is not an injurious article of food, as many believe. A judicious use of plants of the onion family is quite as important a factor in successful cookery as salt and pepper. When carefully concealed by manipulation in food, it affords zest and enjoyment to many who could not otherwise taste of it were its presence known. A great many successful compounds derive their excellence from the partly concealed flavor of the onion, which imparts a delicate appetizing aroma highly prized by epicures.

CAULIFLOWER

When cleaned and washed, drop them into boiling

water, into which you have put salt and a teaspoonful of flour, or a slice of bread; boil till tender; take off, drain and dish them; serve with a sauce spread over and made with melted butter, salt, pepper, grated nutmeg, chopped parsley and vinegar.

Another way is to make a white sauce (see SAUCES) and when the cauliflowers are dished as above, turn the white sauce over, and serve warm. They may also be served in the same way with a milk, cream, or tomato sauce, or with brown butter.

It is a very good plan to loosen the leaves of a head of cauliflower and let lie, the top downward, in a pan of cold salt water, to remove any insects that might be hidden between them.

FRIED CAULIFLOWER

Boil the cauliflower till about half done. Mix two tablespoonfuls of flour with two yolks of eggs, then add water enough to make a rather thin paste; add salt to taste; the two whites are beaten till stiff, and then mixed with the yolks, flour and water. Dip each branch of the cauliflower into the mixture, and fry them in hot fat. When done, take them off with a skimmer, turn into a colander, dust salt all over and serve warm. Asparagus, celery, egg-plant, oyster plant are all fine when fried in this manner.

CABBAGE BOILED

Great care is requisite in cleaning a cabbage for boiling, as it frequently harbors numerous insects. The large drumhead cabbage requires an hour to boil; the green savory cabbage will boil in twenty minutes. Add considerable salt to the water when boiling. Do not let a cabbage boil too long – by a long boiling it becomes watery. Remove it from the water into a colander to drain and serve with drawn butter, or butter poured over it.

Red cabbage is used for slaw, as is also the white winter cabbage. For directions to prepare these varieties, see articles SLAW and SOURCROUT.

CABBAGE WITH CREAM

Remove the outer leaves from a solid, small-sized head of cabbage, and cut the remainder as fine as for slaw. Have on the fire a spider or deep skillet, and when it is hot put in the cut cabbage, pouring over it right away a pint of boiling water.

Cover closely and allow it to cook rapidly for ten minutes. Drain off the water and add half a pint of new milk, or part milk and cream; when it boils, stir in a large teaspoonful of either wheat or rice flour moistened with milk; add salt and pepper, and as soon as it comes to a boil, serve. Those who find slaw and other dishes prepared from cabbage indigestible will not complain of this.

STEAMED CABBAGE

Take a sound, solid cabbage, and with a large sharp knife shave it *very fine*. Put it in a saucepan, pour in half a teacupful of water, or just enough to keep it from burning; cover it very tightly, so as to confine the steam; watch it closely, add a little water now and then, until it begins to be tender; then put into it a large tablespoonful of butter; salt and pepper to taste, dish it hot. If you prefer to give it a tart taste, just before taking from the fire add a third of a cup of good vinegar.

LADIES' CABBAGE

Boil a firm white cabbage fifteen minutes, changing the water then for more from the boiling tea-kettle. When tender, drain and set aside until perfectly cold. Chop fine and add two beaten eggs, a tablespoonful of butter, pepper, salt, three tablespoonfuls of rich milk or cream. Stir all well together, and bake in a buttered pudding-dish until brown. Serve very hot. This dish resembles cauliflower and is very digestible and palatable.

FRIED CABBAGE

Place in a frying pan an ounce of butter and heat it boiling hot. Then take cold boiled cabbage chopped fine, or cabbage hot, cooked the same as steamed cabbage, put it into the hot butter and fry a light brown, adding two tablespoonfuls of vinegar. Very good.

FRENCH WAY OF COOKING CABBAGE

Chop cold boiled white cabbage and let it drain till perfectly dry: stir in some melted butter to taste; pepper, salt and four tablespoonfuls of cream; after it is heated through add two well-beaten eggs; then turn the mixture into a buttered frying pan, stirring until it is very hot and becomes a delicate brown on the under side. Place a hot dish over the pan, which must be reversed when turned out to be served.

SOURCROUT

Barrels having held wine or vinegar are used to prepare

sauerkraut in. It is better, however, to have a special barrel for the purpose. Strasburg, as well as all Alsace, has a well-acquired fame for preparing the cabbages. They slice very white and firm cabbages in fine shreds with a machine made for the purpose. At the bottom of a small barrel they place a layer of coarse salt and alternately layers of cabbage and salt, being careful to have one of salt on the top. As each layer of cabbage is added, it must be pressed down by a large and heavy pestle and fresh layers are added as soon as the juice floats on the surface. The cabbage must be seasoned with a few grains of coriander, juniper berries, etc. When the barrel is full it must be put in a dry cellar, covered with a cloth, under a plank, and on this heavy weights are placed. At the end of a few days it will begin to ferment, during which time the pickle must be drawn off and replaced by fresh, until the liquor becomes clear. This should be done every day. Renew the cloth and wash the cover, put the weights back and let stand for a month. By that time the sauerkraut will be ready for use. Care must be taken to let the least possible air enter the sauerkraut and to have the cover perfectly clean. Each time the barrel has to be opened it must be properly closed again. These precautions must not be neglected.

This is often fried in the same manner as fried cabbage, excepting it is first boiled until soft in just water enough to cook it, then fry and add vinegar.

TO BOIL RICE

Pick over the rice carefully, wash it in warm water, rubbing it between the hands, rinsing it in several waters, then let it remain in cold water until ready to be cooked.

Have a saucepan of water slightly salted; when it is boiling hard, pour off the cold water from the rice, and sprinkle it in the boiling water by degrees, so as to keep the particles separated. Boil it steadily for twenty minutes, then take it off from the fire and drain off all the water. Place the saucepan with the lid partly off, on the back part of the stove, where it is only moderately warm, to allow the rice to dry. The moisture will pass off and each grain of rice will be separated, so that if shaken the grains will fall apart. This is the true way of serving rice as a vegetable and is the mode of cooking it in the Southern States where it is raised.

PARSNIPS, BOILED

Wash, scrape and split them. Put them into a pot of boiling water; add a little salt, and boil them till quite tender, which will be in from two to three hours, according to their size. Dry them in a cloth when done and pour melted butter or white sauce (see SAUCES) over them in the dish. Serve them up with any sort of boiled meat or with salt cod.

Parsnips are very good baked or stewed with meat.

FRIED PARSNIPS

Boil tender in a little hot water salted; scrape, cut into long slices, dredge with flour; fry in hot lard or dripping, or in butter and lard mixed; fry quite brown. Drain off fat and serve.

Parsnips may be boiled and mashed the same as potatoes.

STEWED PARSNIPS

After washing and scraping the parsnips slice them

about half of an inch thick. Put them in a saucepan of boiling water containing just enough to barely cook them; add a tablespoonful of butter, season with salt and pepper, then cover closely. Stew them until the water has cooked away, watching carefully and stirring often to prevent burning, until they are soft. When they are done they will be of a creamy light straw color and deliciously sweet, retaining all the goodness of the vegetable.

PARSNIP FRITTERS

Boil four or five parsnips; when tender take off the skin and mash them fine; add to them a teaspoonful of wheat flour and a beaten egg; put a tablespoonful of lard or beef drippings in a frying pan over the fire, add to it a half teaspoonful of salt; when boiling hot put in the parsnips; make it in small cakes with a spoon; when one side is a delicate brown turn the other; when both are done take them on a dish, put a very little of the fat in which they were fried over and serve hot.

These resemble very nearly the taste of the salsify or oyster plant, and will generally be preferred.

CREAMED PARSNIPS

Boil tender, scrape and slice lengthwise. Put over the fire with two tablespoonfuls of butter, pepper and salt and a little minced parsley. Shake until the mixture boils. Dish the parsnips, add to the sauce three tablespoonfuls of cream or milk in which has been stirred a quarter of a spoonful of flour. Boil once and pour over the parsnips.

STEWED TOMATOES

Pour boiling water over a dozen sound ripe tomatoes; let them remain for a few moments; then peel off the skins, slice them and put them over the fire in a well-lined tin or graniteware saucepan. Stew them about twenty minutes, then add a tablespoonful of butter, salt and pepper to taste; let them stew fifteen minutes longer and serve hot. Some prefer to thicken tomatoes with a little grated bread, adding a teaspoonful of sugar; and others who like the flavor of onion chop up one and add while stewing; then again, some add as much green corn as there are tomatoes.

TO PEEL TOMATOES

Put the tomatoes into a frying basket and plunge them into hot water for three or four minutes. Drain and peel. Another way is to place them in a flat baking-tin and set them in a hot oven about five minutes; this loosens the skins so that they readily slip off.

SCALLOPED TOMATOES

Butter the sides and bottom of a pudding-dish. Put a layer of breadcrumbs in the bottom; on them put a layer of sliced tomatoes; sprinkle with salt, pepper and some bits of butter, and a very *little* white sugar. Then repeat with another layer of crumbs, another of tomato and seasoning until full, having the top layer of slices of tomato, with bits of butter on each. Bake covered until well cooked through; remove the cover and brown quickly.

STUFFED BAKED TOMATOES

From the blossom end of a dozen tomatoes – smooth, ripe and solid – cut a thin slice and with a small spoon scoop out the pulp without breaking the rind surrounding it; chop a small head of cabbage and a good-sized onion fine and mix with them fine breadcrumbs and the pulp; season with pepper, salt and sugar and add a cup of sweet cream; when all is well mixed, fill the tomato shells, replace the slices and place the tomatoes in a buttered baking dish, cut ends up and put in the pan just enough water to keep from burning; drop a small lump of butter on each tomato and bake half an hour or so, till well done; place another bit of butter on each and serve in same dish. Very fine.

Another stuffing which is considered quite fine. Cut a slice from the stem of each and scoop out the soft pulp. Mince one small onion and fry it slightly; add a gill of hot water, the tomato pulp and two ounces of cold veal or chicken chopped fine, simmer slowly and season with salt and pepper. Stir into the pan cracker dust or breadcrumbs enough to absorb the moisture; take off from the fire and let it cool; stuff the tomatoes with this mass, sprinkle dry crumbs over the top; add a small piece of butter to the top of each and bake until slightly browned on top.

BAKED TOMATOES (Plain)

Peel and slice quarter of an inch thick; place in layers in a pudding-dish, seasoning each layer with salt, pepper, butter and a very little white sugar. Cover with a lid or large plate and bake half an hour. Remove the lid and brown for fifteen minutes. Just before taking from the oven pour over the top three or four tablespoonfuls of whipped cream with melted butter.

TO PREPARE TOMATOES (Raw)

Carefully remove the peelings. Only perfectly ripe tomatoes should ever be eaten raw and if ripe the skins easily peel off. Scalding injures the flavor. Slice them and sprinkle generously with salt, more sparingly with black pepper, and to a dish holding one quart, add a light tablespoonful of sugar to give a piquant zest to the whole. Lastly, add a gill of best cider vinegar; although, if you would have a dish yet better suited to please an epicurean palate, you may add a teaspoonful of made mustard and two tablespoonfuls of rich sweet cream.

FRIED AND BROILED TOMATOES.

Cut firm, large, ripe tomatoes into thick slices, rather more than a quarter of an inch thick. Season with salt and pepper, dredge well with flour, or roll in egg and crumbs, and fry them brown on both sides evenly, in hot butter and lard mixed. Or, prepare them the same as for frying, broiling on a well-greased gridiron, seasoning afterward the same as beefsteak. A good accompaniment to steak. Or, having prepared the following sauce, a pint of milk, a tablespoonful of flour and one beaten egg, salt, pepper and a very little mace; cream an ounce of butter, whisk into it the milk and let it simmer until it thickens; pour the sauce on a hot side-dish and arrange the tomatoes in the center.

SCRAMBLED TOMATOES

Remove the skins from a dozen tomatoes; cut them up in a saucepan; add a little butter, pepper and salt; when sufficiently boiled, beat up five or six eggs and just before you serve turn them into the saucepan with the tomatoes, and stir one way for two minutes, allowing them time to be done thoroughly.

CUCUMBER Á LA CRÊME

Peel and cut into slices (lengthwise) some fine cucumbers. Boil them until soft; salt to taste, and serve with delicate cream sauce. For Tomato Salad, see SALADS, also for Raw Cucumbers.

FRIED CUCUMBERS

Pare them and cut lengthwise in very thick slices; wipe them dry with a cloth; sprinkle with salt and pepper, dredge with flour, and fry in lard and butter, a tablespoonful of each mixed. Brown both sides and serve warm.

GREEN CORN, BOILED

This should be cooked on the same day it is gathered; it loses its sweetness in a few hours and must be artificially supplied. Strip off the husks, pick out all the silk and put it in boiling water; if not entirely fresh, add a tablespoonful of sugar to the water, but *no salt*; boil twenty minutes, fast, and serve; or you may cut it from the cob, put in plenty of butter and a little salt, and serve in a covered vegetable dish. The corn is much sweeter when cooked with the husks on, but requires longer time to boil. Will generally boil in twenty minutes.

Green corn left over from dinner makes a nice breakfast dish, prepared as follows: Cut the corn from the cob, and put into a bowl with a cup of milk to every cup of corn, a half cup of flour, one egg, a pinch of salt, and a little butter. Mix well into a thick batter, and fry in small cakes in very hot butter. Serve with plenty of butter and powdered sugar.

CORN PUDDING

This is a Virginia dish. Scrape the substance out of twelve ears of tender, green, uncooked corn (it is better scraped than grated, as you do not get those husky particles which you cannot avoid with a grater); add yolks and whites, beaten separately, of four eggs, a teaspoonful of sugar, the same of flour mixed in a tablespoonful of butter, a small quantity of salt and pepper, and one pint of milk. Bake about half or three-quarters of an hour.

STEWED CORN

Take a dozen ears of green sweet corn, very tender and juicy; cut off the kernels, cutting with a large sharp knife from the top of the cob down; then scrape the cob. Put the corn in a saucepan over the fire with just enough water to make it cook without burning; boil about twenty minutes, then add a teacupful of milk or cream, a tablespoonful of cold butter, and season with pepper and salt. Boil ten minutes longer and dish up hot in a vegetable dish. The corn would be much sweeter if the scraped cobs were boiled first in the water that the corn is cooked in.

Many like corn cooked in this manner, putting half corn and half tomatoes; either way is very good.

FRIED CORN

Cut the corn off the cob, taking care not to bring off any of the husk with it and to have the grains as separate as possible. Fry in a little butter – just enough to keep it from sticking to the pan; stir very often. When nicely browned, add salt and pepper and a little rich cream. Do not set it near the stove after the cream is added, as it will be apt to turn. This makes a nice dinner or breakfast dish.

ROASTED GREEN CORN

Strip off all the husk from green corn and roast it on a gridiron over a bright fire of coals, turning it as one side is done. Or, if a wood fire is used, make a place clean in front of the fire, lay the corn down, turn it when one side is done; serve with salt and butter.

SUCCOTASH

Take a pint of fresh shelled Lima beans, or any large fresh beans, put them in a pot with cold water, rather more than will cover them. Scrape the kernels from twelve ears of young sweet corn; put the cobs in with the beans, boiling from half to three-quarters of an hour. Now take out the cobs and put in the scraped corn; boil again fifteen minutes, then season with salt and pepper to taste, a piece of butter the size of an egg and half a cup of cream. Serve hot.

FRIED EGGPLANT

Take fresh, purple eggplants of a middling size; cut them in slices a quarter of an inch thick, and soak them for half an hour in cold water, with a teaspoonful of salt in it. Have ready some cracker or breadcrumbs and one beaten egg; drain off the water from the slices, lay them on a napkin, dip them in the crumbs and then in the egg, put another coat of crumbs on them and fry them in butter to a light brown. The frying pan must be hot before the slices are put in – they will fry in ten minutes.

You may pare them before you put them into the frying

pan, or you may pull off the skins when you take them up. You must not remove them from the water until you are ready to cook them, as the air will turn them black.

STUFFED EGGPLANT

Cut the egg-plant in two; scrape out all the inside and put it in a saucepan with a little minced ham; cover with water and boil until soft; drain off the water; add two tablespoonfuls of grated crumbs, a tablespoonful of butter, half a minced onion, salt and pepper; stuff each half of the hull with the mixture; add a small lump of butter to each and bake fifteen minutes. Minced veal or chicken in the place of ham, is equally as good and many prefer it.

STRING BEANS

Break off the end that grew to the vine, drawing off at the same time the string upon the edge; repeat the same process from the other end; cut them with a sharp knife into pieces half an inch long, and boil them in *just enough* water to *cover* them. They usually require one hour's boiling; but this depends upon their age and freshness. After they have boiled until tender and the water *boiled nearly out*, add pepper and salt, a tablespoonful of butter and a half a cup of cream; if you have not the cream add more butter.

Many prefer to drain them before adding the seasoning; in that case they lose the real goodness of the vegetable.

LIMA AND KIDNEY BEANS

These beans should be put into boiling water, a little more than enough to cover them, and boiled till tender – from half an hour to two hours; serve with butter and salt upon them.

These beans are in season from the last of July to the last of September. There are several other varieties of beans used as summer vegetables, which are cooked as above.

For Baked Beans, see PORK AND BEANS.

CELERY

This is stewed the same as green corn, by boiling, adding cream, butter, salt and pepper.

STEWED SALSIFY OR OYSTERPLANT

Wash the roots and scrape off their skins, throwing them, as you do so, into cold water, for exposure to the air causes them to immediately turn dark. Then cut crosswise into little thin slices; throw into fresh water, enough to cover; add a little salt and stew in a covered vessel until tender, or about one hour. Pour off a little of the water, add a small lump of butter, a little pepper, and a gill of sweet cream and a teaspoonful of flour stirred to a paste. Boil up and serve hot.

Salsify may be simply boiled and melted butter turned over them.

FRIED SALSIFY

Stew the salsify as usual till very tender; then with the back of a spoon or a potato jammer mash it very fine. Beat up an egg, add a teacupful of milk, a little flour, butter and seasoning of pepper and salt. Make into little cakes, and fry a light brown in boiling lard.

BEETS (Boiled)

Select small-sized, smooth roots. They should be carefully washed, but not cut before boiling, as the juice will escape and the sweetness of the vegetable be impaired, leaving it white and hard.

Put them into boiling water, and boil them until tender, which requires often from one to two hours. Do not probe them, but press them with the finger to ascertain if they are sufficiently done. When satisfied of this, take them up, and put them into a pan of cold water, and slip off the outside. Cut them into thin slices, and while hot season with butter, salt, a little pepper and very sharp vinegar.

BEETS (Baked)

Beets retain their sugary, delicate flavor to perfection if they are baked instead of boiled. Turn them frequently while in the oven, using a knife, as the fork allows the juice to run out. When done remove the skin, and serve with butter, salt and pepper on the slices.

BEETS (Stewed)

Boil them first and then scrape and slice them. Put them into a stew pan with a piece of butter rolled in flour, some boiled onion and parsley chopped fine, and a little vinegar, salt and pepper. Set the pan on the fire, and let the beets stew for a quarter of an hour.

FRIED OKRA

This grows in the shape of pods, and is of a gelatinous character, much used for soup, and is also pickled; it may be boiled as follows: Put the young and tender pods of long white okra in salted boiling water in granite, porcelain or a tin-lined saucepan – as contact with Iron will discolor it; boil fifteen minutes; remove the stems, and serve with butter, pepper, salt and vinegar if preferred.

ASPARAGUS

Scrape the stems of the asparagus lightly, but very clean; throw them into cold water and when they are all scraped and very clean, tie them in bunches of equal size; cut the large ends evenly, that the stems may be all of the same length, and put the asparagus into plenty of boiling water, well salted. While it is boiling, cut several slices of bread half an inch thick, pare off the crust and toast it a delicate brown on both sides. When the stalks of the asparagus are tender (it will usually cook in twenty to forty minutes) lift it out directly, or it will lose both its color and flavor and will also be liable to break; dip the toast quickly into the liquor in which it was boiled and dish the vegetable upon it, the heads all lying one way. Pour over white sauce, or melted butter.

ASPARAGUS WITH EGGS

Boil a bunch of asparagus twenty minutes; cut off the tender tops and lay them in a deep-pie plate, buttering, salting and peppering well. Beat up four eggs, the yolks and whites separately to a stiff froth; add two tablespoonfuls of milk or cream, a tablespoonful of warm butter, pepper and salt to taste. Pour evenly over the asparagus mixture. Bake eight minutes or until the eggs are set. Very good.

GREEN PEAS

Shell the peas and wash in cold water. Put in boiling

water just enough to cover them well and keep them from burning; boil from twenty minutes to half an hour, when the liquor should be nearly boiled out; season with pepper and salt and a good allowance of butter; serve very hot.

This is a very much better way than cooking in a larger quantity of water and draining off the liquor, as that diminishes the sweetness, and much of the fine flavor of the peas is lost.

The salt should never be put in the peas before they are tender, unless very young, as it tends to harden them.

STEWED GREEN PEAS

Into a saucepan of boiling water put two or three pints of young green peas and when nearly done and tender drain in a colander dry; then melt two ounces of butter in two of flour; stir well and boil five minutes longer; should the pods be quite clean and fresh boil them first in the water, remove and put in the peas. The Germans prepare a very palatable dish of sweet young pods alone by simply stirring in a little butter with some savory herbs.

SQUASHES (Cymblings)

The green or summer squash is best when the outside is beginning to turn yellow, as it is then less watery and insipid than when younger.

Wash them, cut them into pieces and take out the seeds. Boil them about three-quarters of an hour, or till quite tender. When done, drain and squeeze them well till you have pressed out all the water; mash them with a little butter, pepper and salt. Then put the squash thus prepared into a stew pan, set it on hot coals and stir it very frequently till it becomes dry. Take care not to let it burn.

Summer squash is very nice steamed, then prepared the same as boiled.

WINTER SQUASH (Boiled)

This is much finer than the summer squash. It is fit to eat in August, and, in a dry warm place, can be kept well all winter. The color is a very bright yellow. Pare it, take out the seeds, cut it in pieces, and stew it slowly till quite soft in a very little water. Afterwards drain, squeeze and press it well; then mash it with a very little butter, pepper and salt. They will boil in from twenty to forty minutes.

WINTER SQUASH (Baked)

Cut open the squash, take out the seeds and without paring cut it up into large pieces; put the pieces on tins or in a dripping-pan, place in a moderately hot oven and bake about an hour. When done, peel and mash like mashed potatoes, or serve the pieces hot on a dish, to be eaten warm with butter like sweet potatoes. It retains its sweetness much better baked this way than when boiled.

VEGETABLE HASH

Chop rather coarsely the remains of vegetables left from a boiled dinner, such as cabbage, parsnips, potatoes, etc.; sprinkle over them a little pepper, place in a saucepan or frying pan over the fire; put in a piece of butter the size of a hickory nut; when it begins to melt, tip the dish so as to oil the bottom and around the sides; then put in the chopped vegetables, pour in a spoonful or two of hot water from the tea-kettle, cover quickly so as to keep in the steam.

When heated thoroughly take off the cover and stir occasionally until well cooked. Serve hot. Persons fond of vegetables will relish this dish very much.

SPINACH

It should be cooked so as to retain its bright green color and not sent to table, as it so often is, of a dull brown or olive color; to retain its fresh appearance, do not cover the vessel while it is cooking.

Spinach requires dose examination and picking, as insects are frequently found among it and it is often gritty. Wash it through three or four waters. Then drain it and put it in boiling water. Fifteen to twenty minutes is generally sufficient time to boil spinach. Be careful to remove the scum. When it is quite tender, take it up, and drain and squeeze it well. Chop it fine, and put it into a saucepan with a piece of butter and a little pepper and salt. Set it on the fire and let it stew five minutes, stirring it all the time, until quite dry. Turn it into a vegetable dish, shape it into a mound, slice some hard-boiled eggs and lay around the top.

GREENS

About a peck of greens are enough for a mess for a family of six, such as dandelions, cowslips, burdock, chicory and other greens. All greens should be carefully examined, the tough ones thrown out, then be thoroughly washed through several waters until they are entirely free from sand. The addition of a handful of salt to each pan of water used in washing the greens will free them from insects and worms, especially if after the last watering they are allowed to stand in salted water for a half hour or longer. When ready to boil the greens, put them into a large pot half full of boiling water, with a handful of salt, and boil them steadily until the stalks are tender; this will be in from five to twenty minutes, according to the maturity of the greens; but remember that long-continued boiling wastes the tender substances of the leaves, and so diminishes both the bulk and the nourishment of the dish; for this reason it is best to cut away any tough stalks before beginning to cook the greens. As soon as they are tender drain them in a colander, chop them a little and return them to the fire long enough to season them with salt, pepper and butter; vinegar may be added if it is liked; the greens should be served as soon as they are hot.

All kinds of greens can be cooked in this manner.

CARROTS (Stewed)

Wash and scrape the carrots and divide them into strips; put them into a stew pan with water enough to cover them; add a spoonful of salt and let them boil slowly until tender; then drain and replace them in the pan, with two tablespoons of butter rolled in flour, shake over a little pepper and salt, then add enough cream or milk to moisten the whole; let it come to a boil and serve hot.

CARROTS (Mashed)

Scrape and wash them; cook them tender in boiling water salted slightly. Drain well and mash them. Work in a good piece of butter and season with pepper and salt. Heap up on a vegetable dish and serve hot.

Carrots are also good simply boiled in salted water and dished up hot with melted butter over them.

TURNIPS

Turnips are boiled plain with or without meat, also mashed like potatoes and stewed like parsnips. They should always be served hot. They require from forty minutes to an hour to cook.

PUMPKINS (Stewed)

See stewed pumpkin for pie. Cook the same, then after stewing season the same as mashed potatoes. Pumpkin is good baked in the same manner as baked winter squash.

ENDIVE (Stewed)

Ingredients – Six heads of endive, salt and water, one pint of broth, thickening of butter and flour, one tablespoonful of lemon juice, a small lump of sugar.

Mode – Wash and free the endive thoroughly from insects, remove the green part of the leaves, and put it into boiling water, slightly salted. Let it remain for ten minutes; then take it out, drain it till there is no water remaining and chop it very fine. Put it into a stew pan with the broth, add a little salt and a lump of sugar, and boil until the endive is perfectly tender. When done, which may be ascertained by squeezing a piece between the thumb and finger, add a thickening of butter and flour and the lemon juice; let the sauce boil up and serve.

Time – Ten minutes to boil, five minutes to simmer in the broth.

MUSHROOMS (Baked)

Prepare them the same as for stewing. Place them in a

baking-pan in a moderate oven. Season with salt, pepper, lemon juice and chopped parsley. Cook in the oven fifteen minutes, baste with butter. Arrange on a dish and pour the gravy over them.

Serve with sauce made by heating a cup of cream, two ounces of butter, a tablespoonful of chopped parsley, a little cayenne pepper, salt, a tablespoonful of white sauce and two tablespoonfuls of lemon juice. Put in a saucepan and set on the fire. Stir until thick, but do not let boil. Mushrooms are very nice placed on slices of well-buttered toast when set into the oven to bake. They cook in about fifteen minutes.

MUSHROOMS (Stewed)

Time, twenty-one minutes. Button mushrooms, salt to taste, a little butter rolled in flour, two tablespoonfuls of cream or the yolk of one egg. Choose buttons of uniform size. Wipe them clean and white with a wet flannel; put them in a stew pan with a little water and let them stew very gently for a quarter of an hour. Add salt to taste, work in a little flour and butter, to make the liquor about as thick as cream, and let it boil for five minutes. When you are ready to dish it up, stir in two tablespoonfuls of cream or the yolk of an egg; stir it over the fire for a minute, but do not let it boil, and serve. Stewed button mushrooms are very nice, either in fish stews or ragouts, or served apart to eat with fish. Another way of doing them is to stew them in milk and water (after they are rubbed white), add to them a little veal gravy, mace and salt and thicken the gravy with cream or the yolks of eggs.

Mushrooms can be cooked in the same manner as the recipes for oysters, either stewed, fried, broiled, or as a soup.

They are also used to flavor sauces, ketchups, meat gravies, game and soups.

MUSHROOMS (Canned)

Canned mushrooms may be served with good effect with game and even with beefsteak if prepared in this way: Open the can and pour off every drop of the liquid found there; let the mushrooms drain, then put them in a saucepan with a little cream and butter, pepper and salt; let them simmer gently for from five to ten minutes, and when the meat is on the platter pour the mushrooms over it. If served with steak, that should be very tender and be broiled, never in any case fried.

MUSHROOMS FOR WINTER USE

Wash and wipe free from grit the small fresh button mushrooms. Put into a frying pan a quarter of a pound of the very best butter. Add to it two whole cloves, a half teaspoonful of salt and a tablespoonful of lemon juice. When hot add a quart of the small mushrooms, toss them about in the butter for a moment only, then put them in jars; fill the top of each jar with an inch or two of the butter and let it cool. Keep the jars in a cool place, and when the butter is quite firm add a top layer of salt. Cover to keep out dust.

The best mushrooms grow on uplands or in high open fields, where the air is pure.

TRUFFLES

The truffle belongs to the family of the mushrooms; they are used principally in this country as a condiment for boned turkey and chicken, scrambled eggs, fillets of beef, game and fish. When mixed in due proportion, they add a peculiar zest and flavor to sauces that cannot be found in any other plant in the vegetable kingdom.

ITALIAN STYLE OF DRESSING TRUFFLES

Ten truffles, a quarter of a pint of salad oil, pepper and salt to taste, one tablespoonful of minced parsley, a very little finely minced garlic, two blades of pounded mace, one tablespoonful of lemon juice.

After cleansing and brushing the truffles, cut them into thin slices and put them in a baking dish, on a seasoning of oil or butter, pepper, salt, parsley, garlic and mace in the above proportion. Bake them for nearly an hour, and just before serving add the lemon juice and send them to the table very hot.

TRUFFLES AU NATUREL

Select some fine truffles; cleanse them by washing them in several waters with a brush until not a particle of sand or grit remains on them; wrap each truffle in buttered paper and bake in a hot oven for quite an hour; take off the paper; wipe the truffles and serve them in a hot napkin.

Eat Like a President: Book I

SANDWICHES

HAM SANDWICHES

Make a dressing of half a cup of butter, one tablespoonful of mixed mustard, one of salad oil, a little red or white pepper, a pinch of salt and the yolk of an egg; rub the butter to a cream, add the other ingredients and mix thoroughly; then stir in as much chopped ham as will make it consistent and spread between thin slices of bread. Omit salad oil and substitute melted butter if preferred.

HAM SANDWICHES (Plain)

Trim the crusts from thin slices of bread; butter them and lay between every two some thin slices of cold boiled ham. Spread the meat with a little mustard if liked.

CHICKEN SANDWICHES

Mince up fine any cold boiled or roasted chicken; put it into a saucepan with gravy, water or cream enough to soften it; add a good piece of butter, a pinch of pepper; work it very smooth while it is heating until it looks almost like a paste. Then spread it on a plate to cool. Spread it between slices of buttered bread.

WATER CRESS SANDWICHES

Wash well some water cress and then dry them in a cloth, pressing out every atom of moisture as far as possible; then mix with the cress hard-boiled eggs chopped fine, and seasoned with salt and pepper. Have a stale loaf and some fresh butter, and with a sharp knife cut as many thin slices as will be required for two dozen sandwiches; then cut the cress into small pieces, removing the stems; place it between each slice of bread and butter, with a slight sprinkling of lemon juice; press down the slices hard, and cut them sharply on a board into small squares, leaving no crust.

Nantasket Beach.

EGG SANDWICHES.

Hard boil some very fresh eggs and when cold cut them into moderately thin slices and lay them between some bread and butter cut as thin as possible; season them with pepper, salt and nutmeg. For picnic parties, or when one is traveling, these sandwiches are far preferable to hard-boiled eggs *au naturel.*

MUSHROOM SANDWICHES.

Mince beef tongue and boiled mushrooms together, add French mustard and spread between buttered bread.

SARDINE SANDWICHES

Take two boxes of sardines and throw the contents into hot water, having first drained away all the oil. A few minutes will free the sardines from grease. Pour away the water and dry the fish in a cloth; then scrape away the skins and pound the sardines in a mortar till reduced to paste; add pepper, salt and some tiny pieces of lettuce, and spread on the sandwiches, which have been previously cut as above. The lettuce adds very much to the flavor of the sardines.

Or chop the sardines up fine and squeeze a few drops of lemon juice into them, and spread between buttered bread or cold biscuits.

CHEESE SANDWICHES.

These are extremely nice and are very easily made. Take one hard-boiled egg, a quarter of a pound of common cheese grated, half a teaspoonful of salt, half a teaspoonful of pepper, half a teaspoonful of mustard, one tablespoonful of melted butter, and one tablespoonful of vinegar or cold water. Take the yolk of the egg and put it into a small bowl and crumble it down, put into it the butter and mix it smooth with a spoon, then add the salt, pepper, mustard and the cheese, mixing each well. Then put in the tablespoonful of vinegar, which will make it the proper thickness. If vinegar is not relished, then use cold water instead. Spread this between two biscuits or pieces of oat-cake, and you could not require a better sandwich.

Some people will prefer the sandwiches less highly seasoned

Eat Like a President: Book I

BUTTER AND CHEESE

TO MAKE BUTTER

Thoroughly scald the churn, then cool well with ice or spring water. Now pour in the thick cream; churn fast at first, then, as the butter forms, more slowly; always with perfect regularity; in warm weather, pour a little cold water into the churn, should the butter form slowly; in the winter, if the cream is too cold, add a little warm water to bring it to the proper temperature. When the butter has "come", rinse the sides of the churn down with cold water and take the butter up with a perforated dasher or a wooden ladle, turning it dexterously just below the surface of the buttermilk to catch every stray bit; have ready some very cold water in a deep wooden tray; and into this plunge the dasher when you draw it from the churn; the butter will float off, leaving the dasher free. When you have collected all the butter, gather behind a wooden butter ladle and drain off the water, squeezing and pressing the butter with the ladle; then pour on more cold water and work the butter with the ladle to get the milk out, drain off the water, sprinkle salt over the butter – a tablespoonful to a pound; work it in a little and set in a cool place for an hour to harden, then work and knead it until not another drop of water exudes, and the butter is perfectly smooth, and close in texture and polish; then with the ladle make up into rolls, little balls, stamped pats, etc.

The churn, dasher, tray and ladle should be well scalded before using, so that the butter will not stick to them, and then cooled with very cold water.

When you skim cream into your cream jar, stir it well into what is already there, so that it may all sour alike; and no *fresh cream should be put with it* within twelve hours before churning, or the butter will not come quickly; and perhaps, not at all.

Butter is indispensable in almost all culinary preparations. Good fresh butter, used in moderation, is easily digested; it is softening, nutritious and fattening, and is far more easily digested than any other of the oleaginous substances sometimes used in its place.

TO MAKE BUTTER QUICKLY

Immediately after the cow is milked, strain the milk into clean pans, and set it over a moderate fire until it is scalding hot; do not let it boil; then set it aside; when it is cold, skim off the cream; the milk will still be fit for any ordinary use; when you have enough cream put it into a clean earthen basin; beat it with a wooden spoon until the butter is made, which will not be long; then take it from the milk and work it with a little cold water, until it is free from milk; then drain off the water, put a small tablespoonful of fine salt to each pound of butter and work it in. A small teaspoonful of fine white sugar, worked in with the salt, will be found an improvement – sugar is a great preservative. Make the butter in a roll; cover it with a bit of muslin and keep it in a cool place. A reliable recipe.

A BRINE TO PRESERVE BUTTER

First work your butter into small rolls, wrapping each one carefully in a clean muslin cloth, tying them up with a string. Make a brine, say three gallons, having it strong enough of salt to bear up an egg; add half a teacupful of pure, white sugar, and one tablespoonful of saltpeter; boil the brine, and when cold strain it carefully. Pour it over the rolls so as to more than cover them, as this excludes the air. Place a weight over all to keep the rolls under the surface.

PUTTING UP BUTTER TO KEEP

Take of the best pure common salt two quarts, one ounce of white sugar and one of saltpeter; pulverize them together completely. Work the butter well, then thoroughly work in an ounce of this mixture to every pound of butter. The butter is to be made into half-pound rolls, and put into the following brine – to three gallons of brine strong enough to bear an egg, add a quarter of a pound of white sugar.

Orange Co., N. Y. Style

CURDS AND CREAM

One gallon of milk will make a moderate dish. Put one spoonful of prepared rennet to each quart of milk, and when you find that it has become curd, tie it loosely in a thin cloth and hang it to drain; do not wring or press the cloth; when drained, put the curd into a mug and set in cool water, which must be frequently changed (a refrigerator saves this trouble).

When you dish it, if there is whey in the mug, lie it gently out without pressing the curd; lay it on a deep dish, and pour fresh cream over it; have powdered loaf-sugar to eat with it; also hand the nutmeg grater.

Prepared rennet can be had at almost any druggist's, and at a reasonable price.

NEW JERSEY CREAM CHEESE

First scald the quantity of milk desired; let it cool a little, then add the rennet; the directions for quantity are given on the packages of "Prepared Rennet." When the curd is formed, take it out on a ladle without breaking it; lay it on a thin cloth held by two persons; dash a ladleful of water over each ladleful of curd, to separate the curd; hang it up to drain the water off, and then put it under a light press for one hour; cut the curd with a thread into small pieces; lay a cloth between each two, and press for an hour; take them out, rub them with fine salt, let them lie on a board for an hour, and wash them in cold water; let them lie to drain, and in a day or two the skin will look dry; put some sweet grass under and over them, and they will soon ripen.

COTTAGE CHEESE

Put a pan of sour or clabbered milk on the stove or range where it is not too hot; let it scald until the whey rises to the top (be careful that it does not boil, or the curd will become hard and tough). Place a clean doth or towel over a sieve and pour this whey and curd into it, living it covered to drain two or three hours; then put it into a dish and chop it fine with a spoon, adding a teaspoonful of salt, a tablespoonful of butter and enough sweet cream to make the cheese the consistency of putty. With your hands make it into little balls flattened. Keep it in a cool place.

Many like it made rather thin with cream, serving it in a deep dish. You may make this cheese of sweet milk by forming the curd with prepared rennet.

SLIP

Slip is bonny-clabber without its acidity, and so delicate is its flavor that many persons like it just as well as ice cream. It is prepared thus: Make a quart of milk moderately warm; then stir into it one large spoonful of the preparation called rennet; set it by, and when cool again it will be as stiff as jelly.

It should be made only a few hours before it is to be used, or it will be tough and watery; in summer set the dish on ice after it has jellied. It must be served with powdered sugar, nutmeg and cream.

CHEESE FONDU

Melt an ounce of butter and whisk into it a pint of boiled milk. Dissolve two tablespoonfuls of flour in a gill of cold milk, add it to the boiled milk and let it cool. Beat the yolks of four eggs with a heaping teaspoonful of salt, half a teaspoonful of pepper and five ounces of grated cheese. Whip the whites of the eggs and add them, pour the mixture into a deep tin lined with buttered paper, and allow for the rising, say four inches. Bake twenty minutes and serve the moment it leaves the oven.

CHEESE SOUFFLÉ

Melt an ounce of butter in a saucepan; mix smoothly with it one ounce of flour, a pinch of salt and cayenne and a quarter of a pint of milk; simmer the mixture gently over the fire, stirring it all the time, till it is as thick as melted butter, stir into it about three ounces of finely-grated parmesan, or any good cheese. Turn it into a basin and mix with it the yolks of two well-beaten eggs. Whisk three whites to a solid froth, and just before the soufflé is baked put them into it, and pour the mixture into a small round tin. It should be only half filled, as the fondue will rise very high. Pin a napkin around the dish in which it is baked, and serve the moment it is baked. It would be well to have a metal cover strongly heated. Time twenty minutes. Sufficient for six persons.

SCALLOPED CHEESE

Any person who is fond of cheese could not fail to favor this recipe.

Take three slices of bread well-buttered, first cutting off the brown outside crust. Grate fine a quarter of a pound of any kind of good cheese; lay the bread in layers in a buttered baking dish, sprinkle over it the grated cheese, some salt and pepper to taste. Mix four well-beaten eggs with three cups of milk; pour it over the bread and cheese. Bake it in a hot oven as you would cook a bread pudding. This makes an ample dish for four people.

PASTRY RAMAKINS

Take the remains or odd pieces of any light puff paste left from pies or tarts; gather up the pieces of paste, roll it out evenly, and sprinkle it with grated cheese of a nice flavor. Fold the paste in three, roll it out again, and sprinkle more cheese over; fold the paste, roll it out, and with a paste-cutter shape it in any way that may be desired. Bake the ramekins in a brisk oven from ten to fifteen minutes; dish them on a hot napkin and serve quickly. The appearance of this dish may be very much improved by brushing the ramekins over with yolk of egg before they are placed in the oven. Where expense is not objected to, Parmesan is the best kind of cheese to use for making this dish. Very nice with a cup of coffee for a lunch.

CAYENNE CHEESE STRAWS

A quarter of a pound of flour, two ounces butter, two ounces grated Parmesan cheese, a pinch of salt and a few grains of cayenne pepper. Mix into a paste with the yolk of an egg. Roll out to the thickness of a silver quarter, about four or five inches long; cut into strips about a third of an inch wide, twist them as you would a paper spill and lay them on a baking-sheet slightly floured. Bake in a moderate oven until crisp, but they must not be the least brown.

If put away in a tin these straws will keep a long time. Serve cold, piled tastefully on a glass dish. You can make the straws of remnants of puff pastry, rolling in the grated cheese.

CHEESE CREAM TOAST

Stale bread may be served as follows: Toast the slices

and cover them slightly with grated cheese; make a cream for ten slices out of a pint of milk and two tablespoonfuls of plain flour. The milk should be boiling, and the flour mixed in a little cold water before stirring in.

When the cream is nicely cooked, season with salt and butter; set the toast and cheese in the oven for three or four minutes and then pour the cream over them.

WELSH RAREBIT

Grate three ounces of dry cheese and mix it with the yolks of two eggs, put four ounces of grated bread and three of butter; beat the whole together in a mortar with a half teaspoonful of made mustard, a little salt and some pepper; toast some slices of bread, cut off the outside crust, cut it in shapes and spread the paste thick upon them, and put them in the oven, let them become hot and slightly browned, serve hot as possible.

Eat Like a President: Book I

EGGS AND OMELETS

There are so many ways of cooking and dressing eggs, that it seems unnecessary for the ordinary family to use those that are not the most practical.

To ascertain the freshness of an egg, hold it between your thumb and forefinger in a horizontal position, with a strong light in front of you. The fresh egg will have a clear appearance, both upper and lower sides being the same. The stale egg will have a clear appearance at the lower side, while the upper side will exhibit a dark or cloudy appearance.

Another test is to put them in a pan of cold water; those that are the first to sink are the freshest; the stale will rise and float on top; or, if the large end turns up in the water, they are not fresh.

The best time for preserving eggs is from July to September.

TO PRESERVE EGGS

There are several recipes for preserving eggs and we give first one which we know to be effectual, keeping them fresh from August until Spring. Take a piece of quicklime as large as a good-sized lemon and two cupfuls of salt; put it into a large vessel and slack it with a gallon of boiling water. It will boil and bubble until thick as cream; when it is cold, pour off the top, which will be perfectly clear. Drain off this liquor, and pour it over your eggs; see that the liquor more than covers them. A stone jar is the most convenient – one that holds about six quarts.

Another manner of preserving eggs is to pack them in a jar with layers of salt between, the large end of the egg downward, with a thick layer of salt at the top; cover tightly and set in a cool place.

Some put them in a wire basket or a piece of mosquito net and dip them in boiling water half a minute; then pack in sawdust. Still another manner is to dissolve a cheap article of gum arabic, about as thin as mucilage, and brush over each egg with it; then pack in powdered charcoal; set in a cool, dark place.

Eggs can be kept for some time by smearing the shells with butter or lard; then packed in plenty of bran or sawdust, the eggs not allowed to touch one another; or coat the eggs with melted paraffin.

BOILED EGGS.

Eggs for boiling cannot be too fresh, or boiled too soon after they are laid; but rather a longer time should be allowed for boiling a new-laid egg than for one that is three or four days old. Have ready a saucepan of boiling water;

put the eggs into it gently with a spoon, letting the spoon touch the bottom of the saucepan before it is withdrawn, that the egg may not fall and consequently crack. For those who like eggs lightly boiled, three minutes will be found sufficient; three and three-quarters to four minutes will be ample time to set the white nicely; and if liked hard, six or seven minutes will not be found too long. Should the eggs be unusually large, as those of black Spanish fowls sometimes are, allow an extra half-minute for them. Eggs for salad should be boiled for ten or fifteen minutes, and should be placed in a basin of cold water for a few minutes to shrink the meat from the shell; they should then be rolled on the table with the hand and the shell will peel off easily.

SOFT BOILED EGGS

When properly cooked eggs are done evenly through, like any other food. This result may be obtained by putting the eggs into a dish with a cover, or a tin pail, and then pouring upon them *boiling* water – two quarts or more to a dozen of eggs – and cover and set them away where they will keep *hot* and *not* boil for ten to twelve minutes. The heat of the water cooks the eggs slowly, evenly and sufficiently, leaving the center or yolk harder than the white, and the egg tastes as much richer and nicer as a fresh egg is nicer than a stale egg.

SCALLOPED EGGS.

Hard-boil twelve eggs; slice them thin in rings; in the bottom of a large well-buttered baking dish place a layer of grated breadcrumbs, then one of eggs; cover with bits of butter and sprinkle with pepper and salt. Continue thus to blend these ingredients until the dish is full; be sure, though, that the crumbs cover the eggs upon top. Over the whole pour a large teacupful of sweet cream or milk and brown nicely in a moderately heated oven.

SHIRRED EGGS

Set into the oven until quite hot a common white dish large enough to hold the number of eggs to be cooked, allowing plenty of room for each. Melt in it a small piece of butter, and breaking the eggs carefully in a saucer, one at a time, slip them into the hot dish; sprinkle over them a small quantity of pepper and salt and allow them to cook four or five minutes. Adding a tablespoonful of cream for every two eggs, when the eggs are first slipped in, is a great improvement.

This is far more delicate than fried eggs.

Or prepare the eggs the same and set them in a steamer over boiling water.

They are usually served in hotels baked in individual dishes, about two in a dish, and in the same dish they were baked in.

SCRAMBLED EGGS

Put a tablespoonful of butter into a hot frying pan; tip around so that it will touch all sides of the pan. Having ready half a dozen eggs broken in a dish, salted and peppered, turn them (without beating) into the hot butter; stir them one way briskly for five or six minutes or until they are mixed. Be careful that they do not get too hard. Turn over toast or dish up without.

POACHED OR DROPPED EGGS

Have one quart of *boiling* water and one tablespoonful of salt in a frying pan. Break the eggs, one by one, into a saucer, and slide carefully into the salted water. Dash with a spoon a little water over the egg, to keep the top white.

The beauty of a poached egg is for the yolk to be seen blushing through the white, which should only be just sufficiently hardened to form a transparent veil for the egg.

Cook until the white is firm, and lift out with a griddle cake turner and place on toasted bread. Serve immediately.

A tablespoonful of vinegar put into the water keeps the eggs from spreading.

Open gem rings are nice placed in the water and an egg dropped into each ring.

FRIED EGGS (Traditional)

Break the eggs, one at a time, into a saucer, and then slide them carefully off into a frying pan of lard and butter mixed, dipping over the eggs the hot grease in spoonfuls, or turn them over, frying both sides without breaking them. They require about three minutes' cooking.

FRIED EGGS (Balls)

Eggs can be fried round like balls, by dropping one at a time into a quantity of hot lard, the same as for fried cakes, first stirring the hot lard with a stick until it runs round like a whirlpool; this will make the eggs look like balls. Take out with a skimmer. Eggs can be poached the same in boiling water.

EGGS AUX FINES HERBES

Roll an ounce of butter in a good teaspoonful of flour; season with pepper, salt and nutmeg; put it into a cupful of fresh milk, together with two teaspoonfuls of chopped parsley; stir and simmer it for fifteen minutes, add a teacupful of thick cream. Hard-boil five eggs and halve them; arrange them in a dish with the ends upwards, pour the sauce over them, and decorate with little heaps of fried breadcrumbs round the margin of the dish.

POACHED EGGS Á LA CRÊME

Put a quart of hot water, a tablespoonful of vinegar and a teaspoonful of salt into a frying pan, and break each egg separately into a saucer; slip the egg carefully into the hot water, simmer three or four minutes until the white is set, then with a skimmer lift them out into a hot dish. Empty the pan of its contents, put in half a cup of cream, or rich milk; if milk, a large spoonful of butter; pepper and salt to taste, thicken with a very little cornstarch; let it boil up once, and turn it over the dish of poached eggs. It can be served on toast or without.

It is a better plan to warm the cream in butter in a separate dish that the eggs may not have to stand.

EGGS IN CASES

Make little paper cases of buttered writing paper; put a small piece of butter in each, and a little chopped parsley or onion, pepper and salt. Place the cases upon a gridiron over a moderate fire of bright coals, and when the butter melts, break a fresh egg into each case. Strew in upon them a few seasoned breadcrumbs, and when nearly done, glaze the tops with a hot shovel. Serve in the paper cases.

MINCED EGGS

Chop up four or five hard-boiled eggs; do not mince them too fine. Put over the fire in a suitable dish a cupful of milk, a tablespoonful of butter, salt and pepper, and some savory chopped small. When this comes to a boil stir into it a tablespoonful of flour, dissolved in a little cold milk. When it cooks thick like cream put in the minced eggs. Stir it gently around and around for a few moments and serve, garnished with sippits of toast. Any particular flavor may be given to this dish, such as that of mushrooms, truffles, ketchup, essence of shrimps, etc., or some shred anchovy may be added to the mince.

SCRAMBLED EGGS AND BACON

Take a nice rasher of mild bacon; cut it into squares no larger than dice; fry it quickly until nicely browned; but on no account burn it. Break half a dozen eggs into a basin, strain and season them with pepper, add them to the bacon, stir the whole about and, when sufficiently firm, turn it out into a dish. Decorate with hot pickles.

SCRAMBLED EGGS (Savory or Sweet)

Much the same method is followed in mixed eggs generally, whatever may be added to them; really it is nothing more than an omelet which is stirred about in the pan while it is being dressed, instead of being allowed to set as a pancake. Chopped tongue, oysters, shrimps, sardines, dried salmon, anchovies, herbs, may be used.

COLD EGGS FOR A PICNIC

This novel way of preparing cold egg for the lunch-basket fully repays one for the extra time required. Boil hard several eggs, halve them lengthwise; remove the yolks and chop them fine with cold chicken, lamb, veal or any tender, roasted meat; or with bread soaked in milk and any salad, as parsley, onion, celery, the bread being half of the whole; or with grated cheese, a little olive oil, drawn butter, flavored. Fill the cavity in the egg with either of these mixtures, or any similar preparation. Press the halves together, roll twice in beaten egg and breadcrumbs, and dip into boiling lard. When the color rises delicately, drain them and they are ready for use.

OMELETS

In making an omelet, care should be taken that the omelet pan is hot and dry. To insure this, put a small quantity of lard or suet into a clean frying pan, let it simmer a few minutes, then remove it; wipe the pan dry with a towel, and then put in a tablespoonful of butter. The smoothness of the pan is most essential, as the least particle of roughness will cause the omelet to stick. As a general rule, a small omelet can be made more successfully than a large one, it being much better to make two small ones of four eggs each, than to try double the number of eggs in one omelet and fail. Allow one egg to a person in making an omelet and one tablespoonful of milk; this makes an omelet more puffy and tender than one made without milk. Many prefer them without milk.

Omelets are called by the name of what is added to give them flavor, as minced ham, salmon, onions, oysters, etc., beaten up in the eggs in due quantity, which gives as many different kind of omelets.

They are also served over many kinds of thick sauces or purees, such as tomato, spinach, endive, lettuce, celery, etc.

If vegetables are to be added, they should be already cooked, seasoned and hot; place in the center of the omelet, just before turning; so with mushroom, shrimps, or any cooked ingredients. All omelets should be served the moment they are done, as they harden by standing, and care taken that they do not *cook too much*.

Sweet omelets are generally used for breakfast or plain desserts.

PLAIN OMELET

Put a smooth, clean, iron frying pan on the fire to heat; meanwhile, beat four eggs very light, the whites to a stiff froth and the yolks to a thick batter. Add to the yolks four tablespoonfuls of milk, pepper and salt; and, lastly, stir in the whites lightly. Put a piece of butter nearly half the size of an egg into the heated pan; turn it so that it will moisten the entire bottom, taking care that it does not scorch. Just as it begins to boil, pour in the eggs. Hold the frying pan handle in your left hand, and, as the eggs whiten, carefully, with a spoon, draw up lightly from the bottom, letting the raw part run out on the pan, till all be equally cooked; shake with your left hand, till the omelet be free from the pan, then turn with a spoon one half of the omelet over the other; let it remain a moment, but continue shaking, lest it adhere; toss to a warm platter held in the right hand, or lift with a flat, broad shovel; the omelet will be firm around the edge, but creamy and light inside.

MEAT OR FISH OMELETS

Take cold meat, fish, game or poultry of any kind; remove all skin, sinew, etc., and either cut it small or pound it to a paste in a mortar, together with a proper proportion of spices and salt; then either toss it in a buttered frying pan over a clear fire till it begins to brown and pour beaten eggs upon it, or beat it up with the eggs, or spread it upon them after they have begun to set in the pan.

In any case serve hot, with or without a sauce, but garnish with crisp herbs in branches, pickles, or sliced lemon. The right proportion is one tablespoonful of meat to four eggs. A little milk, gravy, water, or white wine, may be advantageously added to the eggs while they are being beaten.

VEGETABLE OMELET

Make a purée by mashing up ready-dressed vegetables, together with a little milk, cream or gravy and some seasoning. The most suitable vegetables are cucumbers, artichokes, onions, sorrel, green peas, tomatoes, lentils, mushrooms, asparagus tops, potatoes, truffles or turnips.

Prepare some eggs by beating them very light. Pour them into a nice hot frying pan, containing a spoonful of butter; spread the purée upon the upper side; and when perfectly hot, turn or fold the omelet together and serve. Or cold vegetables may be merely chopped small, then tossed in a little butter, and some beaten and seasoned eggs poured over.

OMELET OF HERBS

Parsley, thyme and sweet marjoram mixed gives the

famous *omelette aux fines herbes* so popular at every wayside inn in the most remote corner of sunny France. An omelet "jardinière" is two tablespoonfuls of mixed parsley, onion, chives, shallots and a few leaves each of sorrel and chervil, minced fine and stirred into the beaten eggs before cooking. It will take a little more butter to fry it than a plain one.

CHEESE OMELET

Beat up three eggs, and add to them a tablespoonful of milk and a tablespoonful of grated cheese; add a little more cheese before folding; turn it out on a hot dish; grate a little cheese over it before serving.

ASPARAGUS OMELET

Boil with a little salt, and until about half cooked, eight or ten stalks of asparagus, and cut the eatable part into rather small pieces; beat the egg and mix the asparagus with them. Make the omelet as above directed. Omelet with parsley is made by adding a little chopped parsley.

TOMATO OMELET No. 1

Peel a couple of tomatoes, which split into four pieces; remove the seeds and cut them into small dice; then fry them with a little butter until nearly done, adding salt and pepper. Beat the eggs and mix the tomatoes with them, and make the omelet as usual. Or stew a few tomatoes in the usual way and spread over before folding.

TOMATO OMELET No. 2

Cut in slices and place in a stew pan six peeled

tomatoes; add a tablespoonful of cold water, a little pepper and salt. When they begin to simmer, break in six eggs, stir well, stirring one way, until the eggs are cooked, but not too hard. Serve warm.

HAM OMELET

Cut raw ham into dice, fry with butter and when cooked enough, turn the beaten egg over it and cook as a plain omelet.

If boiled ham is used, mince it and mix with the egg after they are beaten. Bacon may be used instead of raw ham.

CHICKEN OMELET

Mince rather fine one cupful of cooked chicken, warm in a teacupful of cream or rich milk a tablespoonful of butter, salt and pepper; thicken with a large tablespoonful of flour. Make a plain omelet, then add this mixture just before turning it over. This is much better than the dry minced chicken. Tongue is equally good.

MUSHROOM OMELET

Clean a cupful of large button mushrooms, canned ones may be used; cut them into bits. Put into a stew pan an ounce of butter and let it melt; add the mushrooms, a teaspoonful of salt, half a teaspoonful of pepper and half a cupful of cream or milk. Stir in a teaspoonful of flour, dissolved in a little milk or water to thicken, if needed. Boil ten minutes, and set aside until the omelet is ready.

Make a plain omelet the usual way, and just before doubling it, turn the mushrooms over the center and serve hot.

RICE OMELET

Take a cup of cold boiled rice, turn over it a cupful of warm milk, add a tablespoonful of butter melted, a level teaspoonful of salt, a dash of pepper; mix well, then add three well-beaten eggs. Put a tablespoonful of butter in a hot frying pan, and when it begins to boil pour in the omelet and set the pan in a hot oven. As soon as it is cooked through, fold it double, turn it out on a hot dish, and serve at once. Very good.

OYSTER OMELET

Parboil a dozen oysters in their own liquor, skim them out and let them cool; add them to the beaten eggs, either whole or minced. Cook the same as a plain omelet.

Thicken the liquid with butter rolled in flour; season with salt, cayenne pepper and a teaspoonful of chopped parsley. Chop up the oysters and add to the sauce. Put a few spoonfuls in the center of the omelet before folding; when dished, pour the remainder of the sauce around it.

ONION OMELET

Make a plain omelet, and when ready to turn spread over it a teaspoonful each of chopped onion and minced parsley; then fold, or, if preferred, mix the minces into the eggs before cooking.

JELLY OMELET

Make a plain omelet, and just before folding together, spread with some kind of jelly. Turn out on a warm platter.

Dust it with powdered sugar.

BREAD OMELET No. 1

Break four eggs into a basin and carefully remove the treadles; have ready a tablespoonful of grated and sifted bread; soak it in either milk, water, cream, white wine, gravy, lemon juice, brandy or rum, according as the omelet is intended to be sweet or savory.

Well beat the eggs together with a little nutmeg, pepper and salt; add the bread, and, beating constantly (or the omelet will be crumbly), get ready a frying pan, buttered and made thoroughly hot; put in the omelet; do it on one side only; turn it upon a dish, and fold it double to prevent the steam from condensing.

Stale sponge cake, grated biscuit, or pound cake, may replace the bread for a sweet omelet, when pounded loaf sugar should be sifted over it, and the dish decorated with lumps of currant jelly.

This makes a nice dessert.

BREAD OMELET No. 2

Let one teacupful of milk come to a boil, pour it over one teacupful of breadcrumbs and let it stand a few minutes. Break six eggs into a bowl, stir (not beat) till well mixed; then add the milk and bread, season with pepper and salt, mix all well together and turn into a hot frying pan, containing a large spoonful of butter boiling hot.

Fry the omelet slowly, and when brown on the bottom cut in squares and turn again, fry to a delicate brown and serve hot.

Cracker omelet may be made by substituting three or

four rolled crackers in place of bread.

BAKED OMELET

Beat the whites and yolks of four or six eggs separately; add to the yolks a small cup of milk, a tablespoonful of flour or cornstarch, a teaspoonful of baking powder, one-half teaspoonful of salt, and, lastly, the stiff-beaten whites. Bake in a well-buttered pie tin or plate about half an hour in a steady oven. It should be served the moment it is taken from the oven, as it is liable to fall.

OMELET SOUFFLÉ

Break six eggs into separate cups; beat four of the yolks, mix with them one teaspoonful of flour, three tablespoonfuls of powdered sugar, very little salt. Flavor with extract lemon or any other of the flavors that may be preferred. Whisk the whites of six eggs to a firm froth; mix them lightly with the yolks; pour the mixture into a greased pan or dish; bake in a quick oven. When well-risen and lightly browned on the top, it is done; roll out in warm dish, sift pulverized sugar over, and send to table.

RUM OMELET

Put a small quantity of lard into the pan; let it simmer a few minutes and remove it; wipe the pan dry with a towel, and put in a little fresh lard in which the omelet may be fried. Care should be taken that the lard does not burn, which would spoil the color of the omelet. Break three eggs separately; put them into a bowl and whisk them thoroughly with a fork. The longer they are beaten, the lighter will the omelet be. Beat up a teaspoonful of milk with the eggs and continue to beat until the last moment before pouring into the pan, which should be over a hot fire. As soon as the omelet sets, remove the pan from the hottest part of the fire. Slip a knife under it to prevent sticking to the pan. When the center is almost firm, slant the pan, work the omelet in shape to fold easily find neatly, and when slightly browned, hold a platter against the edge of the pan and deftly turn it out on to the hot dish. Dust a liberal quantity of powdered sugar over it, and singe the sugar into neat stripes with a hot iron rod, heated in the coals; pour a glass of warm Jamaica rum around it, and when it is placed on the table set fire to the rum. With a tablespoon dash the burning rum over the omelet, put out the fire and serve. Salt *mixed* with the eggs prevents them from rising, and when it is so used the omelet will look flabby, yet without salt it will taste insipid.

Add a little salt to it just before folding it and turning out on the dish.

"The Cook."

THE VARIETIES OF
SEASONABLE FOOD

JANUARY.

MEATS – Beef, mutton, pork, lamb.

POULTRY AND GAME – Rabbits, hares, partridges, woodcocks, grouse or prairie chickens, snipes, antelope, quails, swans, geese, chickens, capons, tame pigeons, wild ducks, the canvas-back duck being the most popular and highly prized; turkeys.

FISH – Haddock, fresh codfish, halibut, flounders, bass, fresh salmon, turbot. Frozen fresh mackerel is found in our large cities during this month; also frozen salmon, red-snapper, shad, frozen bluefish, pickerel, smelts, green turtle, diamond-back terrapin, prawns, oysters, scallops, hard crabs, white bait, finnan haddie, smoked halibut, smoked salmon.

VEGETABLES – Cabbage, carrots, turnips, parsnips, beets, pumpkins, chives, celery, winter squash, onions, white and sweet potatoes, Jerusalem artichokes, chicory, Brussels-sprouts, kale-sprouts, oyster plant, leeks, cress, cauliflower. Garden herbs, both dry and green, being chiefly used in stuffing and soups, and for flavoring and garnishing certain dishes, are always in season, such as sage, thyme, sweet basil, borage, dill, mint, parsley, lavender, summer savory, etc., may be procured green in the summer and dried in the winter.

FEBRUARY.

MEATS – Beef, mutton, pork, lamb, antelope.

POULTRY AND GAME – Partridges, hares, rabbits, snipes, capons, pheasants, fowls, pullets, geese, ducks, turkeys, wild ducks, swan, and pigeons.

FISH – Halibut, haddock, fresh codfish, striped bass, eels, fresh salmon, live lobsters, pompano, sheep's-head, red-snapper, white perch, a panfish, smelts – green and frozen; shad, herring, salmon-trout, whitefish, pickerel, green turtle, flounders, scallops, prawns, oysters, soft-shell crabs – which are in excellent condition this month; hard crabs, white bait, boneless dried codfish, finnan haddie, smoked halibut, smoked salmon.

VEGETABLES – White potatoes, sweet potatoes, cabbage, onions, parsnips, oyster plant, okra, celery, chicory, carrots, turnips, Jerusalem artichokes, French artichokes, Brussels-sprouts, beets, mushrooms raised in hot houses, pumpkins, winter squash, dry shallots and garden herbs for seasoning put up in the dried state.

MARCH.

MEATS – Beef, veal, mutton, lamb, pork.

POULTRY AND GAME – Chickens, turkeys, ducks, rabbits, snipes, wild pigeons, capons.

FISH – Striped bass, halibut, salmon, live codfish, chicken halibut, live lobster, Spanish mackerel, flounders, sheep's-head, pompano, grouper, red-snapper. Shad are plentiful this month. Herring, salmon-trout, sturgeon, whitefish, pickerel, yellow perch, catfish, green turtle, terrapin, scallops, soft-shell clams, oysters, prawns, smoked salmon, smoked halibut, smoked haddock, salt codfish.

VEGETABLES – Cabbage, turnips, carrots, parsnips, artichokes, white potatoes, sweet potatoes, onions, leeks, radishes, Brussels-sprouts, celery, mushrooms, salsify-chives, cress, parsley and other garden herbs, greens, rhubarb and cucumbers raised in hot beds.

APRIL.

MEATS – Beef, veal, pork, mutton, lamb.

POULTRY AND GAME – Chickens, fowls, green geese, young ducks, capons, golden plover, squabs, wild ducks.

FISH – Haddock, fresh cod, striped bass, halibut, eels, chicken halibut, live lobsters, salmon, white perch, flounders, fresh mackerel, sheep's-head, smelts, red-snapper, bluefish, skate or ray fish, shad, whitefish, brook trout, salmon-trout, pickerel, catfish, prawns, crayfish, green turtle, oysters, scallops, frogs' legs, clams, hard crabs, white bait, smoked halibut, smoked salmon, smoked haddock, salt mackerel, salt codfish.

VEGETABLES – Onions, white and sweet potatoes, kale-sprouts, rhubarb, artichokes, turnips, radishes, Brussels-sprouts, okra, cabbage, parsnips, mushrooms, cress, carrots, beets, dandelion, egg plant, leeks, lettuce, cucumbers, asparagus, string beans, peas, chives.

MAY.

MEATS – Beef, veal, mutton, lamb, pork.

POULTRY AND GAME – Fowls, pigeons, spring chickens, young ducks, chickens, green geese, young turkeys.

FISH – Halibut, haddock, striped bass, salmon, flounders, fresh mackerel, Spanish mackerel, blackfish, pompano, butterfish, weakfish, kingfish, porgies, shad, bluefish, clams, brook-trout, whitefish, carp, crayfish, prawns, green turtle, soft crabs, frogs' legs, smoked fish.

VEGETABLES – New potatoes, sweet potatoes, cabbage, young onions, asparagus, beets, carrots, kidney beans, string beans, lettuce, tomatoes, cauliflower, peas, turnips, squash, rhubarb, spinach, radishes, artichokes, sorrel, egg-plant, cucumbers, salads generally.

JUNE.

MEATS – Beef, veal, mutton, lamb.

POULTRY AND GAME – Chickens, geese, ducks, young turkeys, plovers, Pigeons.

FISH – Fresh salmon, striped bass, halibut, fresh mackerel, flounders, kingfish, blackfish, weakfish, butterfish, pompano, Spanish mackerel, porgies, sheepshead, sturgeon, sea bass, bluefish, skate or rayfish, carp, black bass, crayfish, lobsters, eels, white bait, frogs' legs, soft crabs, clams.

VEGETABLES – Potatoes, spinach, cauliflower, string beans, peas tomatoes, asparagus, carrots, artichokes, parsnips, onions, cucumbers, lettuce, radishes, cress, oyster plant, egg plant, rhubarb and all kinds of garden herbs, sorrel, horse-radish.

JULY.

MEATS – Beef, veal, mutton, lamb, pork.

POULTRY AND GAME – Fowls, chickens, pigeons, plovers, young geese, turkey-plouts, squabs, doe-birds,- tame rabbits.

FISH – Spanish mackerel, striped bass, fresh mackerel, blackfish, kingfish, flounders, salmon, cod, haddock, halibut, pompano, butterfish, a sweet panfish, sheep's-head, porgies, sea bass, weakfish, swordfish, tantog, bluefish skate, brook trout, crayfish, black bass, moonfish – a fine baking or boiling fish; pickerel, perch, eels, green turtle, frogs' legs, soft crabs, white bait, prawns, lobsters, clams.

VEGETABLES – Potatoes, asparagus, peas, green string beans, butter beans, artichokes, celery, lettuce, carrots, salsify, tomatoes, spinach, mushrooms, cabbage onions, endive, radishes, turnips, mint, various kinds of greens and salads.

AUGUST.

MEATS – Beef, veal, mutton, lamb, pork.

POULTRY AND GAME – Venison, young ducks, green geese, snipe, plover, turkeys, guinea-fowls, squabs, wild pigeons, woodcock, fowls.

FISH – Striped bass, cod, halibut, haddock, salmon, flounders, fresh mackerel, ponito, butterfish, sea bass, kingfish, sheep's-head, porgies, bluefish, moonfish, brook trout, eels, black bass, crayfish, skate or rayfish, catfish, green turtle, white bait, squid, frogs' legs, soft crabs, prawns, clams.

VEGETABLES – Carrots, artichokes, onions, string beans, lima beans, cauliflower Irish potatoes, sweet potatoes, green corn, tomatoes, peas, summer squash, cucumbers, radishes, lettuce, celery, rhubarb, beets, greens, mushrooms, chives.

SEPTEMBER.

MEAT – Beef, veal, mutton, lamb, pork, venison.

POULTRY AND GAME – Larks, woodcock, snipe, wild pigeons, squabs, young geese, young turkeys, plover, wild ducks, wild geese, swans and brant fowls, reed-birds, grouse, doe-birds, partridges.

FISH – Salmon, halibut codfish, pompano, striped bass, haddock, cero, a large fish similar to the Spanish mackerel; flounders, fresh mackerel, blackfish, Spanish mackerel, butterfish, whitefish, weakfish, smelts, porgies, squids, pickerel, crayfish, catfish, bluefish, wall-eyed pike, sea bass, skate, carp, prawns, white bait, frogs' legs, hard crabs, moonfish, soft crabs, herrings, lobsters, clams.

VEGETABLES – Potatoes, cabbages, turnips, artichokes, peas, beans, carrots, onions, salsify, mushrooms, lettuce, sorrel, celery, cauliflower, Brussels sprouts, sweet potatoes, squash, rhubarb, green-peppers, parsnips, beets, green corn, tomatoes, cress.

OCTOBER.

MEATS – Beef, veal, mutton, lamb, pork, venison, antelope.

POULTRY AND GAME – Turkeys, geese, fowls, pullets,

chickens, wild ducks, the canvas-back duck being the most highly prized, for its delicate flavor; woodcock, grouse, pheasants, pigeons, partridges, snipes, reed-birds, golden plover, gray plover, squabs.

FISH – Striped bass, fresh cod, halibut, haddock, Spanish mackerel, fresh mackerel, cero, flounders, pompano, weakfish, white perch, grouper, sheep's-head, whitefish, bluefish, pickerel, red-snapper, yellow perch, smelts, sea bass, black bass, cisco, wall-eyed pike, crayfish, carp, salmon-trout, spotted bass, terrapin, frogs' legs, hard crabs, soft crabs, white bait, green turtle, scallops, eels, lobsters, oysters.

VEGETABLES – Potatoes, cabbages, turnips, carrots, cauliflowers, parsnips, string beans, peas, lima beans, corn, tomatoes, onions, spinach, salsify, egg plant, beets, pumpkins, endive, celery, parsley, squash, cucumbers, mushrooms, sweet herbs of all kinds, salads of all kinds, garlic, shallots.

NOVEMBER.

MEATS – Beef, veal, mutton, pork, venison, antelope.

POULTRY AND GAME – Rabbits, hares, pheasants, woodcock, partridges, quails, snipe, grouse, wild ducks, wild geese, fowls, turkeys, pigeons.

FISH – Striped bass, fresh cod, halibut, haddock, salmon, fresh mackerel, blackfish, whitefish, bluefish, catfish, redfish or spotted bass, black bass, yellow perch, skate, red-snapper, salmon-trout, pickerel, shad, wall-eyed pike, cisco, crayfish, terrapin, green turtle, scallops, prawns, white bait, frogs' legs, hard crabs, oysters.

VEGETABLES – Potatoes, carrots, parsnips, turnips,

onions, dried beans, artichokes, cabbages, beets, winter squash, celery, parsley, pumpkins, shallots, mushrooms, chicory, all sorts of salads and sweet herbs.

DECEMBER.
MEATS – Beef, veal, mutton, pork, venison.
POULTRY AND GAME – Rabbits, hares, grouse, pheasants, woodcock, snipe, partridges, turkey, fowls, chickens, pullets, geese, wild geese, ducks, wild duck, tame duck, canvas-back duck, quails.
FISH – Turbot, sturgeon, haddock, halibut, eels, striped bass, flounders, salmon, fresh cod, blackfish, whitefish, grouper, cusk, shad, mullet, a sweet panfish, black bass, yellow perch, salmon-trout, pickerel, cisco, skate, wall-eyed pike, terrapin, crayfish, green turtle, prawns, hard crabs, soft crabs, scallops, frogs' legs, oysters.
VEGETABLES – - Potatoes, cabbages, onions, winter squash, beets, turnips, pumpkins, carrots, parsnips, dried beans, dried peas, mushrooms, parsley, shallots, Brussels-sprouts, leeks, horse-radish, garlic, mint, sage and small salads. Garden herbs which are mostly used for stuffings and for flavoring dishes, soups, etc., or for garnishing, may be found either green or dried the year round, always in season.

Melons can be had at most of our markets from July 1st until the 15th of October; they are received from the South in the early part of the season, and are not as fresh and good as those ripened in our own vicinity.

WHITE HOUSE COOKBOOK
APPENDIX

Eat Like a President: Book I

CARVING

Carving is one important acquisition in the routine of daily living, and all should try to attain a knowledge or ability to do it well, and withal gracefully.

When carving use a chair slightly higher than the ordinary size, as it gives a better purchase on the meat, and appears more graceful than when standing, as is often quite necessary when carving a turkey, or a very large joint. More depends on skill than strength. The platter should be placed opposite, and sufficiently near to give perfect command of the article to be carved, the knife of medium size, sharp with a keen edge. Commence by cutting the slices thin, laying them carefully to one side of the platter, then afterwards placing the desired amount on each guest's plate, to be served in turn by the servant.

In carving fish, care should be taken to help it in perfect flakes; for if these are broken the beauty of the fish is lost. The carver should acquaint himself with the choicest parts and morsels; and to give each guest an equal share of those *tidbits* should be his maxim. Steel knives and forks should on no account be used in helping fish, as these are liable to impart a *very* disagreeable flavor. A fish-trowel of silver or plated silver is the proper article to use.

Gravies should be sent to the table very *hot*, and in helping one to gravy or melted butter, place it on a vacant side of the plate, not *pour* it over their meat, fish or fowl, that they may use only as much as they like.

When serving fowls, or meats, accompanied with stuffing, the guests should be asked if they would have a portion, as it is not every one to whom the flavor of stuffing is agreeable; in filling their plates, avoid heaping one thing upon another, as it makes a bad appearance.

A word about the care of carving knives: a fine steel knife should not come in contact with intense heat, because it destroys its temper, and therefore impairs its cutting qualities. Table carving knives should not be used in the kitchen, either around the stove, or for cutting bread, meats, vegetables, etc.; a fine whetstone should be kept for sharpening, and the knife cleaned carefully to avoid dulling its edge, all of which is quite essential to successful carving.

MEAT CLASSIFICATIONS

The following is a classification of the qualities of meat, according to the several joints of beef, when cut up.

First Class – Includes the sirloin with the kidney suet (1), the rump steak piece (2), the fore-rib (11).

Second Class – The buttock or round (4), the thick flank (7), the middle ribs (11).

Third Class – The aitch-bone (3), the mouse-round (5), the thin flank (8, 9), the chuck (12), the shoulder-piece (14), the brisket (13).

Fourth Class – The clod, neck and sticking-piece (15, 16).

Fifth Class – Shin or shank (17).

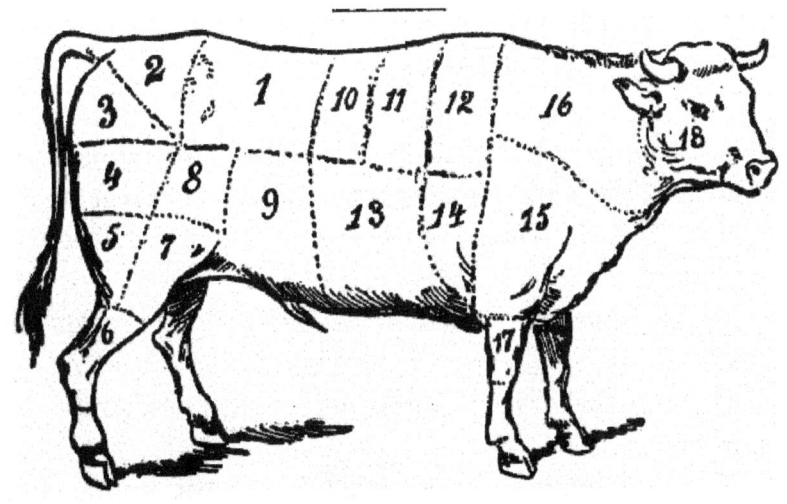

BEEF

HINDQUARTER

No. 1. Used for choice roasts, the porterhouse and sirloin steaks.

No. 2. Rump, used for steaks, stews and corned beef.

No. 3. Aitch-bone, used for boiling-pieces, stews and pot roasts.

No. 4. Buttock or round, used for steaks, pot roasts, beef *á la mode*; also a prime boiling-piece.

No. 5. Mouse-round, used for boiling and stewing.

No. 6. Shin or leg, used for soups, hashes, etc.

No. 7. Thick flank, cut with under fat, is a prime boiling-piece, good for stews and corned beef, pressed beef.

No. 8. Veiny piece, used for corned beef, dried beef.

No. 9. Thin flank, used for corned beef and boiling-pieces.

FOREQUARTER

No. 10. Five ribs called the fore-rib. This is considered the primest piece for roasting; also makes the finest steaks.

No. 11. Four ribs, called the middle ribs, used for roasting.

No. 12. Chuck ribs, used for second quality of roasts and steaks.

No. 13. Brisket, used for corned beef, stews, soups and spiced beef.

No. 14. Shoulder-piece, used for stews, soups, pot-roasts, mincemeat and hashes.

Nos. 15, 16. Neck, clod or sticking-piece used for stocks, gravies, soups, mince-pie meat, hashes, bologna sausages, etc.

No. 17. Shin or shank, used mostly for soups and stewing.

No. 18. Cheek.

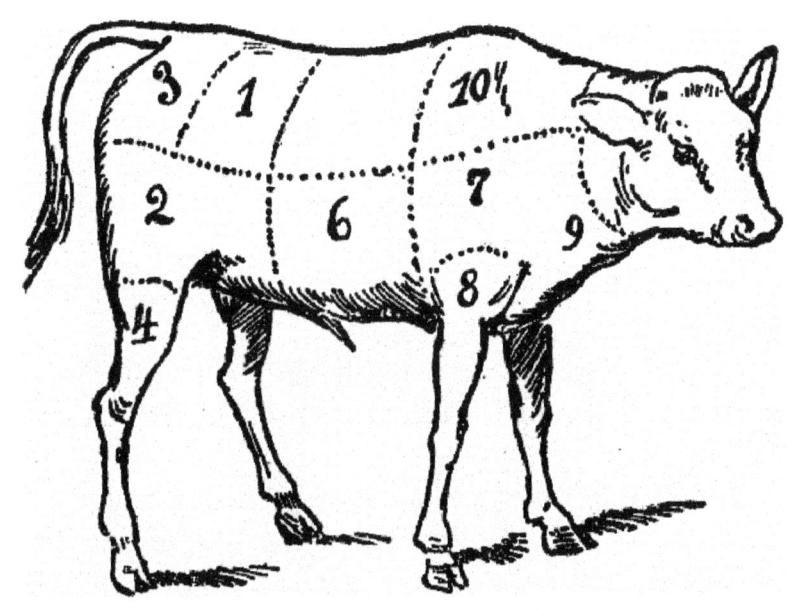

VEAL

HINDQUARTER

No. 1. Loin, the choicest cuts used for roasts and chops.
No. 2. Fillet, used for roasts and cutlets.
No. 3. Loin, chump-end used for roasts and chops.
No. 4. The hind-knuckle or hock, used for stews, potpies, meat-pies.

FOREQUARTER

No. 5. Neck, best end used for roasts, stews and chops.

No. 6. Breast, best end used for roasting, stews and chops.

No. 7. Blade-bone, used for pot-roasts and baked dishes.

No. 8. Fore-knuckle, used for soups and stews.

No. 9. Breast, brisket-end used for baking, stews and potpies.

No. 10. Neck, scrag-end used for stews, broth, meat-pies, etc.

In cutting up veal, generally, the hindquarter is divided into loin and leg, and the forequarter into breast, neck and shoulder.

The Several Parts of a Moderately-sized, Well-fed Calf, about eight weeks old, are nearly of the following weights: Loin and chump, 18 lbs.; fillet, 12½ lbs.; hind-knuckle, 5½ lbs.; shoulder, 11 lbs.; neck, 11 lbs.; breast, 9 lbs., and fore-knuckle, 5 lbs.; making a total of 144 lbs. weight.

MUTTON

No. 1. Leg, used for roasts and for boiling.

No. 2. Shoulder, used for baked dishes and roasts.

No. 3. Loin, best end used for roasts, chops.

No. 4. Loin, chump-end used for roasts and chops.

No. 5. Rack, or rib chops, used for French chops, rib chops, either for frying or broiling; also used for choice stews.

No. 6. Breast, used for roast, baked dishes, stews, chops.

No. 7. Neck or scrag-end, used for cutlets, stews and meat-pies.

NOTE – A saddle of mutton or double loin is two loins cut off before the carcass is split open down the back.

French chops are a small rib chop, the end of the bone trimmed off and the meat and fat cut away from the thin end, leaving the round piece of meat attached to the larger end, which leaves the small rib-bone bare. Very tender and sweet.

Mutton is *prime* when cut from a carcass which has been fed out of doors, and allowed to run upon the hillside; they are best when about three years old. The fat will then be abundant, white and hard, the flesh juicy and firm, and of a clear red color.

For mutton roasts, choose the shoulder, the saddle, or the loin or haunch. The leg should be boiled. Almost any part will do for broth.

Lamb born in the middle of the winter, reared under shelter, and fed in a great measure upon milk, then killed in the spring, is considered a great delicacy, though lamb is good at a year old. Like all young animals, lamb ought to be thoroughly cooked, or it is most unwholesome.

PORK

No. 1. Leg, used for smoked hams, roasts and corned pork.

No. 2. Hind-loin, used for roasts, chops and baked dishes.

No. 3. Fore-loin or ribs, used for roasts, baked dishes or chops.

No. 4. Spare-rib, used for roasts, chops, stews.

No. 5. Shoulder, used for smoked shoulder, roasts and corned pork.

No. 6. Brisket and flank, used for pickling in salt and smoked bacon.

The cheek is used for pickling in salt, also the shank or shin. The feet are usually used for souse and jelly.

For family use the leg is the most economical, that is when fresh, and the loin the richest. The best pork is from carcasses weighing from fifty to about one hundred and twenty-five pounds. Pork is a white and close meat, and it is almost impossible to over-roast or cook it too much; when underdone it is exceedingly unwholesome.

VENISON

No. 1. Shoulder, used for roasting; it may be boned and stuffed, then afterwards baked or roasted.

No. 2. Fore-loin, used for roasts and steaks.

No. 3. Haunch or loin, used for roasts, steaks, stews.

The ribs cut close may be used for soups. Good for pickling and making into smoked venison.

No. 4. Breast, used for baking dishes, stewing.

No. 5. Scrag or neck, used for soups.

The choice of venison should be judged by the fat, which, when the venison is young, should be thick, clear and close, and the meat a very dark red. The flesh of a female deer about four years old, is the sweetest and best of venison.

Buck venison, which is in season from June to the end of September, is finer than doe venison, which is in season from October to December. Neither should be dressed at any other time of year, and no meat requires so much care as venison in killing, preserving and dressing.

MEAT CARVING TIPS

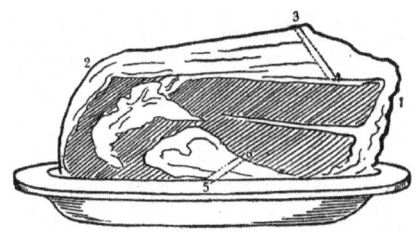

SIRLOIN OF BEEF

This choice roasting-piece should be cut with one good firm stroke from end to end of the joint, at the upper part, in thin, long, even slices in the direction of the line from 1 to 2, cutting across the grain, serving each guest with some of the fat with the lean; this may be done by cutting a small, thin slice from underneath the bone from 5 to 6, through the tenderloin.

Another way of carving this piece, and which will be of great assistance in doing it well, is to insert the knife just above the bone at the bottom, and run sharply along, dividing the meat from the bone at the bottom and end, thus leaving it perfectly flat; then carve in long, thin slices the usual way. When the bone has been removed and the sirloin rolled before it is cooked, it is laid upon the platter on one end, and an even, thin slice is carved across the grain of the upper surface.

Roast ribs should be carved in thin, even slices from the thick end towards the thin in the same manner as the sirloin; this can be more easily and cleanly done if the carving knife is first run along between the meat and the end and rib-bones, thus leaving it free from bone to be cut into slices.

Tongue – To carve this it should be cut crosswise, the middle being the best; cut in very *thin* slices, thereby improving its delicacy, making it more tempting; as is the case of all well-carved meats. The root of the tongue is usually left on the platter.

BREAST OF VEAL

This piece is quite similar to a forequarter of lamb after the shoulder has been taken off. A breast of veal consists of two parts, the rib-bones and the gristly brisket. These parts may be separated by sharply passing the carving knife in the direction of the line from 1 to 2; and when they are entirely divided, the rib-bones should be carved in the direction of the line from 5 to 6, and cutting slices can help the brisket from 3 to 4.

The carver should ask the guests whether they have a preference for the brisket or ribs; and if there be a sweetbread served with the dish, as is frequently with this roast of veal, each person should receive a piece.

Though veal and lamb contain less nutrition than beef and mutton, in proportion to their weight, they are often preferred to these latter meats on account of their delicacy of texture and flavor. A whole breast of veal weighs from nine to twelve pounds.

A FILLET OF VEAL

A fillet of veal is one of the prime roasts of veal; it is taken from the leg above the knuckle; a piece weighing from ten to twelve pounds is a good size and requires about four hours for roasting. Before roasting, it is dressed with a force meat or stuffing placed in the cavity from where the bone was taken out and the flap tightly secured together with skewers; many bind it together with tape.

To carve it, cut in even thin slices off from the whole of the upper part or top, in the same manner as from a rolled roast of beef, as in the direction of the figs. 1 and 2; this gives the person served some of the dressing with each slice of meat.

Veal is very unwholesome unless it is cooked thoroughly, and when roasted should be of a rich brown color. Bacon, fried pork, sausage-balls, with greens, are among the accompaniments of roasted veal, also a cut lemon.

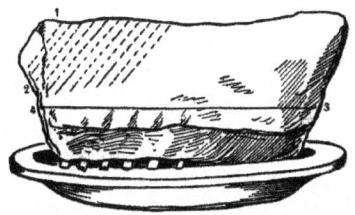

NECK OF VEAL

The best end of a neck of veal makes a very good roasting-piece; it, however, is composed of bone and ribs that make it quite difficult to carve, unless it is done properly. To attempt to carve each chop and serve it, you would not only place *too* large a piece upon the plate of the person you intend to serve, but you would waste much time, and should the vertebrae have not been removed by the butcher, you would be compelled to exercise such a degree of strength that would make one's appearance very ungraceful, and possibly, too, throwing gravy over your neighbor sitting next to you. The correct way to carve this roast is to cut diagonally from fig. 1 to 2, and help in slices of moderate thickness; then it may be cut from 3 to 4, in order to separate the small bones; divide and serve them, having first inquired if they are desired.

This joint is usually sent to the table accompanied by bacon, ham, tongue, or pickled pork, on a separate dish and with a cut lemon on a plate. There are also a number of sauces that are suitable with this roast.

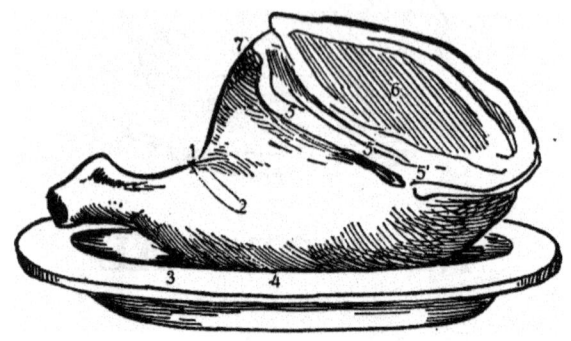

LEG OF MUTTON

The best mutton, and that from which most nourishment is obtained is that of sheep from three to six years old, and which have been fed on dry, sweet pastures; then mutton is in its *prime*, the flesh being firm, juicy, dark colored and full of the richest gravy. When mutton is two years old, the meat is flabby, pale and savorless.

In carving a roasted leg, the best slices are found by cutting quite down to the bone, in the direction from 1 to 2, and slices may be taken from either side.

Some very good cuts are taken from the broad end from 5 to 6, and the fat on this ridge is very much liked by many. The cramp-bone is a delicacy, and is obtained by cutting down to the bone at 4, and running the knife under it in a semicircular direction to 3. The nearer the knuckle the drier the meat, but the under side contains the most finely grained meat, from which slices may be cut lengthwise. When sent to the table a frill of paper around the knuckle will improve its appearance.

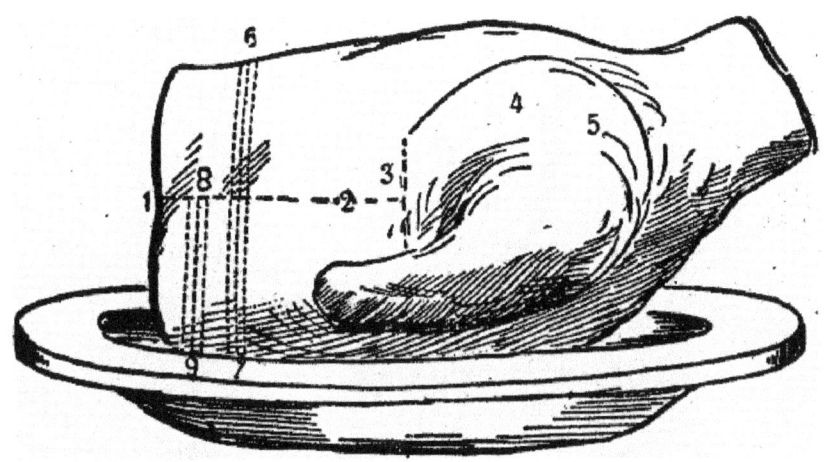

FOREQUARTER OF LAMB

The first cut to be made in carving a fore-quarter of lamb is to separate the shoulder from the breast and ribs; this is done by passing a sharp carving knife lightly around the dotted line as shown by the figs. 3, 4 and 5, so as to cut through the skin, and then, by raising with a little force the shoulder, into which the fork should be firmly fixed, it will easily separate with just a little more cutting with the knife; care should be taken not to cut away too much of the meat from the breast when dividing the shoulder from it, as that would mar its appearance. The shoulder may be placed upon a separate dish for convenience. The next process is to divide the ribs from the brisket by cutting through the meat in the line from 1 to 2; then the ribs may be carved in the direction of the line 6 to 7, and the brisket from 8 to 9. The carver should always ascertain whether the guest prefers ribs, brisket, or a piece of the shoulder.

HAM

The carver in cutting a ham must be guided according as he desires to practice economy, or have at once fine slices out of the prime part. Under the first supposition, he will commence at the knuckle end, and cut off thin slices toward the thick and upper part of the ham.

To reach the choicer portion of the ham, the knife, which must be very sharp and thin, should be carried quite down to the bone through the thick fat in the direction of the line from 1 to 2. The slices should be even and thin, cutting both lean and fat together, always cutting down to the bone. Some cut a circular hole in the middle of a ham gradually enlarging it outwardly. Then again many carve a ham by first cutting from 1 to 2, then across the other way from 3 to 4. Remove the skin after the ham is cooked and send to the table with dots of dry pepper or dry mustard on the top, a tuft of fringed paper twisted about the knuckle, and plenty of fresh parsley around the dish. This will always insure an inviting appearance.

Roast Pig – The modern way of serving a pig is not to send it to the table whole, but have it carved partially by the cook; first, by dividing the shoulder from the body; then the leg in the same manner; also separating the ribs into convenient portions. The head may be divided and placed on the same platter. To be served as hot as possible.

A Spare Rib of Pork is carved by cutting slices from the fleshy part, after which the bones should be disjointed and separated.

A leg of pork may be carved in the same manner as a ham.

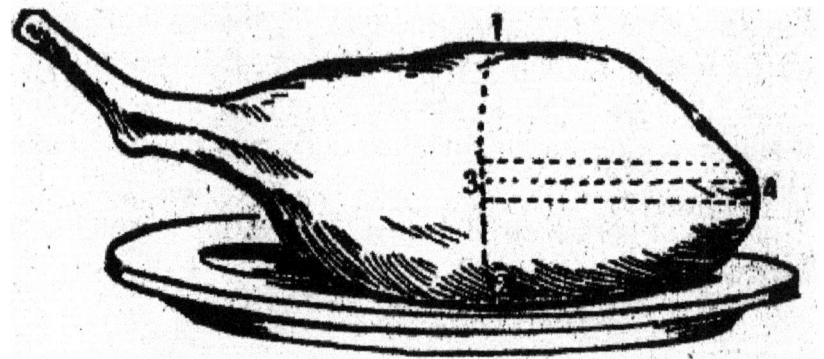

HAUNCH OF VENISON

A haunch of venison is the *prime* joint, and is carved very similar to almost any roasted or boiled leg; it should be first cut crosswise down to the bone following the line from 1 to 2; then turn the platter with the knuckle farthest from you, put in the point of the knife, and cut down as far as you can, in the directions shown by the dotted lines from 3 to 4; then there can be taken out as many slices as is required on the right and left of this.

Slices of venison should be cut thin, and gravy given with them, but as there is a special sauce made with red wine and currant jelly to accompany this meat, do not serve gravy before asking the guest if he pleases to have any. The fat of this meat is like mutton, apt to cool soon, and become hard and disagreeable to the palate; it should, therefore, be served always on warm plates, and the platter kept over a hot-water dish, or spirit lamp. Many cooks dish it up with a white paper frill pinned around the knucklebone. A haunch of mutton is carved the same as a haunch of venison.

FOWLS

First insert the knife between the leg and the body, and cut to the bone; then turn the leg back with the fork, and if the fowl is tender the joint will give away easily. The wing is broken off the same way, only dividing the joint with the knife, in the direction from 1 to 2.

The four quarters having been removed in this way, take off the merry-thought and the neck-bones; these last are to be removed by putting the knife in at figs. 3 and 4, pressing it hard, when they will break off from the part that sticks to the breast.

To separate the breast from the body of the fowl, cut through the tender ribs close to the breast, quite down to the tail.

Now turn the fowl over, back upwards; put the knife into the bone midway between the neck and the rump, and on raising the lower end it will separate readily. Turn now the rump from you, and take off very neatly the two side bones, and the fowl is carved. In separating the thigh from the drumstick, the knife must be inserted exactly at the joint, for if not accurately hit, some difficulty will be experienced to get them apart; this is easily acquired by practice.

There is no difference in carving roast and boiled fowls if full grown; but in very young fowls the breast is usually served whole; the wings and breast are considered the best parts, but in young ones the legs are the juiciest. In the case of a capon or large fowl, slices may be cut off at the breast, the same as carving a pheasant.

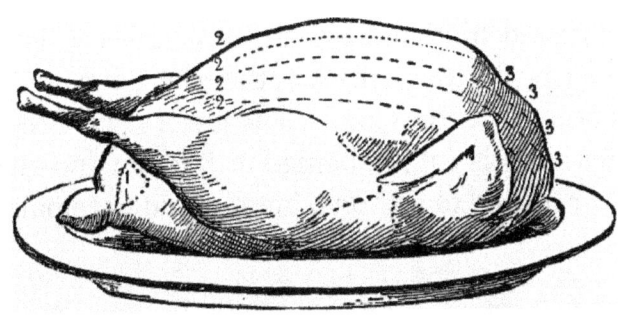

TURKEY

A turkey having been relieved from strings and skewers used in trussing should be placed on the table with the head or neck at the carver's right hand. An expert carver places the fork in the turkey, and does not remove it until the whole is divided. First insert the fork firmly in the lower part of the breast, just forward of fig. 2, then sever the legs and wings on both sides, if the whole is to be carved, cutting neatly through the joint next to the body, letting these parts lie on the platter. Next, cut downward from the breast from 2 to 3, as many even slices of the white meat as may be desired, placing the pieces neatly on one side of the platter. Now unjoint the legs and wings at the middle joint, which can be done very skillfully by a little practice.

Make an opening into the cavity of the turkey for dipping out the inside dressing, by cutting a piece from the rear part 1, 1, called the apron. Consult the tastes of the guests as to which part is preferred; if no choice is expressed, serve a portion of both light and dark meat.

One of the most delicate parts of the turkey are two little muscles, lying in small dish-like cavities on each side of the back, a little behind the leg attachments; the next most delicate meat fills the cavities in the neck bone, and next to this, that on the second joints. The lower part of the leg (or drumstick, as it is called) being hard, tough and stringy, is rarely ever helped to any one, but allowed to remain on the dish.

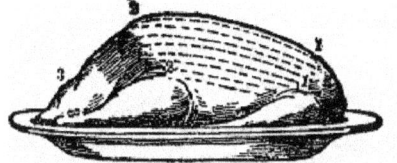 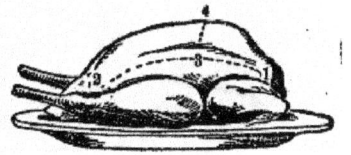

ROAST GOOSE

To carve a goose, first begin by separating the leg from the body, by putting the fork into the small end of the limb, pressing it closely to the body, then passing the knife under at 2, and turning the leg back as you cut through the joint. To take off the wing, insert the fork in the small end of the pinion, and press it close to the body; put the knife in at fig. 1, and divide the joint. When the legs and wings are off, the breast may be carved in long, even slices, as represented in the lines from 1 to 2. The back and lower side bones, as well as the two lower side bones by the wing, may be cut off; but the best pieces of the goose are the breast and thighs, after being separated from the drumsticks. Serve a little of the dressing from the inside, by making a circular slice in the apron at fig. 3. A goose should never be over a year old; a tough goose is very difficult to carve, and certainly most difficult to eat.

ROAST DUCK

A young duckling may be carved in the same manner as a fowl, the legs and wings being taken off first on either side.

When the duck is full size, carve it like a goose; first cutting it in slices from the breast, beginning close to the wing and proceeding upward towards the breast bone, as is represented by the lines 1 to 2. An opening may be made by cutting out a circular slice, as shown by the dotted lines at number 3.

Some are fond of the feet, and when dressing the duck, these should be neatly skinned and never removed. Wild duck is highly esteemed by epicures; it is trussed like a tame duck, and carved in the same manner, the breast being the choicest part.

PARTRIDGES

Partridges are generally cleaned and trussed the same way as a pheasant, but the custom of cooking them with the heads on is going into disuse somewhat. The usual way of carving them is similar to a pigeon, dividing it into two equal parts. Another method is to cut it into three pieces, by severing a wing and leg on either side from the body, by following the lines 1 to 2, thus making two servings of those parts, leaving the breast for a third plate. The third method is to thrust back the body from the legs, and cut through the middle of the breast, thus making four portions that may be served.

Grouse and prairie chicken are carved from the breast when they are large, and quartered or halved when of medium size.

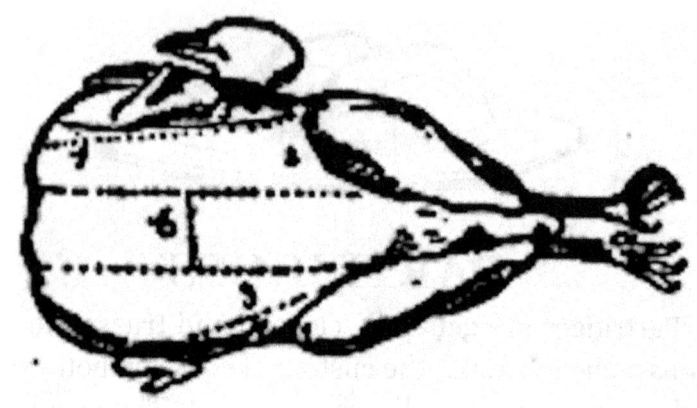

PHEASANT

Place your fork firmly in the center of the breast of this large game bird and cut deep slices to the bone at figs. 1 and 2; then take off the leg in the line from 3 and 4, and the wing 3 and 5, severing both sides the same.

In taking off the wings, be careful not to cut too near the neck; if you do you will hit upon the neck-bone, from which the wing must be separated. Pass the knife through the line 6, and under the merry-thought towards the neck, which will detach it.

Cut the other parts as in a fowl. The breast, wings and merry-thought of a pheasant are the most highly prized, although the legs are considered very finely flavored.

Pheasants are frequently roasted with the head left on; in that case, when dressing them, bring the head round under the wing, and fix it on the point of a skewer.

PIGEONS

A very good way of carving these birds is to insert the knife at fig. 1, and cut both ways to 2 and 3, when each portion may be divided into two pieces, then served. Pigeons, if not too large, may be cut in halves, either across or down the middle, cutting them into two equal parts; if young and small they may be served entirely whole.

Tame pigeons should be cooked as soon as possible after they are killed, as they very quickly lose their flavor. Wild pigeons, on the contrary, should hang a day or two in a cool place before they are dressed.

Oranges cut into halves are used as a garnish for dishes of small birds, such as pigeons, quail, woodcock, squabs, snipe, etc.

These small birds are either served whole or split down the back, making two servings.

FISH

MACKEREL

The mackerel is one of the most beautiful of fish, being known by its silvery whiteness. It sometimes attains to the length of twenty inches, but usually, when fully grown, is about fourteen or sixteen inches long, and about two pounds in weight.

To carve a baked mackerel, first remove the head and tail by cutting downward at 1 and 2; then split them down the back, so as to serve each person a part of each side piece.

The roe should be divided in small pieces and served with each piece of fish. Other whole fish may be carved in the same manner.

The fish is laid upon a little sauce or folded napkin, on a hot dish, and garnished with parsley.

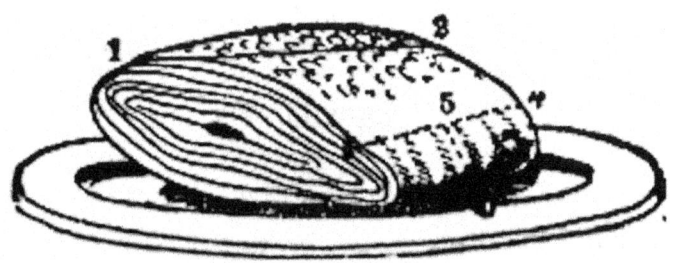

BOILED SALMON

This fish is seldom sent to the table whole, being *too* large for any ordinary sized family; the middle cut is considered the choicest to boil. To carve it, first run the knife down and along the upper side of the fish from 1 to 2, then again on the lower side from 3 to 4. Serve the thick part, cutting it lengthwise in slices in the direction of the line from 1 to 2, and the thin part breadthwise, or in the direction from 5 to 6. A slice of the thick with one of the thin, where lies the fat, should be served to each guest. Care should be taken when carving not to break the flakes of the fish, as that impairs its appearance. The flesh of the salmon is rich and delicious in flavor. Salmon is in season from the first of February to the end of August.

The New Atlantian Library

NewAtlantianLibrary.com
or AbsolutelyAmazingEbooks.com
or AA-eBooks.com

www.ingramcontent.com/pod-product-compliance
Lightning Source LLC
Chambersburg PA
CBHW070733170426
43200CB00007B/512